Entitled
to Power

Entitled to POWER

*Farm Women
and Technology,
1913–1963*

Katherine Jellison

*The University of
North Carolina Press
Chapel Hill & London*

© 1993 The University of North Carolina Press
Manufactured in the United States of America

Library of Congress
Cataloging-in-Publication Data
Jellison, Katherine
     Entitled to power : farm women and
technology, 1913–1963 / by Katherine Jellison.
          p.   cm. — (Gender & American culture)
     Includes bibliographical references and index.
     ISBN 0-8078-2088-1 (alk. paper). —
ISBN 0-8078-4415-2 (pbk.: alk. paper)
          1. Women in agriculture—United States—
History.   2. Rural women—United States—
History.   3. Sociology, Rural—United States.
I. Title.   II. Series.
HD6073.F32U65   1993
338.4'83'0973—dc20   92–46352
                                                          CIP

The paper in this book meets the guidelines for
permanence and durability of the Committee on
Production Guidelines for Book Longevity of the
Council on Library Resources.

97 96 95 94 93   5 4 3 2 1

To David

Contents

Tables

Figures

I am grateful to a number of institutions and individuals for their assistance with this book. The University of Iowa Department of History and the Smithsonian Institution, in particular, provided substantial support at critical times during my research and writing. The University of Iowa Women's Studies Program, the Woodrow Wilson Foundation, the Colonial Dames of America, the Indiana Historical Society, and the State Historical Society, Inc., a private organization promoting scholarship in Iowa history, also generously supported this project.

Staff members at several research facilities also deserve recognition for their assistance with this book. The archivists, librarians, and publications staff at the State Historical Society of Iowa were most helpful in directing me toward sources and encouraging me in my investigation of the experiences of midwestern farm women. In particular, I would like to thank Marvin Bergman, Ginalie Swaim, and my good friend Christie Dailey for providing me with helpful advice and for publishing my scholarship throughout the years. Archivist Mary Bennett also deserves my gratitude for guiding me toward appropriate manuscript sources and for helping me obtain some of the illustrations for this book. The government documents librarians at the University of Iowa Main Library provided patient assistance, as did the archivists and librarians at the Nebraska State Historical Society, the State Historical Society of Wisconsin, the Indiana Historical Society, the Indiana State Library, and the Kansas

Acknowledgments

State Historical Society. In Washington, the staffs of the National Museum of American History, the National Archives, and the Prints and Photographs Division of the Library of Congress provided invaluable assistance. I would also like to thank the personnel of the Haskell County (Kansas) Historical Society, the Shelby County (Iowa) Historical Society, and the Imperial (Nebraska) Public Library. The staff at the University of Iowa Main Library merits a special thank-you for granting me "visiting borrower" status during the last months of this project.

I also owe many thanks to the dozens of women who shared their life stories with me. The women of Haskell and Shelby counties and of Nicodemus, Kansas, deserve my particular gratitude. I owe thanks too to the family of Elizabeth Wherry for sharing information about her life and to Gladys Rife for putting me in touch with the Wherry family.

Members of the University of Iowa Department of History, the University of Iowa Women's Studies Program, and the Iowa City women's community provided me with emotional support and scholarly advice during my work on this book. Other scholars interested in the history of rural women were particularly helpful and included Deborah Fink, Barbara Handy-Marchello, Kim Nielsen, Steven Reschly, and Leslie Taylor. The thoughtful comments and challenging questions of my friends Sharon Wood and Kimberly Jensen helped to make me a better historian of women, and Megan O'Connell was an encouraging friend during the final two years of this project. In addition, I would like to thank Margery Wolf, Ellis Hawley, Malcolm Rohrbough, and Shelton Stromquist. They provided wise advice on significant portions of the book manuscript.

My midwestern support network extends beyond Iowa City to include my sister Sandra Jellison-Knock in South Dakota, my parents, Margaret and Bill Jellison, in Kansas, my mother- and father-in-law, Ella and A. W. Winkelmann, in Nebraska, and my good friend Mary Jo Hrenchir in Minnesota. These people have encouraged me throughout my career as a historian and through the life of this project. In particular, I would like to thank my parents for providing transportation for my research trips in Kansas. I would also like to thank my old friends Bill and Clarelyn Stewart for providing me with a place to stay while doing research at the Kansas State Historical Society.

A number of other individuals have earned my appreciation. Pete Daniel was a helpful adviser during my tenure as a fellow at the Smithsonian Institution. Wayne Knoll was a cheerful landlord and friend during my residence in Washington, D.C., and his interest in my research was gratifying.

Lu Ann Jones was a generous colleague at the Smithsonian, and she has continued to be a very giving friend and scholar. I would like to thank Noralee Frankel, Jack Hurley, and David Danbom for reading portions of my book manuscript and providing useful suggestions. Glenda Riley and Margaret Caffrey referred me to sources on Native American women, and Mary Neth graciously allowed me to read her own book manuscript and gain some valuable insights. I would like to thank Jack Temple Kirby and an anonymous reader for their thought-provoking comments on my manuscript, and I would like to thank the staff of the University of North Carolina Press, particularly Kate Torrey, Sandra Eisdorfer, and Grace Buonocore. Linnea Burwood, Joseph Hawes, Abraham Kriegel, Susan Scheckel, and Linda Borish also deserve thanks for their moral support and general interest in my scholarship during the past year.

My greatest debt is owed to two people: Linda Kerber, my mentor and friend, and my spouse, David Winkelmann. Linda helped nurture this project from its origins to its final form as a much more complex work. As I sit here on her sun porch, I realize that Linda has also provided me with a very pleasant environment in which to create the finishing touches on this book. David too was with me, and the book, every step of the way. My work on this book and our dual careers have necessitated that we frequently live apart. Even at a distance, however, he is my wisest adviser and my most constructive critic. His devotion to me and to this project was perhaps best illustrated last spring when I was sidelined with a spinal injury. David left his busy law practice one weekend to travel over 500 miles to help me lift and sort through boxes of research material for this book. That is only one of a thousand reasons why I have dedicated this book to him.

Iowa City
June 1992

Introduction

In her classic novel of farm life in Nebraska, Willa Cather not only paid homage to the fertile farmland of her home state but also celebrated the woman farm producer. Her heroine, Alexandra Bergson, introduces scientific farming to her neighborhood and becomes a skilled farm manager. In so doing, she expands her interests beyond the small butter-and-egg business her dying father had envisioned as her main enterprise on the farm. She has become the most successful farmer in the community, but her neighbors view her activities with some dismay, and her male relatives downplay her contributions to the farm. By claiming the title of "farmer" for herself, Alexandra Bergson had crossed accepted gender boundaries. As Cather's novel acknowledges, for midwesterners of her day, farm women were not supposed to be farmers; their role as farm producer was understood to be a limited one that remained secondary to their domestic duties.

As historian Joan Jensen has noted, women have been "active participants in every stage of agricultural production and in every period of agricultural history."[1] In a society that has recognized farming as a male occupation, however, many of women's contributions to agricultural production have been ignored or misunderstood. The work that real-life Alexandra Bergsons historically performed in the farmhouse, the barn, and the fields, often unacknowledged during their own lifetime, has been further rendered "invisible" by historians' failure to examine the history of farm women's experience.[2]

There was something individual about the great farm, a most unusual trimness and care for detail. On either side of the road, for a mile before you reached the foot of the hill, stood tall osage-orange hedges, their glossy green marking off the yellow fields. South of the hill, in a low, sheltered swale, surrounded by a mulberry hedge, was the orchard, its fruit trees knee-deep in timothy grass. Anyone thereabouts would have told you that this was one of the richest farms on the Divide, and that the farmer was a woman.

—Willa Cather,

O Pioneers! (1913)

Scholars' general neglect of farm women's history is not the result of a lack of sources. It is rather the result of historians' failure to acknowledge the significance of farm women's experiences.[3] This is particularly true for farm women's experiences in the twentieth century, which are well documented. Historians have largely neglected these documents, perhaps believing that farm life was an experience that few women encountered in the increasingly urbanized twentieth century. In some parts of the country, however, such as the midwestern Farm Belt, a major proportion of the female population lived on farms well into the twentieth century. In ignoring these women, historians have neglected an event that had a significant impact on American social, political, cultural, and economic history: farm families' adoption of twentieth-century farm, household, and communication technology. Farm women as well as men played a role in modernizing farm life and changing forever the face of rural society and the character of its relationship to urban America. This study retrieves those women's voices, reconstructs their experiences, and examines their motives and choices during a fifty-year period of great change in midwestern farm life.

During the early decades of the twentieth century, the very nature of farm women's work convinced most of them that mechanization was a good thing. In their kitchens, farm women washed the dirty field clothes worn by family members and hired help. They canned fruits and vegetables, preserved meat, baked bread, separated milk, and churned butter—all work that farm women largely performed without the use of electric- or gas-powered mechanical equipment. For much of the twentieth century, farm women's household labor remained untouched by the technological revolution that historians have documented for urban women.[4] Outside the farmhouse, women raised gardens and chickens and often sold their produce for cash or bartered it for other goods. They also periodically worked in the barn and in the farm fields. As key members of the farm family work unit, women had a stake in government policies that affected the agricultural economy, particularly those government programs that began promoting the mechanization of American farming during the Progressive Era as a means to maintain a stable rural society and produce cheaper foods for the urban masses. Such programs remained in place for the next fifty years and had a significant impact on the lives of farm women and their families.

Farm women performed their work under a patriarchal system in which their labor largely belonged to their husbands and fathers. Initially, at least some Progressive Era farm women saw their adoption of "labor-saving" technology as part of a larger process to gain greater status and control within the farm family work unit. In the Midwest, where efforts to industrialize agriculture dominated the experiences of farm families for the next several decades, the participation of women in this movement was crucial to its success, and a vast propaganda network functioned to reinforce women's generally positive attitude toward the adoption of mechanized equipment.

While the modern field and household equipment that this propaganda promoted was attractive to most farm women, an underlying message of this prescriptive literature was not. Government publications, editorials in farm periodicals, and advertisements for mechanical equipment often focused on the idea that adoption of modern equipment would release women from their productive role on the farm and instead allow them to conform more closely to the role of full-time "homemaker." Most farm women did not see this as a worthwhile goal. They valued their work as farm producers and for reasons of economics and family politics wanted to retain that position. In other words, farm women held an alternative vision of modern farm life, one in which their work as farm producers was central.

Against the onslaught of propaganda attempting to make women relinquish their role as farm producer, farm women did not become full-time home-makers in the twentieth century. Although, as the twentieth century unfolded, farm women gave up many of their traditional productive functions in the henhouse, garden, and farm kitchen, in the post–World War II era they adopted a new productive role in the farm field, one that relied on their use of modern field technology. They also took on other new tasks outside the farmhouse, such as employment in off-farm jobs, which circumvented the role of full-time homemaker. As historians of twentieth-century urban women have noted, urban women's rejection of the domestic ideal largely sprang from economic motives.[5] Farm women's experience followed a similar pattern. Their acceptance of modern technology and rejection of the home-maker role ultimately did not represent a conscious feminist challenge to rural patriarchy but was a way to maintain a modicum of economic power and influence within the patriarchal structure of midwestern family farming.

Women's adoption of new equipment and practices thus often had unfore-seen consequences for themselves and their families. Progressive Era women who had seen adoption of new equipment as part of a general plan to improve their status within the farm family saw that goal disappear as economic and political realities dictated other priorities for midwestern farm women during the years of agricultural depression and world war. By the post–World War II era, when improved economic conditions allowed modernization to become a reality, women's goals were more modest. Years of crisis on the farm had made economic survival the paramount concern. That survival, however, depended upon women retaining a role in agricultural production and using new technology to put that role into practice. In the process of modernizing their work, midwestern farm women thus significantly altered the character of American farm life and the continuing role of women in agricultural production. This study tells the story of these women and their transformation of rural society.

When an anonymous Kansas farm woman
made these remarks to the secretary of agriculture, nearly five years had passed since
President Theodore Roosevelt's Commission on Country Life had first noted that
the experience of many farm women bore
little resemblance to the Jeffersonian ideal
of personal independence and spiritual
fulfillment on the farm.[1] Instead, women
often found hard work and frustration
there, and much of their discontent lay in
the knowledge that their work was undervalued and unnecessarily difficult. Under a
gendered work system in which men were
primarily responsible for performing cash-
producing field work, women's labor in the
farmhouse, vegetable garden, and poultry
house was viewed as secondary. As the
comments of this farm woman suggest, one
indication of the subordinate status accorded farm women's labor was farm families' lack of capital investment in the
equipment that women used. By 1913,
technology existed that would ease farm
women's labor, but most women did not yet
possess the appropriate equipment. Farm
women's dissatisfaction with their work
lives was compounded by the fact that they
had intimate contact with persons who did
make use of modern equipment—male
family members. Farm women's discontent
with existing gender hierarchies, therefore,
readily entered into the Progressive Era
debate on the modernization of American
agriculture. In their comments to government officials and farm editors, women
called for greater recognition of their labor
and economic contribution, to be acknowl-

To "Lessen Her Heavy Burdens"

The Country Life Movement and the Smith-Lever Act

*In many homes, life on the
farm is a somewhat one-sided
affair. Many times the spare
money above living expenses is
expended on costly machinery
and farm implements to make
the farmer's work lighter . . .
while little or nothing is done
for home improvement and no
provision made for the comfort
and convenience of the women
in the family.—Kansas farm
woman (1913)*

edged by a fairer investment in the equipment they used to perform their labor.

In 1913, America was an increasingly urban society that nevertheless subscribed to what historian Richard Hofstadter referred to as the "agrarian myth"—the idea that life on the farm represented the ideal American experience. In the early twentieth century, many American leaders still believed that only in Thomas Jefferson's "nation of farmers" could the American virtues of independence and self-sufficiency thrive and prosper. Ignoring the reality that even in Jefferson's own time American farmers had been dependent upon commercial markets, twentieth-century adherents to the agrarian myth harkened back to a time of rural independence and self-fulfillment. At a time when the nation's native-born leadership worried about the influx of foreign immigrants into overcrowded, politically corrupt American cities, the vision of an ideal, rural American past was especially appealing. The idea that the federal government should be particularly concerned about the status of American agriculture and rural life was not new in the early twentieth century, but it took on a heightened sense of importance during this era of Progressive politics.[2]

Progressive reformers were concerned about improving the quality of rural life, believing that a stable rural society lay at the base of a successful America. They believed that a more efficient agriculture, employing fair and sound business principles, would benefit the nation's growing urban population. These reformers equated more efficient agriculture with cheaper food prices for the urban masses. They also hoped that by making farm life more prosperous and attractive for America's farm families, they could help stem the tide of continued rural-to-urban migration, which threatened to compound urban problems of unemployment and inadequate housing.[3]

With these concerns in mind, President Roosevelt appointed his Commission on Country Life to investigate the means by which Progressive goals might be met in America's countryside. In creating his commission, Roosevelt affirmed his belief in the agrarian myth and argued that America's greatness was "based on the well-being of the great farmer class . . . for it is upon their welfare, material and moral, that the welfare of the rest of the nation ultimately rests."[4]

The seven-member commission presented its report to Roosevelt in January 1909. Ironically, the commission argued that one way to improve rural life was to make it more like urban life. The commission suggested that the citizens of rural America emulate urban dwellers by becoming more reliant on the use of modern technology, in the form of mechanized equipment to perform their daily labor and to communicate with the world beyond the farm. According to this view, adoption of steam- and gasoline-powered field equipment, gasoline- and electric-powered household appliances, telephones, and automobiles would lead to a more efficient, prosperous, and stable rural society.[5]

Commission members noted that farm women particularly considered their work to be unduly difficult and were generally less satisfied with farm life than were farm men. Arguing that "the success of country life depends in very large degree on the woman's part," the commission recommended that the mechanization of farm women's housework keep pace with that of men's field work and suggested that women would also benefit from improvements in rural roads and telephone communication. With such technological improvements, argued the commission, farm women would be more satisfied with farm life and would contribute to the prosperity and stability of life in the American countryside.[6]

In recommending that farm women adopt modern domestic and communication equipment, such as washing machines, modern cooking ranges, electric lighting, indoor plumbing systems, and telephones, commission members were in essence suggesting that farm women adopt the standards and equipment of middle-class urban women. Commission members, who were themselves male and primarily members of the urban upper middle class, evidently believed that the role of the urban middle-class housewife was appropriate for all women. In this regard, they resembled Progressives who encouraged urban immigrant women to adopt the housekeeping standards of the native-born middle class. Like many middle-class settlement house workers, the members of the Commission on Country Life, who had little regular contact with the nation's farm women, apparently did not realize the extent to which their recommendations ignored the cultural and economic realities of the women they were attempting to aid.[7]

Commission members stated that the "routine work of women on the farm [was] to prepare three meals a day."[8] In reality, farm women's responsibilities were much more diverse. While the farm man worked in the fields, the farm woman cooked, cleaned, and washed and mended clothing not only for family members but for hired help. She also preserved meat, baked bread and pastry, churned butter, tended the garden, canned fruits and vegetables, raised chickens, and periodically worked in the fields herself. It was also largely her responsibility to market surplus dairy, garden, and poultry products. In addition to these duties, she reproduced the farm family work unit, maintaining a higher birthrate than did women in American cities. The diversity of her work and the importance of her role as farm producer made her situation significantly different from that of the middle-class, urban housewife, whose work primarily centered on the care and supervision of her own family members.

While commission members failed to acknowledge the diversity of farm women's domestic, economic, and productive responsibilities, they did recognize that women could not achieve the goal of mechanized housekeeping without at least a limited restructuring of rural society. In other words, farm women could not become more like urban housewives without what commission members referred to as "a general elevation of country living," to be accomplished by a national education program "designed to forward not only the business of agriculture, but sanitation, education, home-making, and all interests of country life."[9]

Out of the commission's recommendations emerged the Country Life Movement, the rural arm of American Progressivism. Its goals were twofold. One was to make the business of American agriculture more efficient by encouraging farmers to rely more heavily on mechanized equipment and scientific farming methods. Reformers referred to this modern agrarian ideal as the New Agriculture. Under this system of mechanized farming, fewer family members would be required to perform physical labor on the farm. Farm women, therefore, would become more like urban, middle-class housewives, with their work taking place primarily within the home. Advocates of the New Agriculture envisioned farm women making the transition from a producer role to one that was more consumer oriented. In this role, women would increasingly acquire new pieces of domestic equipment until they had achieved technological parity not only with farm men but also with urban women. Freed from long work hours by the adoption of labor-saving technology, farm women could then aid the Country Life Movement in meeting its second goal—the "elevation" of rural society through the improvement of rural churches, schools, health care facilities, voluntary organizations, and family life. Reformers believed that by strengthening farm business practices and revitalizing rural institutions, farm people would remain on the land and thus ensure that the American value system would continue to be based on the successful practice of agriculture and rural living.[10]

Among the most visible proponents of the agrarian myth, the New Agriculture, and the Country Life Movement were a number of midwestern editors and journalists.[11] Their arguments on behalf of rural reform, including altering the condition of American farm women, often played to large audiences. For example, in a 1913 article appearing in a popular national women's magazine, *Good Housekeeping*, Iowa novelist and journalist Herbert Quick labeled rural-to-urban migration "largely a woman movement" and maintained that farm families would only remain on the land if they adopted equipment that would end women's drudgery. According to Quick, any farm family that could justify mechanized field and barn equipment—such as self-feeders for the cattle, pumping engines to provide water for the livestock, and mechanical corn shredders—could "afford every modern convenience for making the home a good place for a woman to live, work, rear children, and develop in her the love for farm life."[12] Likewise, the "most prominent agricultural editor of the Middle West," Henry Wallace of the Des Moines–based *Wallaces' Farmer*, frequently published editorials that promoted the mechanization of farm women's work.[13] Wallace, a member of Roosevelt's Commission on Country Life, largely encouraged the mechanization of women's work as a means toward keeping families on the farm. In the words of a 1914 *Wallaces' Farmer* editorial on farm home modernization, "Until we make life on the farm satisfying to the farmer's wife, we will labor in vain to check the drift of rural population to the towns and cities."[14]

At the time that Quick and Wallace presented such arguments, agricultural production was a significant component of midwestern life. With the exception of Michigan and Ohio, midwestern states still found their economies heavily reliant on agriculture. From the humid prairies of Indiana, Illinois, Iowa, Minnesota, Missouri, and Wisconsin across the ninety-eighth meridian to the dry plains of Kansas, Nebraska, and North and South Dakota, agriculture remained the primary enterprise. Family-operated general grain and livestock farms dominated the agriculture of this ten-state region, with significant specialization occurring only in Wisconsin and Minnesota dairy operations and on Dakota wheat farms. Corn was still the major cash crop in every state except North Dakota, where wheat had already begun to dominate. Average farm size ranged from approximately 100 acres in humid Indiana, where Euro-Americans had been farming for four generations, to well over 300 acres in dry North Dakota, where white farmers had begun settling only at the end of the nineteenth century (see Table 1.1).[15]

The population of the midwestern Farm Belt was overwhelmingly white and native-born, although in Minnesota and North Dakota immigrant farmers made up slight majorities. Germans dominated the immigrant population in every state except North Dakota, where Norwegians predominated. Native

Table 1.1 Average Farm Size, 1910

Illinois	129.1 acres
Indiana	98.8 acres
Iowa	156.3 acres
Kansas	244.0 acres
Minnesota	177.3 acres
Missouri	124.8 acres
Nebraska	297.8 acres
North Dakota	382.3 acres
South Dakota	335.1 acres
Wisconsin	118.9 acres

Source: U.S. Bureau of the Census, *Thirteenth Census of the United States, 1910: Agriculture* (Washington: Government Printing Office, 1913).

Americans were the major ethnic minority in rural North and South Dakota and in rural Minnesota and Wisconsin, although they made up less than 1 percent of the rural population in each of the latter two states. African Americans were the major ethnic minority in rural areas of the remaining states, although they made up considerably less than 2 percent of the rural population in every state except the border state of Missouri (see Tables 1.2 and 1.3).

The female population of this ten-state region was overwhelmingly white and predominantly rural (see Tables 1.4 and 1.5). Possibly reflecting Herbert Quick's assessment of women's antipathy toward the countryside, the ratio of men to women was significantly skewed throughout the rural areas of each state. Perhaps reflecting its recent frontier status, North Dakota had the highest ratio of men to women in rural areas: 123.2 males to 100 females. Indiana had the lowest ratio of rural males to rural females, with 106.8 males to 100 females (see Table 1.6). Because of the relative scarcity of women in the countryside, the lack of economic opportunities for single women in rural areas, and the existence of a gendered family labor system that demanded the presence of an adult woman on each farm, most women living in rural areas were married. Although independent women farmers in the mold of Willa Cather's Alexandra Bergson existed in the Midwest, they were a distinct minority and, like Cather's heroine, were viewed by their society as an oddity.[16] Rural women were more likely to be married than were members of any other population group in the Midwest (see Table 1.7).

Table 1.2 Ethnicity of All Rural Residents, 1910

	Native-born White (%)	Immigrant White (%)	African American (%)	Native American (%)
Illinois	89.4	9.5	1.1	*
Indiana	96.1	3.1	0.8	*
Iowa	87.8	11.8	0.3	*
Kansas	90.2	8.2	1.5	*
Minnesota	74.9	24.3	*	0.7
Missouri	94.3	2.9	2.8	*
Nebraska	86.0	13.5	0.1	*
North Dakota	71.3	27.4	0.1	1.2
South Dakota	78.8	17.4	0.1	3.8
Wisconsin	80.0	19.2	0.1	0.7

Source: U.S. Bureau of the Census, *Thirteenth Census of the United States, 1910: Population* (Washington: Government Printing Office, 1913).
*Statistically insignificant.

Table 1.3 Ethnicity of Farm Operators, 1910

	Native-born White (%)	Immigrant White (%)	Nonwhite (%)
Illinois	86.2	13.3	0.6
Indiana	95.1	4.5	0.4
Iowa	77.3	22.6	0.1
Kansas	84.5	14.5	1.0
Minnesota	47.9	52.0	0.2
Missouri	93.5	5.2	1.3
Nebraska	72.1	27.5	0.4
North Dakota	48.1	50.9	1.0
South Dakota	63.6	32.8	3.6
Wisconsin	60.5	39.2	0.3

Source: U.S. Bureau of the Census, *Thirteenth Census of the United States, 1910: Agriculture* (Washington: Government Printing Office, 1913).

Table 1.4 Ethnicity of Female Population, 1910

	White (%)	African American (%)	Native American (%)
Illinois	98.1	0.02	*
Indiana	98.0	0.02	*
Iowa	99.3	0.01	*
Kansas	97.0	0.03	*
Minnesota	99.2	*	*
Missouri	95.2	0.05	*
Nebraska	99.1	0.01	*
North Dakota	99.0	*	0.01
South Dakota	96.3	*	0.04
Wisconsin	99.4	*	*

Source: U.S. Bureau of the Census, *Thirteenth Census of the United States, 1910: Population* (Washington: Government Printing Office, 1913).
*Statistically insignificant.

Table 1.5 Place of Residence of Female Population, 1910

	Urban Areas (%)	Rural Areas (%)
Illinois	62.2	37.8
Indiana	43.0	57.1
Iowa	31.5	68.5
Kansas	30.3	69.6
Minnesota	41.4	58.6
Missouri	43.3	56.7
Nebraska	26.7	73.3
North Dakota	11.3	88.7
South Dakota	13.5	86.5
Wisconsin	44.2	55.7

Source: U.S. Bureau of the Census, *Thirteenth Census of the United States, 1910: Population* (Washington: Government Printing Office, 1913).

Table 1.6 Male to Female Ratio, 1910 (number of males per 100 females)

	State as a Whole	Rural Areas
Illinois	106.8	109.9
Indiana	105.0	106.8
Iowa	106.6	109.5
Kansas	110.0	113.5
Minnesota	114.6	116.1
Missouri	105.1	108.0
Nebraska	111.2	113.0
North Dakota	122.4	123.2
South Dakota	118.9	119.7
Wisconsin	107.4	111.9

Source: U.S. Bureau of the Census, *Thirteenth Census of the United States, 1910: Population* (Washington: Government Printing Office, 1913).

Table 1.7 Marital Status, 1910 (percentage of population age 15 and older who were married at time of census)

	Urban Men	Urban Women	Rural Men	Rural Women
Illinois	54.7	56.2	56.1	62.8
Indiana	58.9	59.1	60.4	65.0
Iowa	55.7	55.5	55.9	62.4
Kansas	58.6	60.2	56.1	65.4
Minnesota	46.9	52.3	49.5	59.5
Missouri	54.5	55.0	58.8	64.7
Nebraska	52.8	56.3	54.8	64.3
North Dakota	45.9	53.2	48.9	65.0
South Dakota	50.6	57.0	50.3	64.1
Wisconsin	54.7	54.3	52.8	60.7

Source: U.S. Bureau of the Census, *Thirteenth Census of the United States, 1910: Population* (Washington: Government Printing Office, 1913).

The midwestern women whom Country Life reformers most wanted to reach were those of the white, native-born middle class. Unlike members of other ethnic groups, native-born white women were potentially capable of becoming full-time homemakers on industrialized farms. European immigrant women were less likely to do so because they were often members of ethno-religious communities that resisted the entrepreneurial focus of the New Agriculture. Members of immigrant communities tended to view farming not as a business but as a traditional way of life that was to be passed on to their children. For these women, maintenance of the family farm and a rural way of life frequently necessitated their active involvement in farm production. Likewise, Native American women were rarely the targets of New Agriculture propaganda because their families had largely abandoned the system of private land ownership that had been urged upon them by the Dawes Act of 1887. Lacking capital to invest in farming supplies and finding Euro-American agricultural practices unfamiliar and culturally unsuitable, Native Americans in the Midwest frequently chose instead to lease their government land allotments to white farmers. African American women were also inappropriate recipients of propaganda that promoted modernized agriculture and homemaking. Sharecropping women in Missouri, members of the Nicodemus exoduster community in Kansas, and black farm women elsewhere in the Midwest generally lacked the income to spend on technological improvements. Native-born white women, however, could possibly have the resources and desire to acquire mechanical devices.[17]

Native-born white women in the rural Midwest were a highly literate group (see Table 1.8), a fact reflected in the large number of letters and diaries that they left to historians.[18] Discussion of farm and household technology is prominent in the written sources that these women left behind, including the letters that they addressed to Woodrow Wilson's secretary of agriculture, David F. Houston, in 1913.[19]

Recognizing "that problems that the farm woman [was] interested in ha[d] been in no little measure neglected," Houston, a supporter of the Country Life Movement, believed that the federal government should intervene to upgrade farm women's working and living conditions. Although a skeptical observer of feminist politics, Houston did believe that farm women themselves should have a voice in determining U.S. Department of Agriculture (USDA) policies that would affect them. In October 1913, Houston sent letters to the wives of USDA volunteer crop correspondents in an attempt to receive feedback from women who were supposedly the best-informed members of their farming communities. These women were predominantly white, middle class, and native-born. Houston asked them to comment on farm women's concerns and how the federal government might respond to those problems. The secretary requested that respondents submit descriptive let-

Table 1.8 Illiteracy, 1910 (percentage of population
age 10 and older who were illiterate)

	General Population	Rural White Females*
Illinois	3.7	2.0
Indiana	3.1	2.5
Iowa	1.7	0.7
Kansas	2.2	0.9
Minnesota	3.0	0.6
Missouri	4.3	4.0
Nebraska	1.9	0.6
North Dakota	3.1	0.6
South Dakota	2.9	0.3
Wisconsin	3.2	1.0

Source: U.S. Bureau of the Census, *Thirteenth Census of the United States, 1910:*
Population (Washington: Government Printing Office, 1913).
*White women who were born in the United States.

ters about their experiences as farm women and also include information on
the opinions of their neighbors and acquaintances in women's clubs, farm
organizations, and churches. Based on the 2,241 replies that Houston received from women throughout the country, the U.S. Department of Agriculture began publishing its summaries of the survey results in 1915.[20]

Superficially, midwestern farm women seemed to complain chiefly that
their work was undermechanized. At a time when men increasingly employed
steam- or gasoline-powered equipment, including the newly available gasoline tractor, most midwestern farm women relied on their own physical labor
to perform their daily tasks.[21] They attributed this situation in part to men's
failure to recognize the economic importance of farm women's work and
women's desire for improved domestic and communication technology. One
of their chief complaints was that farmhouses frequently lacked a safe, convenient water supply. Although women expressed concern about health and
hygiene, their main reason for wanting modern plumbing was a desire to
reduce their own work load. Embedded in their comments about a convenient
water supply were complaints about men's indifference to this issue. One
Kansas woman asserted that farm husbands frequently located wells for the
convenience of their livestock rather than that of their wives. According to

her, farm women often had to haul water 100 to 200 yards from the barnyard into the farm home. Another Kansas woman described the plight of farm women, and male indifference, in dramatic language:

> Oh, the weary arms that pump water, carry it down step[s], around the corner, up two steps, through two doors, giving the pail a final hoist to a high shelf, table, or sink. Then the water must be carried out. Few men can see a slop pail. The same arms carry a larger pail, its weight enhanced with floating peelings and kitchen refuse, carry it down the same steps, around the corner, and 4 rods through mud to the pigpen, handily arranged for a lift over a stock fence.[22]

Arid conditions on the Kansas plains further magnified the farm woman's work load in terms of the dust problem that existed there even before the "Dirty Thirties." Without electric vacuum cleaners or an adequate water supply, women's task of keeping the farm home clean was severely hampered. One woman's response to the 1913 survey provides a graphic and insightful picture of the problem:

> I am going to write of the women [sic] of western Kansas. Her greatest difficulty and hardest work and least profit comes with the dust that seeps over this region and that every high wind drives into every crack and crevice and that penetrates everywhere. Cleaning may be thorough and next day may fill the house from cellar to attic with the fine dirt that continues to sift everywhere. Food is ruined, beds are filled with the choking dust, and the walls and ceiling so loaded that a thorough cleaning is necessary, and it may be just completed when another dust storm is on and the house be filled as bad as ever. . . . Too much stirring of the surface soil during dry times seems to be the chief cause, and the remedy will have to be in direct opposition to the cause. Less plowing in dry times and more moisture on the surface of our country . . . [are] the greatest need[s] just now.[23]

As these comments suggest, the farm woman's recognition of her own labor needs often led to criticism of male behavior—in this case, existing farming practices. Criticism of male indifference to women's water procurement problems was not limited to the remarks of women on the arid plains, as the comments of a Minnesota woman indicate:

> This summer a neighbor dug a large cistern. The mother wanted the pump put in the kitchen; but the son (and he was a good boy) said, "With

the separator and everything in there this winter there would not be room for the pump," so it was put outside, and the mother has to run out and get the water, and it will freeze and be of no use during the winter. That boy should be educated to look at things differently and that mother should be educated to demand her rights.[24]

Many of the survey respondents suggested that the federal government support an educational program that would teach farm families the importance of using new equipment to aid women in their work. Others suggested that the federal government intervene by providing farm people with inexpensive electric power that could, in the words of a Wisconsin woman, "furnish lights and do away with so much work cleaning lamps and lanterns and also to furnish motor power to run the washing machine, the vacuum cleaner, and to pump water and air into the pressure tank."[25]

According to many respondents, electricity would solve numerous labor problems on the farm, including problems of water procurement. With an electric pumping system, farm homes could enjoy the advantages of running water. As a Kansas farm woman argued:

The thing [the farm woman] needs in this day and time is electricity. Then when her house is lighted, her cream separated and churned, her washing, ironing, and sweeping, her sewing machine run by the same power, and she relieved from the drudgery of washing and filling lamps, lifting and washing jars, pans, and all these other hard old things, she can have some time for a social life and the improvement of her mind. The only way I can see is for the Government to furnish, at a reasonable price, electricity to every farm.[26]

Other respondents looked to the federal government for aid in improving rural roads. More than one respondent suggested that federal money spent on construction of the Panama Canal would have been better invested in the improvement of rural roads. Most respondents suggested that improved transportation would not lead farm women away from the farm but would instead make them more content with staying in the countryside. Women not only commented on the need for improved roads but also expressed their desire for inexpensive automobiles. Henry Ford's Model T, introduced five years earlier, would revolutionize transportation in the countryside during the next decade. In 1913, however, the price of a Model T had not yet fallen into an affordable range for many farm families. An Iowa woman commented, "I long for an auto cheap enough to be available and simple in construction. . . . I would have the country women [sic] get away from home more that she may be glad to get back and realize her blessings." In other words, access to an automobile would allow women some recreational time away from the farm and thus make their daily work there more bearable. A Missouri mother of six daughters perhaps best expressed the desire for better roads and inexpensive automobiles: "Why, when we get good roads we can buy an automobile as we did our piano—on the installment plan—and raise turkeys and poultry to pay for it, and one of my girls can drive it; then nothing is far."[27]

Another general theme among the survey responses was a call for cooperative efforts in farm neighborhoods. Cooperation, suggested by members of Roosevelt's Commission on Country Life as a possible cure for the economic ills of the countryside, became a cornerstone of the Country Life Movement's program for rural reform—even in the face of reformers' reverence for rural "independence." Many respondents to the USDA survey apparently agreed that cooperation was the key to easing farm women's work and called on the government to encourage the establishment of cooperative dairies, bakeries, canneries, and hatcheries and cooperative efforts in butchering and house-cleaning. A Wisconsin woman suggested that members of rural neighborhoods collectively "invest in a vacuum cleaner and go around each spring and fall and clean the homes; it would be another saving of work."[28]

The most frequently mentioned cooperative innovation, however, was the cooperative laundry. Many respondents agreed with a Minnesota woman's assessment of farm women's work: "I have always lived on a farm except the first five years of my marriage, and I think I might almost as soon have been in jail, because the work is so hard and is never done. The hardest is the washing."[29] Several respondents recommended the elimination of privatized laundry work by establishing cooperative laundries in conjunction with existing creameries. In Wisconsin and Minnesota, farm families did successfully organize cooperative laundries on this model. A Wisconsin woman suggested that cooperative bakeries could also be established along with creamery and laundry facilities: "Three heavy tasks would thus be taken out of the home, as I think, to the advantage of family life in the country. The women would have more time to work out of doors, to garden, to beautify the yard, and to build up a better social atmosphere in the community."[30]

As expressed in responses to the Department of Agriculture's 1913 survey, women's dissatisfaction with farm life seemingly centered around their use of outdated equipment. In arguing for improvement of rural women's technology, farm women themselves pointed out that easing women's work would benefit both women and, perhaps more important, the larger society. Not only would women who used modern equipment be more productive members of the farm labor force, but they would also be able to devote additional time to the supervision of their families and the improvement of their communities. Of course, in editing responses for publication, Department of Agriculture writers chose those comments that best represented the department's own position—a position firmly in line with that of the Country Life Movement. In his annual report for 1913, Secretary Houston outlined the department's position on farm women: "The woman on the farm is a most important economic factor in agriculture. . . . On her rests largely the moral and mental development of the children, and on her attitude depends in great part the important question of whether the succeeding generation will continue to farm or will seek the allurements of life in the cities."[31]

Echoing reformers who a century earlier had argued that the new American republic required educated mothers who would school their sons in the ways of self-government, Houston believed that the New Agriculture required well-informed farm wives and mothers who could persuade their families to adopt the ways of modern farm life. In a December 1913 address to farm boys and girls, Houston went so far as to state that Department of Agriculture educational programs should be targeted primarily at women; he reasoned, "While many educated men might tolerate an uneducated woman, I think very few educated women would tolerate for a long time an uneducated man. There is not much danger of the boys being uneducated if the mothers are educated."[32]

Throughout the waning months of 1913, USDA policymakers debated the form that an educational program aimed at farm women might take. In the same month that Houston sent out his letters requesting information from farm women, Department of Agriculture researcher Dr. C. F. Langworthy had sent an outline of the department's proposed program for farm women to various high-ranking officials within the USDA. The October 1913 report stressed the use of traveling female teachers who would use automobiles to visit farm women in their communities and conduct lessons in improved food preparation, home money-making projects, and more efficient work methods. The key to farm women's successful implementation of many of the lessons they would learn, however, lay in their adoption of new technology. A major task of Langworthy's traveling teachers, therefore, would be to urge the adoption of such equipment. According to Langworthy, "Perhaps nothing would help so much to make the homes in rural regions . . . more comfortable and pleasant and better workshops, as adequate light, water, heating and cooking devices, and convenient household equipment."[33]

Langworthy's emphasis on technology, reinforced by the results of Houston's survey of farm women, ensured that the modernization of farm women's work would be a central feature of the Department of Agriculture's educational extension program for women established under the Smith-Lever Act of 1914. The Smith-Lever Act created a voluntary system through which the federal government provided matching funds on the basis of rural population to states and counties that desired the services of county farm and home demonstration agents. The Department of Agriculture and the nation's agricultural colleges would cooperatively carry out the work of this newly created national Agricultural and Home Economics Extension Service. By dividing extension services into two categories—farm work and housework—the Smith-Lever Act promoted the idea of separate spheres on American farms, with men's work taking place out of doors and women's work being performed in the house.

The Smith-Lever Act did not invent the concept of extension services to farm families. The state agricultural colleges created by the Morrill Land-Grant Act of 1862 had begun providing farm families with advice on farming techniques and equipment during the latter decades of the nineteenth century. These so-called land-grant colleges had also begun developing home economics departments in the nineteenth century; the State College of Iowa established a home economics program in 1869, and the Kansas State Agricultural College followed suit in 1873. College home economics courses began in Illinois in the 1870s and in South Dakota in 1890. By 1905, almost all of the nation's land-grant colleges had established home economics departments, and some of them had begun small-scale efforts at extension work in the farmhouse. An early focus of these fledgling extension programs was promoting the use of modern household equipment.[34]

Before passage of the Smith-Lever Act, extension work had been supported by limited funds from state and local organizations, private foundations, public-spirited individuals, and commercial institutions—such as Sears, Roebuck and Company and International Harvester—that sold mechanized equipment and wanted to promote its use on American farms.[35] By providing for federal financial support, the Smith-Lever Act expanded existing extension services, including services aimed at farm women. In a speech to Congress before passage of the bill, Asbury F. Lever of South Carolina, chairman of the House Committee on Agriculture and cosponsor of the bill, commented on the significance of the Smith-Lever bill for farm women:

> Our efforts heretofore have been given in aid of the farm man, his horses, cattle, and hogs, but his wife and girls have been neglected almost to a point of criminality. This bill provides the authority and the funds for inaugurating a system of teaching the farm wife and farm girl the elementary principles of home making and home management, and your committee believes there is not more important work in the country than is this.[36]

As Lever's comments indicate, the federally supported Extension Service would not seek to upset the existing gender hierarchy on American farms. Lever stated that Extension Service programs would provide aid to the farm woman and "lessen her heavy burdens" not only for her own sake but also because, in her subordinate role in the farm family, she exerted some "influence upon rural life." While previously the federal government had directed its attention to the farm man and *his* livestock, now the government would also attend to *his* wife and *his* daughter. In bettering the lives of farm women, the Extension Service would thus improve the overall quality and efficiency of patriarchal farm life in the nation's rural counties.[37]

Officials' creation of this agenda was based on a flawed use of the evidence before them. First, they treated the women who wrote to Houston as spokespersons for all farm women. In selecting women who were married to volunteer crop correspondents, however, Houston ensured that he would receive responses from women whose families had already accepted—but perhaps not yet achieved—the progressive farming ideal. Women from families who held an alternative point of view were not represented in the sample. With their primary focus on the native-born middle class, USDA officials made no attempt to solicit the opinions of women who did not fit the desired demographic profile. Absent from the sample, for instance, were immigrant women whose families wanted to maintain traditional practices on the family farm.[38]

USDA officials based their agenda not only on the responses of an elite segment of the rural population but also on a selective reading of those responses. As women's letters suggested in their criticism of male behavior, their desire for new equipment often went beyond simply wanting to ease the performance of their daily household chores. While male reformers like Quick, Wallace, Houston, and Lever saw farm women's acquisition of new technology as a way to increase their satisfaction with farm life by making them more like urban housewives, some midwestern farm women viewed it as part of a larger restructuring of their existing role on the farm. Even though responses to the 1913 survey exist only in edited form, their frequent challenge to the patriarchal nature of midwestern farm life remains apparent.[39]

In his study of the Country Life Movement, historian David Danbom acknowledges that the women who wrote to Houston did not enjoy independence—the "rural trait" so admired by Country Life reformers—but argues that because adult farm women "had grown up in families like those they formed, rural women probably viewed male domination as normal, and perhaps as correct." Certainly, many of the women who criticized male behavior in their responses to Houston did not find fault with patriarchy itself but rather with the failure of men to live up to their patriarchal responsibilities of economic support and physical protection. On the other hand, a number of the women who wrote to Houston were critical of rural patriarchy.[40]

For these women, Houston's survey served as a forum to comment on patriarchal control. When a Minnesota woman wrote of her neighbor's attempt to have her son locate a pump in the kitchen, the letter writer's focus was less on the need for a pump than on the need for women's greater control over their own tools and labor. When another woman complained about the difficulty of her laundry work and compared her life on the farm to life in jail, her concern centered less on upgrading her laundry equipment than on improving her status within the farm family. Although these women wanted equipment that would ease their work, few of them expressed a desire to abandon their traditional tasks entirely and instead engage in full-time, mechanized homemaking. In fact, when discussing acquisition of the equipment they wanted, many of these women proudly spoke of stepping up their efforts at poultry raising and gardening in order to afford modern machinery. For the most part, they desired that the effort they put into their work on the farm be better recognized by a fairer investment in the equipment they used to perform that labor. They did not want to relinquish their role in farm production; they wanted a larger voice in determining the priorities of the farm family work unit. This argument was expressed in the year following passage of the Smith-Lever Act by a Nebraska woman who forcefully reminded Secretary Houston that women's call for new equipment often represented their desire to alter family politics.[41]

In 1915, Minnie Boyer Davis of Holt County, Nebraska, lived in a sod house 30 miles from the nearest railroad. Here, the former Iowan raised her son and daughter, cared for hired men, cooked, cleaned, sewed, gardened, and periodically worked in the fields. Davis, who characterized herself as a "good deal of a radical," also earned cash by writing articles for a number of farm periodicals. In "a moment of despondency," this middle-aged farm woman took time to write down her thoughts about life on the farm and send them to Secretary Houston, asking him to "give recognition to the original agriculturalist, the farm woman."[42]

According to Davis, the letters that Houston had received "from women all over the country tell the story, not complaint of work or lack of conveniences, but of *unequal status*." In her opinion, the greatest service Houston could perform for farm women would be to support women's suffrage. In asking for vacuum cleaners and bathtubs in the farmhouse, she reasoned, women were really asking for greater power and influence within the farm family and the rural community. Davis's remarkable letter emphasized many of the themes presented in the responses to Houston's survey. Davis wrote of her skills as a farm producer and stressed the importance of her contributions to the family economy. She wrote of hard work, lack of a social life, the struggle to educate her children, and her displeasure at having to care for "ignorant coarse hired men." Such conditions, however, were not the result of outdated technology but of outdated politics. Until women challenged the patriarchal system that lay behind their lack of modern technology, their lives would remain difficult:

> On the farm man's law is supreme. Woman's influence is exerted over dirt, drudgery, calves, small children, rents and tears in clothing, cabbage worms and the conversion of raw products into manufactures. When there are beans to pick or thresh, with the garden, the chickens, or at butchering time, or when enormous amounts of cooking are to be done, then I am not asked to keep out of it. I do not want to leave any work undone that I now do but I have a very large share in making our land what it is, and I have a right to be something more than a drudge. And that is what women are when they do nothing but work, work, work, from year's end to year's end.[43]

Davis's letter ended with a skeptical assessment of the Smith-Lever Act, a discussion of her belief in the agrarian myth—and women's exclusion from it—and a final call for the dismantling of rural patriarchy:

> I see no ray of hope or promise of help from that Smith-Lever bill. . . . I do not want any visiting nurse, or economist from the state university. I do not need any more bulletins than those already published. . . . The

greatest thing for the improvement of farm life is the elevation of women to an equal status. Never until she is counted as a citizen of the state, the peer of any, her opinion and influence counted as one, expressed by herself, never until she has the *ballot* will she have that equality in the home which makes for the best home life. You do not see women flocking from city farmward, but on every hand I see women leaving the farms and many others demanding to go. And when they cannot go themselves they help the children to go. I can write up many pounds of good paper telling of the beauties of farm life—and it is true too, but the women's part—that is another story. . . . Is it a national question? I ask you is not our nation founded upon the prosperity of agriculture? Anything that concerns agriculture and farm women is a national question.[44]

Davis's letter to Houston demonstrates the optimism of the era's feminists in their belief that women's suffrage would logically result in a challenge to patriarchal control in all aspects of American society. Houston's own ambivalence on the suffrage issue indicates that he found this a foreign concept. Many of the other themes that Davis presented, though, were ones that Houston himself espoused: that the success of agriculture was key to the prosperity of the nation, that contented farm women were vital to the success of agriculture, and that the tide of rural-to-urban migration must be stemmed. Houston's response to Davis's letter, however, reaffirmed his own more conservative approach to the problems of farm women and reiterated his faith in the Smith-Lever Act:

Without entering into a discussion of the matter of woman's suffrage, I may say that some of the difficulties that you speak of are clearly incident to a somewhat sparsely settled community and others to the personal attitude of men which it is difficult to correct. . . . I am inclined to think that you underrate the possibilities under the Smith-Lever [A]ct. While it is true that the work for women . . . has not been well developed, the indications are that it will be expanded somewhat rapidly from now on. . . . I deeply sympathize with the difficulties you labor under, and while I recognize that great changes can not be made quickly, I believe in time changes will come.[45]

With Houston at the helm of the USDA, then, programs to aid farm women did not attempt to challenge patriarchal control on the farm but instead emphasized "the devising and demonstrating of labor-saving machinery and methods for the farm housewife." Despite his pledge thereby to improve women's life on the farm, however, Houston reported that at the time of Minnie B. Davis's letter only 11.5 percent of the state and federal funds available for extension work under the Smith-Lever Act were going to projects aimed at improving women's access to modern technology. Although influential women's organizations, including the General Federation of Women's Clubs and the International Congress of Farm Women, urged the secretary and other officials to spend more money and effort on programs for farm women, women's extension work under the Smith-Lever Act was underfinanced and narrowly focused when the first midwestern home demonstration agent began her work in 1915.[46]

In order for a home demonstration agent to be assigned to a county, local women had to request her services, usually by a petition to the state agricultural college. The first home demonstration agent assigned to a midwestern county under the Smith-Lever Act, Eva Benefiel, began serving the women of Kankakee County, Illinois, on 1 July 1915. Fifteen hundred women in the county each pledged a dollar a year for three years to provide their county's share of the expenses to support home demonstration work in the area. In line with Henry Wallace's belief that farm women's work should be modernized, an editorial appearing in his periodical praised the women of Kankakee County and encouraged similar efforts throughout the Midwest: "We would very much like to hear of a county adviser for women in every county in which *Wallaces' Farmer* circulates. We are ready to give the movement a boost, but, mind you, only a boost. . . . We can only help; the women themselves must lead."[47]

The image of the home demonstration agent, however, even as set forth in the Extension Service's own literature, could be a troubling one to the farm women she was to serve. As an agricultural-college graduate and as a single woman, the agent differed greatly in educational background and marital status from most of her clientele. Perhaps more important, the home demonstration agent presented an image of technological and economic independence that was foreign to many of her would-be clients. Extension Service literature consistently emphasized that the "majority of the home demonstration agents use[d] automobiles for travel about the country" and noted that although home agents often traveled with male agricultural agents, the "most satisfactory arrangement [was] for the home demonstration agent to have an automobile for her exclusive use." This type of publicity appeared at a time when, according to the results of Houston's survey, many farm women desired but could not attain such freedom of movement about the countryside. Citing the supposed independence and attractive yearly salary of Kankakee County's Eva Benefiel, the *Wallaces' Farmer* editorialist commented: "We imagine we see the eyes of some of our farm girls snap when they think of the eighteen hundred dollars a year, and of the fun there would be in riding around in an automobile over the country."[48]

The reality of an agent's life and work contrasted with this image of a carefree "girl." Four years after the appearance of the *Wallaces' Farmer* editorial, only 3 percent of the home agents employed outside the South were under the age of twenty-five. Thirty-six percent were between twenty-five and thirty years of age, and the majority of agents, about 61 percent, were between the ages of thirty and forty-five. In appointing home agents, the Extension Service gave preference to applicants who were "familiar with rural home conditions." In most cases this meant women who themselves had grown up on farms or who at some other time had lived on a farm. The average salary of demonstration agents outside the South was $1,545 a year but could range as low as $1,140. Demonstration agents frequently encountered problems "in riding around in an automobile" and had to improvise with available technology. For example, when Florence Atwood became a home agent in Nebraska in 1919, the county agricultural agent taught her how to drive a car. Atwood obtained a Model T but could not crank it, so she and the county agent had to construct "some kind of starter" for the car.[49]

The image of home extension agents as impractical, overpaid, inexperienced young women, however, was one that many farm women held strongly. While historians have characterized *Wallaces' Farmer* in the 1910s as "well represent[ing] rural opinion in the Middle West," it represented a largely male perspective on midwestern farm life, as numerous critical letters from women readers demonstrate.[50] For example, in a letter to the editor published a month after the 1915 editorial supporting home demonstration work, a female reader argued that most Corn Belt farm women had no desire to take the lead in extension work. In criticizing the Smith-Lever Act, the reader expressed skepticism that college-educated single women would be capable of teaching appropriate homemaking practices to women who resided on farms. Among home agents' impractical suggestions, argued the reader, was the idea that every farm home should have modern appliances, no matter the cost. In the reader's words: "We don't . . . like the idea of having a woman come into our home and tell us we ought to have a gasoline engine to 'do' the washing, an oil stove to cook on, a fireless cooker, a bread mixer, water piped into our houses, a bath room, etc., for we are going to have these things as fast as we can afford it."[51]

The question of affordability loomed large at a time when USDA economists estimated that the average annual income for farm-owning families in the Corn Belt was $1,938. For tenant families, the average income was nearly half, $992. At the same time, a 10-horsepower gasoline engine cost $231, and the Sears catalog advertised its Ever Ready Pneumatic Water Supply Outfit for as much as $248. Other types of modern household equipment, though, fell within a more reasonable price range. For instance, an oil-powered cooking range cost from $11 to $21 in the mid-1910s. The strain of purchasing most types of household equipment on a limited income, however, caused many farm dwellers to be skeptical of Extension Service advice recommending farm home modernization.[52]

Resistance to home extension work, in fact, remained widespread until the wartime emergency of 1917–18, although little organized opposition ever took place. Resentment of outside intervention, concern over the cost of supporting extension work at the county level, and skepticism about household modernization faded under the wartime conditions of unusually high farm prices, fervent rural patriotism, and the expanded power of the federal government. The emphasis of home extension work during the war, however, was not on the acquisition of new household equipment but on increased food production and conservation for the war cause. Relying on federal war emergency funds, home extension services expanded rapidly during the war. In 1916–17, the total allotment of funds from all sources for home demonstration work across the nation was $741,680. That figure jumped to $2,226,228 in 1917–18. The number of counties nationwide employing home extension agents rose from 430 in 1916 to 1,715 in 1918. In the thirty-three states lying outside the South, the total number of county home demonstration agents rose from 4 in 1916 to 803 in 1918. In Iowa alone, the number of county home demonstration agents increased from 2 in the summer of 1917 to 99— 1 in every county in the state—by the summer of 1918. During that summer, the major focus of home extension work in Iowa was the saving of sugar and wheat. Home demonstration agents also emphasized the canning and drying of surplus vegetables. As a result, women in forty Iowa counties saved 3,646,623 pounds of sugar during the summer of 1918, women in forty-one counties saved 13,721,465 pounds of flour during that summer, and 35,558 people in fifty-two counties reported drying fruits and vegetables. In July 1918 alone, 88,426 Iowa women attended home demonstration meetings. In contrast, a total of only 4,000 Iowa women had attended such meetings during the entire 1914–17 period.[53]

Under government pressure to expand production, and with economic incentives to do so, farm families who had previously rejected Extension Service advice now sought the guidance of experts who could provide them with information on new farming and home production methods and technology. In other words, the war had brought extension agents "new respect and attention" from farm families.[54] The Extension Service thus achieved legitimacy among farm people during the First World War, but its basic aims had not changed. The Extension Service still sought to remake rural life in the image of urban, industrial America, and this goal remained a problematic one for farm women, as events in the postwar era would demonstrate.

Without emergency wartime funding and the impetus of wartime patriotism and economic incentives, extension services diminished following World War I. Total funds for the support of home demonstration work nationwide dropped from $2,889,210 in 1918–19 to $2,177,024 in 1919–20. The number of counties nationwide employing home extension agents fell from 1,715 in 1918 to 1,049 in 1919. The number of home demonstration agents employed in the thirty-three states outside the South declined from 803 in 1918 to 609 in 1919. Decreases in home extension services, however, affected primarily urban counties, where a commitment to such services had been viewed only as a temporary wartime measure, dependent upon federal emergency funds. In contrast, as a result of their wartime experiences with home demonstration work, farm women had grown more used to the presence of extension services, and agents remained in most rural counties, including counties throughout the midwestern Farm Belt. In 1919, home demonstration agents provided services to 2,132,699 people in states lying outside the South. In the year following the war, the Extension Service continued to promote efficient food preservation methods and provided women with instruction in other home production activities, including sewing, baking, and small carpentry projects. The Extension Service also renewed efforts to encourage women to modernize their homes by acquiring mechanized equipment—equipment that had been unavailable during the wartime emergency. Ironically, however, a drop in farm income following the war made it difficult for many farm families to purchase the equipment that extension agents and publications suggested.[55]

The experiences of midwestern wheat producers illustrate the general problems faced by American farmers in the post–World War I period. High farm prices had motivated many farmers to expand their wheat operations during the war. This expansion caused wheat producers to invest heavily in mechanized equipment—particularly gasoline tractors—to plant and harvest their additional acres, and it set off a period of major land speculation on the Great Plains. Within a few years, however, the wartime wheat boom had ended. By the summer of 1920, Europe had sufficiently recovered to resume its own production of wheat. In addition, the domestic market for wheat had decreased from its prewar size, owing in part to dietary changes that resulted from wartime restrictions on wheat products. Americans who had substituted other foods for bread during the war did not automatically revert to their old habits. As a result of these developments, wheat prices plummeted drastically. Land prices also fell. But farming costs—machinery, labor, taxes—remained high. In 1920, many farmers who had invested in mechanized equipment and additional acres during the war now found themselves heavily in debt, with little hope of soon remedying this situation.[56]

Wheat farming presents the most dramatic example of postwar decline, but livestock and corn farming in the Midwest met with similar problems. One reaction to this swift change of fortunes was the development of a greater emphasis among reformers on the rehabilitation of farm business practices. Although the goal of rural social reform did not disappear, its importance diminished as postwar conditions heightened the resolve of reformers to improve farm business. The decline of the Country Life reformers' parent movement, Progressivism, also contributed to the diminished emphasis on rural social reform. In the years following the war, government criticism of the excesses of industrial capitalism and their deleterious effect on American society became muted as government and business formed a new partnership in the 1920s. Many items on the Progressive reform agenda were thus abandoned. Warren G. Harding's call for a "return to normalcy" in the postwar era left less room for social criticism, or social engineering, in the city or in the countryside.[57]

Instead, government officials in the postwar era focused their attention on constructing managerial and bureaucratic institutions, based upon those that had arisen to meet the recent wartime emergency, that would enlist public and private policymakers in an "enlightened partnership" to deal with the nation's peacetime problems.[58] Within the Department of Agriculture, this meant the creation in the early 1920s of new institutions, including the Bureau of Agricultural Economics and the Bureau of Home Economics, designed to oversee the implementation of policies to improve farm business and homemaking practices. In the postwar era, then, bureaucrats assumed the goal of farm business reform that Country Life reformers promoted.[59] In the 1920s, these bureaucrats entered into an "enlightened partnership" with a new private organization—the American Farm Bureau.

Historian David Kennedy has characterized the formation of the American Farm Bureau in 1919 as possibly the best example of the postwar era's "newly articulate agrarian conservatism." Indeed, its formation resulted in part from the concern of USDA officials and large farmers that organizations such as the radical Non-Partisan League were gaining too much influence among American farmers, especially in the Midwest. It was also formed as an institution to oversee the organization of federally funded extension work. In essence, the bureau was a private organization composed primarily of prosperous owners of large farms, whose major goal was to improve the commercial interests of American farming. In meeting that goal, the organization supported most of the conservative causes of the 1920s. Among the resolutions passed at the organization's first conventions were ones condemning labor militancy, offering the bureau's aid in the government's drive "to rid the country of Bolshevism," and praising the American Legion as "one of the most important factors in the life of America."[60] Henry C. Wallace, who had inherited the editorship of *Wallaces' Farmer* from his father Henry, voiced the sentiments of most major farm reformers of the era when he hoped that the bureau would "not degenerate into an educational or social institution." He felt that it should be made "the most powerful business institution in the country."[61] In the 1920s, the business of farm reform was business.

The Farm Bureau quickly became the largest farm organization in the nation and one that carried great influence within the Department of Agriculture. By 1921, the bureau found itself in the advantageous position of having one of its major cheerleaders, Henry C. Wallace, serving as secretary of agriculture. Throughout the 1920s, bureau policies significantly influenced Department of Agriculture programs, including those that dealt with farm women. During this period, the bureau gave no attention to issues involving farm women's health, education, or economic status. Instead, Farm Bureau policies regarding women centered on making them into better homemakers. Again, the target population was primarily women of the white, native-born middle class.[62]

The difference between prewar and postwar reform efforts was subtle but significant. While in the prewar era the improvement of farm business had been a component of a larger program of rural reform, in the postwar era this goal often stood alone. Many officials within the USDA now viewed creation of an efficient, mechanized New Agriculture as an end in itself; they no longer viewed it as part of a general program of rural "uplift." For farm women, the goal remained to make them more like middle-class women in the city—the wives of urban businessmen—but this was now more likely to be a self-contained objective. It was less likely than in the prewar era to be viewed by reformers as part of a larger scheme of "uplift" for rural citizens. In the postwar era, reformers wanted women to become full-time modern home-makers and companions who created a domestic haven for farm businessmen. References to releasing women from drudgery, and lessening "their heavy burdens," often disappeared from the pages of USDA literature.

One example of officials' changed attitude toward farm women was a series of USDA reports issued in the early 1920s that softened the harsh image of farm women that the USDA itself had once promoted. In the early 1920s, USDA associate economist Emily F. Hoag solicited responses from "happy and forward-looking farm women" who would refute current "misrepresen-tations" of American farm life. Hoag interviewed "capable, optimistic" farm women around the country, and based on these interviews, and on her reading of several thousand letters that women had written to the St. Paul–based *Farmer's Wife* magazine, Hoag compiled a report that in many ways countered the image of farm life presented in the Commission on Country Life report and in D. F. Houston's survey of farm women. While acknowledg-ing that the complaints made by farm women in the 1913 survey had been valid a decade earlier, Hoag argued that in 1923, "with the movement for improvement of conditions well under way," farm women were no longer living under desperate circumstances. According to Hoag, however, the pub-lic perception of farm life lagged behind the reality of improved rural condi-tions. Hoag wrote her positive assessment, therefore, because, in her words, "farm people now resent characterization and cartooning as ignorant objects of misguided pity."[63]

Although Hoag personally interviewed women in at least one midwestern state, she based most of her discussion of midwestern farm women on information obtained from women's letters to the *Farmer's Wife*. In 1922, the magazine's editors had sponsored a contest that asked women to write letters answering the question "Do I want my daughter to marry a farmer?" The authors of the "best letters" received prizes and had their letters excerpted in the pages of the magazine. Given the nature of the project, most of the letters were positive in tone and answered the question affirmatively. Seventy-five

Table 1.9 Percentage of Farm Households with
Certain Types of Modern Equipment, 1923

	Automobiles	Telephones	Water Piped into House	Gas or Electricity
Illinois	52.9	73.2	11.2	9.8
Indiana	46.4	65.4	11.4	10.0
Iowa	73.1	86.1	15.9	15.3
Kansas	62.0	77.9	9.3	8.7
Minnesota	57.1	62.0	6.4	7.6
Missouri	30.9	62.2	4.5	5.5
Nebraska	75.6	76.4	16.6	9.7
North Dakota	56.6	46.8	6.0	5.8
South Dakota	69.4	59.4	12.3	8.6
Wisconsin	49.6	59.1	7.1	8.8

Source: Emily F. Hoag, "The Advantages of Farm Life: A Study by Correspondence and Interviews with Eight Thousand Farm Women" (1923), Manuscript File (1917–35), Records of the Bureau of Agricultural Economics, Record Group 83, National Archives, Washington, D.C.

percent of the women who wrote letters to the magazine were midwestern-ers. The vast majority of these midwestern letter writers were middle-aged women who were members of middle-income families that owned their own farms, which were primarily general grain and livestock operations. A large proportion of these women, 52 percent, had at least a high school education. Like the women who had responded to Houston's survey, these letter writers represented an elite group of farm women. Nevertheless, their work lives represented the typical experience of most midwestern farm women. Of those women who reported on daily work activities in their letters, 68 percent raised poultry and 41 percent raised gardens. Most of these midwestern farm women still lacked conveniences in their homes but did have access to modern communication equipment, a situation that they shared with the majority of midwestern farm residents (see Table 1.9). In fact, the letter writers cited lack of modern conveniences as their chief complaint about life in the farm home and considered "over work" the main disadvantage of their labor on the farm. Hoag, however, presented these complaints, which had loomed so large in government reports on farm life a decade earlier, as relatively minor inconveniences. In Hoag's report, the joys and challenges of farm life clearly outweighed the problems that resulted from long work hours and a lack of mechanized equipment.[64]

In contrast to the women quoted in reports on Houston's survey, the women quoted in Hoag's study spoke favorably of their life and labor in the midwestern countryside. The remarks of a Wisconsin woman were representative: "The very fact that many farm women are working calmly, patiently along, without moving pictures, fashions, electrical conveniences, and all modern improvements shows that they are deriving a certain other satisfaction from life. . . . We the farm woman [sic] are where we belong. I feel that this close-to-nature elemental existence, is the fullest, richest source of emotional satisfaction."[65]

Women's resentment of farm men's access to superior equipment also largely disappeared in the pages of Hoag's study. The women she quoted accepted the priority given to improvement of farm equipment as a necessary part of life on the farm. In the words of an Iowa woman, "Naturally, if the outbuildings are modernized, it enables the farmer to work faster and realize more capital with which to make further improvements. There's truth in the old saying: 'A barn can build a house sooner than a house can build a barn.' "[66]

Complaints about long work hours were also absent in the quotations that Hoag presented. Women quoted in the earlier reports had resented the fact that they frequently performed field work in addition to their daily household chores; Hoag now quoted an Illinois woman as saying she was "sorry for the woman who [did not] get a chance to help her husband once in a while." Women quoted in the Hoag report seemed to view their multiple tasks as a challenge and a way for farm women to display their varied talents. A frequent complaint among respondents to the 1913 survey had been the extra work that women were required to perform for non–family members, particularly for hired help. The women whom Hoag quoted, however, did not view these experiences negatively. One midwestern woman reported that she had cooked for fifteen to twenty hired hands on a regular basis and that last-minute dinner guests were never a problem because she "could get ready for extra people without any bother."[67]

Hoag's portrayal of farm women showed them as contented helpmates who, although they still lacked modern equipment, were patiently waiting for the day when technology would transform their lives. Like the Wisconsin woman who spoke glowingly of her "close-to-nature elemental existence," most of the women whom Hoag quoted apparently believed that women as well as men shared in the benefits of life on the farm. As historian Mary Neth has noted, Hoag's study presented a more accurate view of midwestern farm people than the stereotype of farm women as victimized drudges and farm men as selfish brutes. As Neth's own research demonstrates, men and women in a number of midwestern farm families developed systems of cooperation, reciprocity, and mutual dependence that allowed for a more equitable distribution of labor and resources among farm family members. On the other hand, the experience of women in these families contrasted with the reality of women like Minnie B. Davis and many of those who answered Houston's 1913 survey. For these women, life on the family farm was more difficult. They were not mindless victims or drudges but thinking women who criticized male behavior, demanded greater recognition of women's work, called for a share of the farm income, and requested greater decision-making power within the farm family. The acquisition of new equipment was more than a means by which to ease their work. It would be a tangible symbol of their improved status within the farm home. Women who advocated such views, however, were largely excluded from USDA literature in the 1920s. Instead, Hoag's portrait became the more prominent depiction of farm women in USDA literature of the period.[68]

This more positive representation of farm women resulted from a number of factors. First, the USDA no longer needed to publicize women's complaints about farm life to garner support for the Smith-Lever Act and the Extension Service. They were already realities. Second, a continuing decline in farm income during the 1920s caused the Department of Agriculture to put a more optimistic face on its picture of the American farm woman. Acquisition of the equipment that Extension Service personnel had once told women would soon be within their grasp was delayed until an improvement in farm prices would make such purchases feasible. In line with its goal of keeping farm women and their families on the farm—after all, efficient, modern farm business still required that the farm family remain in the countryside—the USDA had to revise its rhetoric. To boost the morale of farm people under worsening economic conditions, the USDA needed to portray women as leading satisfactory lives *without* the equipment that they would nevertheless someday enjoy. Additionally, in the years following passage of the suffrage amendment in 1920, the American feminist movement was no longer unified behind a single issue, and feminists branched off into a greater variety of interest groups and causes. Without the weight of a unified, highly visible feminist movement behind them, and with the demise of Progressive Era social criticism in the years following World War I, rural women lacked a political context for their criticism of patriarchal farm life. Farm women's criticism of the conditions under which they lived and worked thus became increasingly muted in official literature as the 1920s progressed.

By the time an editorial writer for the *Nation* presented an essay entitled "Feminism on the Farm" in 1921, the USDA was already working to soften women's criticism of male behavior within its own publications. Commenting on a "Declaration of Independence" recently written by a group of Nebraska farm women, the writer noted that these women had demanded a power washing machine in the house for every tractor purchased for the farm, a bathtub in the house for every binder on the farm, running water in the kitchen for every riding plow in the fields, a kerosene cook stove for every motor truck, a fireless cooker for every new mowing machine, and a share of the farm income.[69]

Evaluating the women's document, the *Nation* editorialist commented: "This declaration is neither a petulant outburst nor an amiable jest. Backed up by the home demonstration service of the Department of Agriculture the farm women of Nebraska are going to see to it that 100 per cent of their number are supplied with water in the kitchen, kerosene stoves, fireless cookers, linoleum kitchen floors, bread mixers, screened porches."[70]

In reality, the authors of the declaration had gone beyond USDA policy in demanding their share of the total farm income—a necessary prerequisite for acquisition of new equipment and, more important, a means to attain some control over family politics. Instead, in line with its policy of maintaining patriarchal control on the farm, the Department of Agriculture promoted do-it-yourself "pin money" projects by which farm women could earn money for the purchase of household equipment. Women could only undertake such projects, however, when they were not performing the litany of chores that already occupied long hours and contributed significantly to the general farm family income. The policy that the USDA espoused could not reasonably be termed "feminist" in that it did not seek to challenge patriarchal control over the farm family economy or work unit. In reality, the Department of Agriculture largely functioned to diffuse any signs of feminist rebellion on the farm. As the Nebraska "Declaration" suggested, however, the desire of some women to challenge patriarchal authority continued, albeit largely unpublicized, in the postwar era.

The goal of improved farm business and home management had always been part of the Country Life agenda; it simply became a more prominent objective in the postwar era. With less emphasis on the social "uplift" component of the Country Life Movement, reformers' efforts were now more focused on modernizing and urbanizing household equipment and management practices. The importance the Department of Agriculture placed on modern homemaking in the postwar era is perhaps best illustrated by the formation in 1923 of a Bureau of Home Economics designed, in the words of Secretary Wallace, to "strengthen the scientific work of the Department as it may be related to home economics."[71] An entire bureau within the department was now committed to the objective of making farm women better domestic managers.

One result of the narrowed focus of postwar reform efforts was that women's voices of protest, although never fully acknowledged or understood by reformers, disappeared almost entirely from the pages of reform literature. The effect was a further obscuring of farm women's preferences and needs, making it less likely that women's desire to retain a productive role would be heard. In the prewar period, the call for modern domestic equipment had included the voices of women who wanted to challenge rural patriarchy. In the 1920s, calls for the improvement of farm women's technology instead appeared to originate with individuals and institutions whose faith in the patriarchal family, farm modernization, and the USDA separate spheres policy never wavered.

With these comments, Smith, chief of the Department of Agriculture's Office of Co-operative Extension Work, made clear that the goal of extension work for farm women in the 1920s was to make them into the image of urban, middle-class homemakers.[1] As full-time homemakers, women would ensure the happiness, efficiency, and stability of farm families. And a major key to making farm women better homemakers was to encourage their use of modern domestic equipment. In the dozen years following World War I, private organizations, mail-order catalogs, and periodical and radio advertisements joined the Extension Service in reminding farm women of the world beyond their farm homes, where urban, middle-class women enjoyed a variety of household conveniences. These sources told farm women, however, that they too deserved such equipment and reinforced many of the Extension Service's arguments on behalf of farm home modernization. Farm women of the 1920s, therefore, were exposed to extensive propaganda that pushed for their adoption of the modern domestic ideal.

Extension Service policymakers promoted the use of modern household equipment in part as a response to the expressed needs of farm women themselves. In the first major survey of farm women since 1913, the Department of Agriculture, in cooperation with the land-grant colleges and County Farm Bureaus, questioned ten thousand northern and western farm women in the summer and fall of 1919. Survey takers attempted to question

"Mother Must Have Every Labor-Saving Convenience"

The Modernization Message of the 1920s

When the farmer returns weary from the field at night to a modest, attractive home, it makes him feel that the day's work has not been in vain. . . . But, to have such a home, to sit down to the evening meal with joy on every face demands that mother . . . must have every labor-saving convenience. . . . Home life in the country will never reach its highest ideals until farm women have more of the things that they really desire.
—C. B. Smith (ca. 1925)

"typical" farm women, but because "progressive" farm women provided the most extensive survey responses, the final results probably represented "conditions rather above the average." Once again, USDA officials were hearing from a relatively elite group of farm women. The survey's findings showed that midwestern farm women worked an average of 13.2 hours a day in the summer and 10.5 hours in the winter. Acknowledging—but not questioning—the patriarchal system under which farm women labored, Florence E. Ward, director of extension work for women in the northern and western states, noted that such long work hours in any other industry, "where love and service are not the ruling motives," would have caused workers to call a strike.[2]

Ward's analysis of the survey's results, however, went beyond her recognition of farm women's long work hours. Citing statistics on the increased number of rural young people moving to American cities, Ward noted that more young women than men were drifting away from the farm. Ward's analysis of this phenomenon presumed that women left the farm in greater numbers primarily because they disliked the conditions under which they lived and worked. She neglected to note that young women also left the farm because they faced limited economic options under a patriarchal system in which young men primarily inherited management of the family farm. Echoing the sentiments of other rural reformers of the era, Ward suggested a familiar solution to women's abandonment of farm life. Using the 1919 survey as a guide, Ward suggested that women might find farm life more pleasant "if the average farmhouse were as well equipped as . . . the up-to-date barn."[3]

Statistics gathered in the 1919 survey indicated that midwestern farm women performed a variety of tasks on a weekly, if not daily, basis. Seventy-nine percent of midwestern farm women cleaned and cared for kerosene lamps on a daily basis, 68 percent hauled water every day from an average distance of 41 feet, 97 percent baked bread at least once or twice a week, and 97 percent of midwestern farm women did the household laundry once a week. Most of these women performed this work without modern equipment. Only 24 percent of these women had running water in their houses; 89 percent used outdoor toilets. Only 22 percent of midwestern farmhouses contained power machinery of any type, but 64 percent owned washing machines, primarily the hand-powered variety.[4]

Although survey results indicated that farmhouses in the Midwest largely lacked modern domestic appliances, midwestern farm families were relatively well off in terms of access to modern communication technology. In 1919, 73 percent of farm families had access to an automobile, and 85 percent had telephones. Such equipment was important in a region where distances averaged 5.1 miles to the nearest high school, 2.6 miles to church, 4.6 miles to market, and 4.9 miles to the family doctor.[5]

Extension Service policymakers acknowledged that midwestern farm women were fortunate in having access to technology that lessened their sense of isolation, although policymakers failed to realize that women's own technological priorities might have been responsible for the gap between domestic technology and communication technology. Although modern communication technology obviously benefited male and family interests, women themselves saw benefits to new communication technology and often played an active role in choosing to use family resources to acquire it. When a USDA official asked one farm woman of the era why her family acquired a car before it obtained modern plumbing, her answer was straightforward: "Why, you can't go to town in a bathtub!"[6]

With their emphasis on domestic technology over communication technology, Extension Service policymakers not only dismissed many farm women's own technological priorities but also ignored negative factors hidden behind the supposedly rosy statistics on ownership of modern communication equipment. First, the fact that most farm families owned automobiles did not mean that most farm women had ready use of automobiles for their own purposes, a situation they had lamented in the 1913 survey. Throughout the period between World War I and World War II, more farm men than farm women knew how to drive, and even those women who did know how to drive cars found their driving activities curtailed by family politics. Business and family needs overrode those of individual women. Even young farm women who worked away from the farm home, such as rural schoolteachers, often relied on fathers or brothers to transport them between farm and workplace in the family car. Those farm women who did have greater access to family cars, such as one young western Nebraskan whose father taught her to drive at an early age, still found male family members setting the transportation priorities. In this instance, the daughter had specifically learned to drive so that she could run errands for her father. Women who had access to cars also often found poor rural roads to be unnavigable—a problem that affected both male and female drivers.[7]

The statistics on rural telephone ownership also masked some problems concerning women's access to this equipment. In many farm families, telephone use was primarily restricted to business and emergency purposes.

Rural phone systems were generally party lines, and many farm neighborhood phone companies enforced time limits on calls. Combined statistics for the midwestern states as a group also hid differences between farm women's access to communication technology in the Corn Belt and on the Great Plains. Just as the greater distance between plains farms meant that more plains families than Corn Belt families came to rely on use of the automobile, fewer plains families than Corn Belt families could rely on telephones. The expense and difficulty of extending telephone wires to widely spaced farm-houses on the plains delayed the use of telephones in much of that region until many years after phones had become commonplace in the Corn Belt.[8]

Not only did Extension Service policymakers ignore farm women's continued need for improved communication technology, they also generally ignored survey results indicating that much of farm women's work took place outside the farmhouse kitchen. In short, they did not perceive the interdependence and fuzzy distinction between the farmhouse and the farm itself. In the Midwest, 67 percent of farm women tended gardens, and 89 percent raised poultry. Forty-five percent of midwestern farm women milked cows, 93 percent washed milk pails, 76 percent washed cream separators, 66 percent made butter, and 33 percent sold butter. Twenty-two percent of midwestern farm women performed field work for an average of 4.9 weeks a year. In addition, 34 percent of midwestern farm women did the bookkeeping for their families' farms. In other words, women devoted a substantial number of hours to their work as farm producers and marketers.[9]

Policymakers largely ignored these statistics, however, in continuing their emphasis on women's work in the farmhouse. Although home demonstration agents offered lessons in poultry-raising practices, for instance, policymakers considered such lessons important because poultry production yielded "money for home improvements"—a recognition of survey results showing that 25 percent of midwestern farm women saved poultry earnings for their own uses.[10]

Based on their analysis of the 1919 survey, Extension Service policymakers determined that the greatest aid to the nation's farm women would not be direction in more efficient production or communication practices outside the farmhouse but would be promotion of household modernization. Commenting on the "fundamental purpose" of extension work directed at farm women in 1919, Florence E. Ward stated: "Better and more permanent agriculture requires that the farm home be equipped with modern conveniences and labor-saving appliances quite as much as that there be improved equipment in the barn, better live stock, and more thorough cultivation of the soil."[11]

Such comments by Extension Service officials emphasized once again that, in their view, the path to rural stability and agricultural efficiency lay firmly within the boundaries of the patriarchal family. Although in their responses to the USDA's 1913 survey farm women had asked for guidance in setting up cooperative housekeeping practices outside the privatized family, policymakers largely ignored such requests. Ironically, at a time when the Extension Service was promoting the cooperative marketing of agricultural products, it did not encourage cooperative housekeeping. In the minds of Extension Service policymakers, taking housework out of individual homes apparently undermined the nuclear family farming unit, which they believed lay at the heart of successful agriculture and rural living. Cooperative housekeeping also threatened American business and its attempt to sell its products to individual families. Bowing to pressures from the business community and demonstrating their faith in the privatized, nuclear family, policymakers rejected the strategy of cooperative housekeeping.[12]

The Extension Service promoted its policy of privatized, mechanized housework in the face of evidence that cooperative efforts to reorganize housekeeping could significantly lessen women's work without any investment in new equipment. For example, before World War I, farm women in Minnesota and Wisconsin had established successful cooperative laundries using the steam plants and water supplies that already operated their neighborhood creameries.[13]

The Extension Service's insistence on adoption of privatized, mechanized housekeeping practices also disadvantaged those farm women on the margins of midwestern rural society. Women whose economic or cultural status excluded them from participation in the New Agriculture were often those who benefited from the "hiring out" system of traditional midwestern farm life. For example, Mennonite women in Haskell County, Kansas, were excluded from mainstream rural society by their unique religious customs, their German language, and their families' reliance on traditional, labor-intensive farming methods. While their neighbors adopted new farming equipment during World War I and increasingly specialized in large-scale, cash-dependent wheat farming, the Haskell County Mennonites retained their diversified, small-scale farming operations. In order to supplement the family economy, young Mennonite women would "hire out" to do household chores for their

English-speaking neighbors, who, unlike Mennonites in the community, might have a little extra cash to pay for such services. Likewise, the descendants of former slaves who settled in Graham County, Kansas, continued to work small-scale farms with horses and mules after their white neighbors began purchasing gasoline-powered field equipment, expanding their farms, and specializing in wheat production during World War I. Women in these families also hired out to perform household tasks for their wealthier white neighbors. In the same way that farm mechanization reduced the need for male field laborers, mechanization of farmhouses meant the displacement of these ethnic minority women from necessary work that aided their family budgets. The Extension Service and its allies, however, were less interested in these women than in their white, English-speaking, ostensibly middle-class counterparts—in other words, those women who were potentially capable of achieving the privatized, mechanized domestic ideal.[14] In a series of articles designed to promote adoption of gasoline-powered farm machinery and electric-powered domestic equipment on Wheat Belt farms, writers working for *Capper's Farmer*, a Topeka-based periodical published by a Republican senator, Arthur Capper, quoted a number of middle-class Kansas women who argued that a chief advantage of the use of modern field and household equipment on their farms was the elimination of "undesirable" hired household and field workers who disturbed the "home circle" and deprived middle-class families of their privacy.[15]

Beginning in 1922, the Extension Service was joined in its call for the modernization of individual farm homes by Secretary of Commerce Herbert Hoover's Better Homes in America movement. As another example of the postwar linkage of private organizations to government bureaucracies, Better Homes in America was a private organization "created specifically to serve as a publicity and 'education' apparatus" of the Division of Building and Housing within the Commerce Department's Bureau of Standards. Members of other government agencies, including the USDA's Bureau of Home Economics, also played a prominent role within the movement. Equating home ownership with responsible citizenship, the Better Homes movement promoted the ownership and improvement of private homes in urban as well as rural America. Like the Extension Service, the Better Homes movement promoted separate roles for men and women: Men were to be home owners, while women were to be homemakers.[16] In their special program for farmhouses, Better Homes supporters emphasized the acquisition of modern appliances, arguing that while public utilities provided water, electricity, and sewage disposal for city and small-town residents, farm homeowners had to supply those services for themselves.[17] Supporters of the Better Homes movement agreed with USDA policymakers that the "four systems needed for making the farmhouse modern, in the order of importance, [were] the water-supply system, the heating plant, the sewage system, and the lighting system."[18]

In 1924, Extension Service agents reported that since the implementation of federally supported extension work in 1914, 52,823 of the nation's farm families had followed Extension Service plans in installing water systems in their homes, and 15,454 farm families had installed sewage disposal systems according to Extension Service instructions. During the same ten-year period, 3,956 farm families had installed heating systems according to Extension Service plans, and 59,308 farm families had followed Extension Service directions in installing lighting systems. Nevertheless, the vast majority of American farm homes still lacked this equipment. The most obvious explanation for farm families' resistance to the use of such equipment was its cost. A Department of Agriculture bulletin promoting the installation of modern equipment in the "typical" farmhouse reported that a self-installed plumbing system in one central Iowa house cost $300, while a heating system was $200.[19]

A USDA study of 2,886 white nuclear families in eleven states, based primarily on the responses of the wives, indicated that most farm families could not afford such equipment in the 1920s. Among those questioned were women who resided in the Corn Belt, including women from three counties in Iowa, six counties in Missouri, and four counties in eastern Kansas. Of the 1,439 midwestern farm families studied, 61 percent owned their own farms. The remainder were farm tenants or the families of hired men. During the 1922–24 period, the average value of all goods and equipment within each of these midwestern farm homes was $1,613. Household equipment and furnishings made up only 2.7 percent of the total value of the farm family's goods on the average midwestern farm. In the Midwest, 72.6 percent of farm homes had no modern household equipment whatsoever. Farm ownership had an impact on the extent to which midwestern farm families modernized their houses. In the Midwest, 67.1 percent of farm owners lacked any modern equipment, but 81.9 percent of nonowners were without any modern conveniences. Figures showed that although midwestern farm families spent an average of $43.50 on household equipment each year, they spent an average of $93.30 on family automobile expenses—once again indicating the priority given to communication/transportation technology. The vast majority of the midwestern farm family budget, however, simply went to feeding the family, which averaged 4.3 persons. At a time when midwestern farms were increasingly specialized in the production of cash grains and livestock, many foods had to be purchased away from the farm.[20]

According to USDA economist E. L. Kirkpatrick, the responsibility for these farm families acquiring modern household equipment lay largely on the shoulders of farm women. According to the results of this survey, farm families in which the wife had more years of formal schooling than the husband were more likely to own modern equipment, leading Kirkpatrick to comment that "formal schooling of the homemaker exert[ed] a greater influence than [did] formal schooling of the farm operator on the [farm family's] standard of living."[21] In other words, farmhouse modernization was dependent upon a well-informed female population—one of the chief short-term goals of the Extension Service.

More important, however, in determining the farm family's standard of living, including the use of modern equipment, was the family's income level. In particular, Kirkpatrick noted that income "from other than farm business sources" was often the means of raising the standard of living. He noted further, "Sources of this additional income include especially prepared home-canned or preserved products, articles of fancy work, boarding and lodging of school teachers or others, teaching or other work performed by different members of the family."[22] When Kirkpatrick referred to "different members of the family," however, he was referring to farm women and the work they performed to extend the family budget. Another short-term goal of the Extension Service in the 1920s was to teach farm women ways in which they could earn money through craft, poultry, gardening, and canning projects. The expectation was that women would use this "pin money" to purchase domestic equipment.

Throughout the 1920s, extension literature emphasized the correlation between women's work for pay and the acquisition of modern household equipment. And the Extension Service attempted to influence all factors of the equation. Extension Service writer Ola Powell Malcolm noted that in 1923 home demonstration agents across the nation had convinced farm women to adopt home appliances and water, light, and sewage disposal systems. According to Malcolm, "much of the money spent for improvements was earned through some home enterprise, such as poultry raising, gardening and orcharding . . . and other similar activities carried on under the direction of the home demonstration agent."[23]

Statistics indicated that women's poultry work was the most profitable of these activities. By marketing eggs and other products, farm women could achieve the Extension Service's ultimate goal. In reviewing the results of home demonstration work in 1923, Malcolm noted that through women's marketing activities, "funds were provided for beautifying and improving the home which resulted in a better satisfied farm family."[24] Malcolm neglected to note, however, that farm families frequently reinvested such funds in the farm or used the money to purchase food or pay bills and taxes.

As agricultural economist E. L. Kirkpatrick noted, money and years of education were not the only quantifiable factors in determining whether or not farm families adopted new technology. The value placed on farm women's time and the number of hours they devoted to household tasks also played a part. In Kirkpatrick's words, "The final decision of the question whether the farm home is to have running water in the kitchen may involve a valuation of the home maker's time, as well as the money necessary to provide the machinery to force the water to the kitchen."[25]

Perhaps ignoring the reality that many farm families undervalued women's work, home demonstration agents in 1924 continued to have as their major goal farm families' acquisition of "home labor-saving equipment." Projects aimed at promoting the use of such equipment were in effect in forty-five of the forty-eight states, the highest number of states participating in any one "home management and improvement" activity.[26]

The Extension Service, though, was taking its household modernization message primarily to families at the top of the rural socioeconomic scale. In a study of farm families in four states, including Iowa, the service found that during the 1923–24 period, extension agents most effectively reached families living on large farms and those who were members of the conservative Farm Bureau, which was the private organization responsible for overseeing Extension Service work in Iowa and most other midwestern states (see Table 2.1). In the years following World War I, however, farm women were also part of a national information network that existed beyond the boundaries of the Extension Service and other federal agencies. This network also carried the message of industrial consumption and farmhouse modernization and thus ensured that even those women who had no direct contact with the Extension Service were well aware of the modern domestic ideal.

Table 2.1 Percentage of Various Farm Family Groups Adopting
Extension Service Advice and Practices, 1923–1924

Families on Small Farms	Families on Medium Farms	Families on Large Farms
69	74	78
Families Not Belonging to Farm Bureau	Families Formerly Belonging to Farm Bureau	Families Belonging to Farm Bureau
55	84	91

Source: M. C. Wilson, *The Effectiveness of Home Economics Extension Work in Reaching Farm Women* (Washington: Federal Extension Service, 1929).

Farm women's access to information about modern equipment was not entirely a development of the twentieth century. Since the late nineteenth century, for example, farm women had been reading mail-order catalogs that displayed a variety of domestic goods, including mechanized household equipment. The Chicago-based Sears, Roebuck and Company, which by the 1920s was billing itself as the "World's Largest Store," had in fact built its business largely by selling its mail-order goods to farm families. From the 1910s onward, the pages of the Sears catalog were increasingly filled with pictures and descriptions of mechanized washing machines, electric irons, gas cooking ranges, and other modern equipment. If many farm women did not yet possess such items themselves, they were certainly aware of the equipment's prominent display in the pages of the Sears catalog. The pages of popular women's magazines and farm life periodicals were also filled with advertisements for mechanized household and communication equipment. And in the 1920s, commercial radio broadcasting joined popular print marketing in reminding farm women of the modern domestic ideal.

As Stuart Ewen has noted in his classic study of American consumer culture, the post–World War I modernization message was not unique to advertising and broadcasting aimed at farm women. As a result of new mass production techniques in this era, American industry found itself with a surplus of manufactured products and thus the need to expand domestic markets. A new type of advertising emerged at this time, therefore, which functioned to draw new members into America's consumer culture, including members of the urban working class and the nation's farm families. One of the chief goals of this advertising was to convince these new consumers that they should emulate the material conditions of the existing consumer class—the urban upper and middle classes. The chief strategy employed in this new type of advertising was to make would-be consumers insecure about the extent to which they were conforming to a "modern" way of life by purchasing the appropriate products of American industry.[27]

Like Extension Service literature, periodical advertisements aimed at farm women often emphasized the acquisition of modern domestic equipment. These advertisements appeared in farm life periodicals side by side with editorials that demanded the acquisition of modern equipment in order to improve the efficiency of the farm home. Many of these advertisements also spoke to a theme that USDA bureaucrats of the 1920s frequently ignored: that adoption of modern technology could also aid women in their role as farm producers.

Cooking range ads were among those that frequently appeared in midwestern farm periodicals. Modernity and technological competence were popular themes in advertisements for cooking ranges that echoed reformers' calls for an efficient, industrialized New Agriculture. The makers of gas, oil, and electric equipment all competed in these twentieth-century range wars, with each range maker claiming that its product was the most modern one on the market.[28] In much of this advertising, modernization was equated with urbanization. A 1929 Skelgas ad showed a fashionably dressed woman lighting the burner of her gas range and thinking of other modern conveniences. The ad's headline read: "What are City Advantages Now? Today in Suburb, Small City, and Country You May Have every City Convenience" (see Figure 2.1). The ad also featured testimony by that most modern of post–World War I figures—the expert. In this case, it was Emma F. Holloway of the Pratt Institute, who advised that a gas-powered stove in the farm home gave "just as satisfactory service as that . . . available to the city dweller."[29]

Perfection oil range ads of the era echoed the tone of Skelgas advertising. The headline of a 1929 Perfection ad, featuring a drawing of a fashionably dressed woman, proclaimed, "Antiques for the rest of the house if you wish . . . but the kitchen must be modern." Along with featuring illustrations of women in flapper fashions, range ads emphasizing the modernity of their product also showed women enjoying increased leisure and the use of other modern equipment. Another Skelgas ad appearing in 1929 stated, "Skelgas in your kitchen will give You Time to Enjoy Other Things Elsewhere," and featured a drawing of a woman driving a car through the countryside. The ad's copy continued this theme: "The time you are spending now in building

Fig. 2.1. A 1929 Skelgas advertisement pictures a young farm woman lighting a gas range and dreaming of other pieces of modern equipment. (Courtesy of *Wallaces' Farmer*)

old fashioned fires or in tending devices for burning gasoline, carbide or kerosene can be yours—yours for rest or pleasure."[30]

An ad appearing in *Wallaces' Farmer* in 1930 combined all the major themes of the era's range advertising, including keeping young people "down on the farm." The ad featured a drawing of a fatigued woman and asked, "Is this your wife?" The ad's copy then went on to explain the drawbacks of old-fashioned cooking equipment:

> Why do farm girls leave the farm? . . . Is it because these farm children know the conveniences that city women enjoy, and move to towns and cities to escape the slavery of old-fashioned kitchens? Home demonstration agents have been saying for years that the lack of city conveniences on the farm is the only drawback to rural life. . . . The coming of Skelgas has revolutionized the farm woman's life. . . . [It is] the greatest of all farm home conveniences.[31]

The appliance manufacturers who benefited most from the recommendations of home demonstration agents were the washing machine companies, including midwestern manufacturers like the Maytag Company of Newton, Iowa, and the Voss Company of Davenport, Iowa. Having rejected the strategy of cooperative laundries, Extension Service personnel focused on the creation of special laundry facilities in individual homes. A 1921 USDA bulletin characterized laundry work as "among the hardest of the regular household tasks" and promoted as the farm housewife's ideal "a separate room for her laundry, with running water and modern labor-saving devices."[32] This bulletin and other publications used and distributed by Extension Service agents argued that farm women particularly deserved modern equipment because they could not rely on laundresses or commercial laundries as city women did and because farm women washed larger and dirtier loads of laundry than their urban counterparts. Capitalizing on the Extension Service's promotion of washing machines, their manufacturers advertised heavily in farm periodicals.

An ad appearing in *Wallaces' Farmer* in 1919 featured an attractive young woman who owned a Maytag washing machine with a gasoline-powered Liberty motor, which "liberated" her "from all the fatiguing work of washday."[33] Like much of post–World War I advertising, this ad used the image of a youthful New Woman to equate its product with modernity and the liberation of women from strenuous household labor (see Figure 2.2). In the 1920s, advertisers frequently featured pictures of the era's ultimate symbol of youth

"There's the real Liberty Motor"

"The power that liberates me from all the fatiguing work of washday. From dependence upon unreliable hired help. From the whims or necessities of the men folks, who always seem to need the farm power plant for something else when washday comes around.

"This Multi-Motor washer has its own independent power plant, a little easily operated gasoline engine built in under the tub, as a part of the washer.

"I *can* belt the washer up to the cream separator, churn or other light machinery and save hand labor in a dozen different ways outside of washing. I even loan it to the men, in a pinch, for shelling corn."

With its swinging, reversible wringer, also operated by the engine, this washer is the one machine that places the farm home on a par with the power operated farm. It does for the home what the truck and tractor does for the farm.

Write for the Maytag Household Manual, telling all about this wonderful machine and containing many helpful suggestions in home management. Sent gratis.

THE MAYTAG COMPANY, DEPT. 488 **Newton, Iowa**

BRANCHES
Philadelphia   Indianapolis   Minneapolis   Kansas City
Atlanta   Portland (Oregon)   Winnipeg   73

DISTRIBUTORS
SEATTLE—Seattle Hardware Co.
SPOKANE—Holley-Mason Hardware Co.
HELENA, MONT.—A. M. Holter Hardware Co.
BILLINGS, MONT.—Billings Hardware Co.
OAKLAND, CALIF.—Creighton-Morris Co.
SALT LAKE CITY—Utah Power & Light Co.
BOISE, IDAHO—Stewart Wholesale Co.
SAN ANTONIO—Smith Bros. Hdwe. Sales Co.
DULUTH—Kelley Hardware Co.
NEWARK, N.J.—Newark Electrical Supply Co.
BALTIMORE, MD.— King Electric Washing
Machine Company.
FOR UTAH AND IDAHO—Consolidated Wagon
& Machine Co., Salt Lake City.

Fig. 2.2. A Clara Bow look-alike points out the Liberty motor attached to her Maytag washing machine in a 1919 advertisement. (Courtesy of *Wallaces' Farmer*)

46   Entitled to Power

and female independence—the flapper. Ironically, advertisers often used this feminist motif, as in the Maytag ad, to convince women that the purchase of new domestic equipment would make them happier in their role as home-maker.[34]

The Maytag advertisement also emphasized the versatility of laundry equipment, a theme that became more prevalent during the agricultural depression, when many farm families were reluctant to purchase such equipment. The Maytag Company used this strategy in its advertising of the early 1930s, which suggested that farm families purchase, "at reasonable cost," butter churn and meat grinder attachments that could be powered by the washing machine motor. Recognizing women's role as farm producer, Maytag advertisements prominently featured these "labor-saving" attachments at a time when women were interested in saving money by preparing more dairy and meat products at home and in making money by selling such products outside the home.[35]

Another strategy that washing machine advertisers employed during this period was to capitalize on some farm women's resentment that family resources were often used to acquire modern field and barn equipment rather than new household devices. A 1930 Maytag advertisement suggested to farm women, "Change places with your husband next washday." The ad featured a drawing of a husband wearing an apron and carrying a full laundry basket as his wife drives by, waving from a tractor (see Figure 2.3). The advertisement told women, "If your husband did the washing, he would insist on having a new Maytag, for the same reason that he buys power machinery for his field work." In 1931, Sears advertised its washers by arguing, "Men wouldn't think of pumping water for their cattle by hand. . . . So women shouldn't be doing their washing by hand when power can do it cheaper and quicker."[36]

During the depths of the agricultural depression, washing machine advertisements continued to stress the theme of modernity, with each washing machine company claiming that its product was the most modern alternative to the old-fashioned washboard. In 1929, the Voss Company claimed, "Farm women have found . . . the Voss has every worth-while feature that you expect in a modern washer," while an advertisement for Thor washing machines promised that with the "World's Lowest Priced Quality Washing Machine . . . every farm home [would] have the most modern of all washers." In another 1929 advertisement, Maytag combined the modernity theme with the home appliance versus field equipment debate: "Farms of today demand modern

Change places
with your *husband*
next washday

IF your husband did the washing, he would insist on having a new Maytag, for the same reason that he buys power machinery for his field work.

The quick-washing Maytag gives you extra hours to spend in other profitable ways. The gentle, water-washing action makes the clothes last longer ... washes everything clean without hand rubbing.

THE NEW MAYTAG

You owe it to yourself to see this latest creation of the world's largest washer factory. The one-piece, cast-aluminum tub is extra roomy. The new-type roller water remover is extra convenient and thorough. The new oil-packed drive is extra quiet and smooth-running.

A Week's Washing FREE

Write or phone the nearest dealer for a trial home washing with the New Maytag. If it doesn't sell itself, don't keep it. Divided payments you'll never miss.

THE MAYTAG COMPANY
Newton, Iowa :: Founded 1893
NORTHWESTERN BRANCH:
615 Washington Ave. North, MINNEAPOLIS, MINN.

For homes with electricity, the Maytag is available with electric motor.

TUNE IN on Maytag Radio Programs over N.B.C. Coast to Coast Network Monday Evenings, Daylight Saving Time — 9:00 E.T., 8:00 C.T., 7:00 Mt.T., 6:00 P.T. — Standard Time is one hour earlier. WJZ, New York; KDKA, Pittsburgh; KYW, Chicago; KSTP, St. Paul; WSM, Nashville; WREN, Kansas City; KOA, Denver; KSL, Salt Lake City; WKY, Oklahoma City; KPRC, Houston; WFAA, Dallas; KECA, Los Angeles; KGW, Portland and Asso. Sta.

THE GASOLINE MULTI-MOTOR

This Maytag engine represents sixteen years development ... half a million in use. It is a woman's engine ... so simple and compact that by removing only four bolts it is interchangeable with the electric motor. A step on the pedal starts it.

The Churn and Meat Grinder Attachments

These two attachments, sold as extra equipment at reasonable cost, add extra usefulness to your Maytag. The Churn Attachment is made of aluminum, sets over the center post and churns the butter with the same power that washes the clothes. The Meat Grinder Attachment grinds meats, nuts, fruits, relish at two pounds an hour.

F-30-7

The *Maytag Aluminum Washer*

Fig. 2.3. A 1930 Maytag advertisement plays upon farm women's presumed resentment of the superior technology used by farm men. (Courtesy of *Wallaces' Farmer*)

labor-saving conveniences in the home as well as in the field. The Maytag is a washer in step with modern farm progress."[37]

Advertising of the 1920s and early 1930s also continued to exploit farm women's supposed distress that they lagged behind urban women in the modernization of their homes. ABC Companion washer ads played on this concern by assuring consumers, "Farm women [are] . . . as modern-minded as those who live in the city [and] . . . need especially to banish the drudgery of wash day." The company's 1930 advertising campaign drove home the point that farm women were just as up-to-date as urban women by featuring pictures of the ABC Companion being used by a stylish young farm woman (see Figure 2.4).[38]

A final theme of early depression-era washing machine advertising was the affordability of laundry equipment. Ads featured such key phrases as "Deferred Payments You'll Never Miss." Recognizing that farm women were using a variety of novel methods to earn money during the depression, the Maytag Company encouraged midwestern farm women to use one such method to purchase a new washing machine. Under the heading "Let your Corn Stalks Buy a Maytag," the 1929 ad urged farm women to take advantage of the new cornstalk paper industry by gathering and selling "a product until now considered waste—[to earn] money for additional home comforts and conveniences."[39]

Advertising for communication technology was also prominent during this period. The Bell Company advertised widely in farm life publications of the late 1920s and early 1930s. During this time, many farm families were abandoning local or neighborhood phone companies, sometimes in favor of Bell service. More frequently, however, farm families were discontinuing phone service altogether because they were finding it too expensive to maintain during "hard times," a phenomenon that also occurred in midwestern towns and cities. Bell's advertising campaign, therefore, was aimed at attracting farm families back to telephone use, arguing, "The Farm Telephone Pays for Itself Many Times Over."[40]

Incorporating a major tactic of post–World War I advertising, many of the Bell ads played on consumers' fears by suggesting that unless they purchased the proper modern equipment, they would be vulnerable to physical catastrophe. For instance, in an advertisement that appeared in *Wallaces' Farmer* in 1929, the theme was household disaster: "Fire broke out in a fine farm home in South Dakota—a mother and her young child were there alone." The drama had a relatively happy ending, however, as the responsible mother took

Fig. 2.4. With her bobbed hair and motorized washing machine, the figure in this 1930 advertisement represented Madison Avenue's image of the modern farm woman. (Courtesy of *Wallaces' Farmer*)

her child to safety and then telephoned her neighbors, who were able to get to the farm in time to help the woman save all of her household belongings. The ad reminded readers, "It is times like this that the telephone is worth most, but every day the farmer can use it to save time and trips; to buy and sell to better advantage; to make life more comfortable and enjoyable for himself and his family."[41]

Bell advertising suggested that it was primarily farm women who would find life more "comfortable and enjoyable" with a telephone. In the early 1930s, ads headed "The Telephone Makes Farm Life More Enjoyable" and "Women on the Farm Prize the Telephone For Talking With Neighbors" pictured women using the phone and stated that the telephone was "a farm woman's delight" because it overcame "isolation and loneliness."[42]

In its final category of advertising aimed at or featuring women, the Bell Company pictured women as knowledgeable farmers. An ad of the early 1930s featured a farm woman who saved a valuable mare, while her husband was away from the farm, by recognizing the horse's symptoms and quickly phoning the veterinarian. Another Bell ad of the period featured the farm woman as businessperson: "One midwestern farm woman calls customers regularly each week by telephone and takes orders for eggs and chickens. Another woman sells fresh fruits, eggs, sweet cream, turkeys by telephone— all above the regular market price by calling selected customers. The money they make in this way pays for the protection and convenience of the telephone many times over."[43]

Automobile manufacturers were the captains of industry who most successfully used modern advertising to create new consumers among the nation's working-class and farm families. Like the phone company ads, automobile advertisements directed at farm consumers frequently acknowledged the diversity of farm women's roles. Automobile ads, however, suggested that cars were less "user friendly" to women than were telephones and initially portrayed women as car passengers rather than car drivers. By the early 1920s, however, advertisers began to picture women as drivers more frequently. In 1923, Chevrolet advertised its $650 Utility coupe as "The Car for the Woman on the Farm." The advertisement pictured a woman in flapper fashions taking a similarly clad passenger on a drive through the countryside. The ad suggested that women needed access to automobiles for their butter-and-egg businesses, as well as for social reasons. Its suggestion that farm families purchase relatively expensive second cars exclusively for women's use, however, remained unrealistic.[44]

℘PLYMOUTH℘

A M E R I C A ' S   L O W E S T - P R I C E D
F U L L - S I Z E   C A R

Fig. 2.5. A 1929 Plymouth advertisement promoted the image of women as competent automobile drivers. (Courtesy of *Wallaces' Farmer*)

Attempting to capture the attention of female consumers, some advertisements of 1920s even pictured women achieving greater technological competence than men. For example, a 1929 Plymouth ad pictured a woman driver and passenger traveling by a field where a farmer and his son were working with horses (see Figure 2.5). A 1929 Buick ad pictured a woman driving through the countryside with her husband and son as passengers. Two years later, an ad for the Chevrolet Six showed a woman behind the wheel of the car while her husband leaned out of the passenger window to talk to a feed store operator. During the same period, however, a Pontiac ad found it necessary to remind would-be customers that female family members were capable of driving cars "with as much safety and comfort as any masculine member of the household."[45]

Although advertising for modern equipment frequently employed gender-role stereotypes, it was more likely than other prescriptive literature to recognize the diversity of farm women's work. Unlike much of the Extension Service's literature, print advertising did not place farm women strictly within the domestic sphere. In order to sell their products, manufacturers of the era cannily employed advertising strategies that not only emphasized the Extension Service's household modernization message but also portrayed farm women as they viewed themselves. In creating their marketing campaigns, advertisers of the era remembered women like Carmen Welch of Fayette County, Illinois, who wrote to *Capper's Farmer* in 1927 saying that she deserved electricity and running water in her farm home and expected to be treated as a partner in her family's farming operation because her duties as poultry keeper, gardener, seamstress, cook, laundress, bookkeeper, and secretary were worth $1,612 a year to the farm.[46]

Welch's view of herself was in line with the self-perception of the farm women who responded to both the 1913 and 1919 surveys. These women devoted much time and effort to their role as farm producers and viewed themselves as farm partners whose work was often undervalued and therefore undermechanized. Advertisers played on this theme frequently and issued their own challenge to rural patriarchy. The depiction of an aproned husband and a tractor-driving wife in a Maytag advertisement showed that women's discontent with their status in the farm family had not disappeared in the 1920s. In employing this role reversal theme, the Maytag Company played on anxieties it certainly believed to exist among midwestern farm women. And the Maytag Company was not alone in employing this strategy in advertising of the era.

When advertising dealt with women's domestic responsibilities, however, it also urged farm women to meet the standards of urban, middle-class domesticity and thus reinforced the Extension Service message that privatized, mechanized housekeeping would guarantee the efficiency of farm women. In advertisement after advertisement, American manufacturers promised farm women that the purchase of new equipment for individual farm homes would save women's labor. Often employing the image of the modern, liberated flapper, these ads promised women emancipation from "monstrous" heating stoves and "old-fashioned" washboards. In reality, this equipment did not

Table 2.2 Percentage of Farm Families Owning Modern Transportation, Field, and Communication Equipment, 1920 and 1930

	Automobiles		Tractors		Telephones	
	1920	1930	1920	1930	1920	1930
Illinois	52.9	79.5	9.2	30.8	73.2	68.8
Indiana	46.4	77.9	4.3	22.3	66.4	60.8
Iowa	73.1	90.2	9.1	29.4	86.1	84.2
Kansas	62.0	87.5	9.8	35.6	77.9	72.8
Minnesota	57.1	86.0	8.3	24.9	62.0	61.9
Missouri	30.9	64.1	2.8	9.2	62.2	53.8
Nebraska	75.6	91.8	8.3	29.3	76.4	72.5
North Dakota	50.6	86.6	15.2	43.8	46.8	40.9
South Dakota	69.4	86.5	16.3	37.2	59.4	53.6
Wisconsin	49.6	83.9	4.8	26.8	59.1	59.1

Source: U.S. Bureau of the Census, *Fifteenth Census of the United States, 1930: Agriculture* (Washington: Government Printing Office, 1932).

save women's labor; it merely changed the type of labor they performed. As time-labor studies demonstrated, women spent no less time performing household tasks when they used modern equipment than when they worked without it.[47]

While the Extension Service urged farm women to view themselves as homemakers, many of these women continued to see themselves as at least junior partners in the farm business. In taking a middle ground that presented women both as modern-minded homemakers and as farm producers who deserved technological parity with men, advertisers of the 1920s cleverly marketed their products to a receptive rural audience. In recognizing the diversity of farm women's lives, advertisements could be more persuasive than other types of prescriptive literature in encouraging women to consider new equipment.

Advertising undoubtedly contributed to the desire of farm women and their families to modernize their farms and houses. And farm families did make technological gains in the two decades following passage of the Smith-Lever Act. With the exception of the telephone, all types of modern equipment that had been on the market in 1914 became more prevalent on midwestern farms in the next two decades, even as the farm economy actually worsened (see Tables 2.2 and 2.3). Nevertheless, the majority of farmhouses still lacked

Table 2.3 Percentage of Farm Families Owning Modern
Household Equipment, 1920 and 1930

	Running Water		Electric Lights	
	1920	1930	1920	1930
Illinois	11.2	19.8	9.8	16.0
Indiana	11.4	19.5	10.0	16.7
Iowa	15.9	24.0	15.3	21.4
Kansas	9.3	16.9	8.7	12.5
Minnesota	6.4	12.5	7.6	12.6
Missouri	4.5	8.3	5.5	7.9
Nebraska	16.6	29.6	9.7	16.5
North Dakota	6.0	7.5	5.8	7.9
South Dakota	12.3	14.5	8.6	10.9
Wisconsin	7.1	15.7	8.8	25.6

Source: U.S. Bureau of the Census, *Fifteenth Census of the United States, 1930:
Agriculture* (Washington: Government Printing Office, 1932).

modern domestic equipment.[48] In the 1920s, however, a new type of communication equipment became a fixture in many midwestern farm homes—the radio.

The radio was a unique piece of household equipment. Once a farm family had acquired a radio, the programming that members received on it often encouraged them to increase their investment in other modern household devices. Within a few years of the inception of commercial radio broadcasting in 1920, the Department of Agriculture and the land-grant colleges began broadcasting advice programs that promoted farm modernization. Household appliance, farm machinery, and automobile manufacturers were often sponsors of this programming. Sears, Roebuck and Company also advertised frequently on these programs. Sears even owned its own radio station in Chicago, station WLS, whose call letters, according to Sears advertising, stood for "World's Largest Store." Midwestern farm women, therefore, were exposed to a variety of radio messages asking them and their families to purchase modern equipment.[49]

During the early 1920s, both *Wallaces' Farmer* and *Capper's Farmer* added radio experts to their staffs and invited readers to write in with inquiries and comments about radio use. Among the readers who wrote letters to both publications about their experiences with radio were farm women. Farm women praised radio for its entertainment value and for its ability to aid farm business by providing timely market reports. A letter from an Illinois woman to *Wallaces' Farmer* in the summer of 1925 also demonstrated radio's instructional value. According to the letter writer, she and her women neighbors frequently listened to advice programs that recommended methods and equipment "for making [women's] work lighter."[50]

Kansas State Agricultural College was the midwestern pioneer in presenting this type of advice programming, as well as credit courses that farm people could participate in "over the air." Beginning in 1924, the college radio station, KSAC, broadcast extension lessons on dairy production, livestock feeding, agricultural engineering—and poultry raising, cooking, home decoration, and home conveniences. By 1926, twenty-four of the nation's agricultural colleges had their own radio stations and broadcast similar programs.[51]

Farm families were willing to spend a sizable amount of money to obtain such programming. A survey of 2,500 farm people in 1923 indicated that the average price they had paid for radios was $175. In 1926, a canvass of radio dealers throughout the country revealed that farm families rarely purchased radios that cost less than $100 because these families had "discovered that they need[ed] good long-distance sets to get the weather and market reports and entertainment they demand[ed]."[52] Nevertheless, radios remained cheaper than $300 plumbing systems, and analysts predicted that manufacturers would soon develop a radio equivalent of the Model T, which would make possible universal radio ownership among farm people. *Wallaces' Farmer* writer I. W. Dickerson predicted that radios would become even more popular than automobiles, reporting that it was already "not at all uncommon to hear a farmer say that he would rather part with his car than to do without his radio."[53]

Recognizing the popularity and influence of radio, the Department of Agriculture, the land-grant colleges, and various private farm organizations—including the Farm Bureau—began broadcasting the "National Farm and Home Hour" on NBC affiliates in October 1928. The forty-five–minute program, broadcast over the noon hour from Chicago every weekday, remained the dominant national farm program for the next decade. Its combination of music, weather and crop forecasts, soil conservation information, and comments about home economics became a regular companion at the farm family dinner table.[54]

Three months after the inception of the "Farm and Home Hour," in January 1929, Elizabeth C. Wherry began writing her "Country Air" column in *Wallaces' Farmer*. Created as a column about radio "from the farm woman's viewpoint," the column later covered other issues of interest to farm women as well, and Wherry remained its author until her death in December 1956. In 1929, Wherry was a thirty-six-year-old former schoolteacher who was living and working on a Jones County, Iowa, dairy farm with her husband and two young sons. In her column, Wherry attempted to speak for all midwestern farm women, as indicated by the fact that until the late 1930s she remained anonymous and signed her columns as "A Farm Woman." Wherry's column provided *Wallaces' Farmer* with the female perspective its reform-minded editorials had lacked.[55]

Wherry's early columns provide an insightful picture of radio's impact on farm women and their families. During the first year of her column, Wherry often cited the "Farm and Home Hour" as an example of positive farm programming and as a unifying force for farmers around the country. During the summer of 1929, Wherry frequently commented that since midwestern farm families were "bound to be educated" as they consumed their noon meal, they should tune in to the nationally broadcast program "to strengthen the bonds of comprehension and brotherhood between widely separated farming districts."[56]

In January 1930, the Department of Agriculture reported that in the previous ten months, the USDA had led all other federal agencies in use of radio, providing approximately one hundred hours of programming, including regular broadcasts of the "Farm and Home Hour." Three weeks later, however, Elizabeth Wherry noted that among the correspondence she regularly received from readers, "not one letter mentioned the National Farm and Home Hour or any other special farm broadcast." She went on to ask, "What does that signify—if anything?"[57]

What it signified, according to the letters Wherry received, was that although records showed that many farm families listened to the "Farm and Home Hour" on a regular basis, entertainment-oriented programs held a greater fascination for them. In particular, Wherry's readers seemed to enjoy music programs and often rearranged their work schedules in order to hear the programs they liked. Women wrote to Wherry saying that they churned butter or made beds while listening to the radio. That women could perform some of their chores while listening to their favorite broadcasts was, in the words of one of Wherry's readers, "the beauty of radio."[58]

Some farm women claimed that listening to the radio even made doing housework more enjoyable. One young farm woman reported in the summer of 1929 that she had come to rely on the radio as a valuable piece of "domestic equipment," which provided music or exercise programs to accompany her housework: "I am the mother of four children, the oldest a boy of seven and the baby a girl of two months old. We are living on a 240-acre farm, and that means that I must spend most of my time in the kitchen, cooking, baking, washing, ironing, mending, scrubbing, canning and caring for the babies. The first thing that I do in the morning, even before I go to the kitchen, is to go into the front room and tune in the radio."[59]

Wherry herself found that the radio was one piece of modern communication equipment that she could take advantage of and still pay full attention to other tasks. On the tenth anniversary of her column's debut, Wherry commented on her early career as a columnist: "I surrounded the radio with the stocking basket and several piles of shirts, overalls and underwear, settled down with the headphones and began my career as a commentator. The most notable result, however, was the commendably mended up appearance of my family."[60]

Wherry even found a way not to miss her favorite radio programs during the spring chick-hatching season. In April 1929, she hooked up a radio extension in the brooder house and listened to programs as she cared for her poultry. The following fall, after the pullets had been housed and the cockerels sold, Wherry removed the radio extension from the brooder house and gave it to her husband Don to use in the milk barn during the winter.[61]

The Wherrys were not the only farm couple who worked cooperatively to enjoy the benefits of radio listening. In February 1930, Wherry reported that one of her readers and his wife had "husked their own corn—2,800 bushels of it—and milked fifteen cows twice a day—and bought a radio with the money saved on hired man's wages." Remarked Wherry, "Can't you just see how they enjoy that radio!"[62]

Advertisers of the era counted on the fact that other farm families were willing to make similar sacrifices in order to acquire radios. For example, an Atwater Kent ad appearing in midwestern magazines during the winter of 1926 implied that farm families should sacrifice other luxuries in order to purchase a radio. Featuring the supposed testimony of a Galesburg, Illinois, farm couple, the ad reported that the couple had given up their annual winter trip to California and had instead purchased an Atwater Kent radio. They "hardly missed the trip," however, because, in the words of the wife, "California is just one trip, but Radio takes you on hundreds."[63]

Other radio manufacturers emphasized the joys of bringing modern, urban life into farm homes. In a 1929 advertisement appearing in *Nebraska Farmer*, the Eveready Company presented this theme along with several other ones emphasized in advertising of the era. The ad featured a drawing of a middle-aged couple and a young man who sat yawning in a rocking chair. According to the ad's copy, the young man, Cousin Harry, had been thoroughly bored on his last trip to the farm five years ago and had returned to the city after only two weeks, leaving his farm relatives, the Marsh family, feeling "lonesomer than ever" and remembering what Harry had said: "The gay shows . . . music . . . entertainment . . . something interesting every evening of the week in the city!" The story of Mr. and Mrs. Marsh and their young cousin, however, had a happy ending:

> Cousin Harry came out again last week. Expected to be bored. But that evening in the Marsh's [*sic*] living room he heard the most magnificent concert he had ever heard in his life! . . . [T]he Marsh's had bought a radio. Now—the day is done in a hurry. The evening brings news from the whole wide world. Music, speeches, educational topics, Sunday evening hymns . . . and John Marsh made enough to pay for his radio by taking advantage of prices broadcast direct from the market.[64]

Along with its emphasis on placating youth, benefiting the farmer's business, and breaking down the monotony and isolation of farm life, the Eveready ad featured another major advertising theme as well: that farm families should avail themselves of the best radio technology on the market. In the closing words of the ad, the Eveready Company urged, "[If] you already have an old set, you don't know how perfect today's radio reception is—get a new set and you will be astonished at the great improvement!"[65]

This theme remained a prominent one in advertising for electric- and battery-powered radios. A series of Radiola ads appearing in *Wallaces' Farmer* in 1930 also argued that farm families should ideally own expensive, high-powered radios. The ads claimed, "Thousands of farmers have learned by experience that a high-power Radiola is a profit-maker. It has become an essential part of modern farm equipment. One quick flash of important weather or market news over the radio often saves more money than the cost of several radio sets." Radiola ads continued to stress other uses for radio, arguing, "Every member of the family gets big value out of this wonderful modern invention. There are special programs on the air for mother, entertainment hours for the children, educational hours for young men and women who can't go to college. . . . [I]n fact a Radiola in the home is a daily wonder box of entertainment."[66] Nevertheless, as the agricultural depression worsened, radio manufacturers more frequently relied on marketing their product as a business expense that would reap financial rewards—and thus justify the sizable cost of investing in a quality radio. In the four-year period between 1926 and 1930, then, radio manufacturers had moved from marketing radio as a desirable farm luxury to promoting it as a necessary piece of farm equipment. This change in attitude, however, went beyond a mere alteration of marketing strategies. Improvements in radio technology and accompanying lower radio prices contributed to the increasingly common attitude that radio was a farm home necessity. Nevertheless, obtaining the money to purchase a radio often remained problematic. A letter from an Illinois reader to Betty Hunter's "Household Shopper's Service" in the Chicago-based *American Farming* magazine demonstrates the attitude of many farm people in 1931:

> I am writing to you about something that has been troubling my conscience for some time. I have been saving and saving—a little here and a little there, until I have enough saved to buy a moderately priced radio. It will have to be a battery operated set because we do not have electricity. I have dreamed and dreamed about having one, and now that it is so near a reality I am wondering if I ought not use the money for something more practical.[67]

Hunter's reply to her worried reader was illustrative of an attitude held by many farm life advisers of the era. In encouraging the reader to go ahead and purchase a radio, Hunter argued, "Lasting enjoyment can come from a radio and the farm home can almost take them out of the luxury classification."[68]

Statistics for radio ownership demonstrated that farm families listened to the advice of farm periodical columnists, the claims of advertisers, and to their own preferences. Radio ownership among midwestern farm families was widespread by 1930, and in one state, Iowa, more farm families than nonfarm families owned radios (see Table 2.4). In the Midwest, radio ownership had outdistanced farm family ownership of every other type of modern equipment except the automobile and telephone. That a radio could be run without electric wiring, that the whole family could benefit from and enjoy its use, and that it was less expensive than many other types of desired equipment undoubtedly contributed to its widespread use on midwestern farms. Moreover, unlike other modern equipment, the radio did not replace any type of existing technology or practice. While farm families might reason that they could

Table 2.4 Percentage of Families Owning Radios, 1930

	Urban Families	Farm Families
Illinois	60.6	40.8
Indiana	47.4	32.4
Iowa	50.0	50.9
Kansas	41.1	38.5
Minnesota	54.8	38.9
Missouri	47.0	23.4
Nebraska	50.1	49.3
North Dakota	46.6	39.5
South Dakota	48.2	44.5
Wisconsin	59.0	38.4

Source: U.S. Bureau of the Census, *Fifteenth Census of the United States, 1930: Population* (Washington: Government Printing Office, 1933).

continue relying on face-to-face communication, horse-drawn wagons, or outhouses rather than invest in telephones, cars, or bathrooms, they purchased radios because their function was unique.

In 1930, Elizabeth C. Wherry commented that radio was "a medium bringing into the home news, commercial advertising, drama, educational lectures, music—good and bad—talks upon every conceivable subject." She noted further, "It may be that it has come so quickly that we are hardly aware ourselves of the weight that the radio has in molding our thoughts and tastes."[69] By the end of the 1920s, then, radio had made great inroads into midwestern farm life. Along with print advertising, radio broadcasting had reinforced the Extension Service's arguments on behalf of farm and farmhouse modernization and had further familiarized farm women with urban, middle-class domestic standards—the standards that government advisers urged farm women to adopt as their own.

Ultimately, advertising and radio broadcasting were perhaps more effective than Extension Service personnel in taking the modernization message to farm women. In 1929, an Extension Service study of farm women in fifteen states found little improvement in reaching the majority of farm women. According to results of this 1929 study, demonstration agents were most successful in influencing the practices of women who lived on large farms and were Farm Bureau members (see Table 2.5). In addition, demonstration

Table 2.5 Percentage of Various Farm Women Groups Adopting
Extension Service Advice and Practices, 1929

Women on Small Farms	Women on Medium Farms	Women on Large Farms
26	32	38
Women in Non-Bureau Families	Women in Former Bureau Families	Women in Bureau Families
20	73	85

Source: M. C. Wilson, *The Effectiveness of Home Economics Extension Work in Reaching Farm Women* (Washington: Federal Extension Service, 1929).

agents were particularly successful in influencing college-educated women, a group that composed only 4 percent of the women in the 10,421 farm families surveyed.

Results of this 1929 survey also showed that for all the Extension Service's efforts, its home improvement program was among the least successful of its projects, in terms of the number of families who actually adopted new equipment. Much more successful were projects that helped to extend farm family resources, such as Extension Service clothing construction and food preservation projects (see Table 2.6).

As the decade of the twenties ended, Extension Service officials also realized that modern equipment was not decreasing the total number of hours that farm women spent performing housework. Although Extension Service publications emphasized that the methods and equipment that they recommended were designed to save labor, this was only a short-term goal. Saving labor and time in washing clothes with a washing machine, for instance, would allow farm women to use that time and energy in other ways. Again, policymakers hoped that women would use their extra time and energy to make the farm home more attractive and thus keep their families "down on the farm." In 1927, extension agent Madge J. Reese reiterated the Extension Service's position:

> Too often the time and energy consumed in housekeeping have made real homemaking impossible. The cooperative extension service offers the farm woman help in bringing about a better balance between the two. . . . [T]he manager of the farm home must have time and energy to

Table 2.6 Number of Home Demonstration Practices Adopted per 100
Farm Homes Participating in Extension Service Programs, 1929

Practices	Number per 100 Homes
Clothing Construction	24
Food Preservation	20
Food Preparation	6
Nutrition	6
Health and Sanitation	3
Home Management	2
Home Improvement	2

Source: M. C. Wilson, *The Effectiveness of Home Economics Extension Work in Reaching Farm Women* (Washington: Federal Extension Service, 1929).

think and plan for real homemaking through cultivation of those qualities of mind and soul which make her an interesting and attractive companion to her whole family. She must have time to associate with her children and teach them the true values of country life.[70]

In commenting on the results of a 1930 study of farm women's domestic work, another proponent of farm home modernization, Maud Wilson, noted that the overall labor-saving advantages of new appliances often evaporated as women changed their housekeeping standards. In the study, farm women who had neither electricity nor modern plumbing in their houses spent 3.3 hours a week more than those who had both utilities on preparing and clearing away meals, cleaning, and washing. On the other hand, women who owned modern equipment spent 2.2 hours more than those who did not on ironing, sewing, care of children, and care of house surroundings. According to Wilson, the study's results showed that with "the 'modernizing' of the home . . . the homemaker [used] that part of her time which it [set] free, in those marginal activities for which she [was] constantly 'trying to find time.'"[71]

Wilson, however, did not criticize this phenomenon. To her, and to other officials affiliated with the Extension Service, this study indicated that the goals of farm home modernization were being met by at least a minority of women; some farm women were becoming full-time homemakers with attractive, improved houses. As a result of their artificial division of farm and home, however, Extension Service policymakers neglected to see that women with access to some new domestic technology could alternatively choose to use their extra time and energy to focus additional attention on productive farm work. Most midwestern farm women certainly could not afford to become the full-time consumers envisioned by proponents of the New Agriculture—and many had no desire to play that role even if economic factors allowed it.

The history of the Extension Service in the 1920s is largely one of policymakers' goals greatly exceeding the reality of most women's lives. In urging women to purchase modern equipment and lead lives that approximated those of women in the urban middle class, the Extension Service ignored women's lack of economic and political power within the farm family. In order for farm women to have achieved the technological goals that the Extension Service set out for them during its first decade and a half, one factor was absolutely necessary—an increase in farm women's purchasing power. In order for that to have occurred, one of two scenarios was necessary—an improvement in the overall farm economy or an improvement in women's access to existing, limited cash resources. Neither scenario occurred. In the fifteen years between 1914 and 1929, with the exception of the war-boom years, the farm economy steadily worsened. And with government policies largely working against the notion of altering farm family politics, women were not able to achieve greater economic power within their families. In the 1920s, therefore, women heard the Extension Service's modernization message, and its reinforcement over the radio and in advertising, but most farm women did not respond to that message.

Twenty years earlier, Progressive reformers had attempted to impose an idealized agrarian ethos on an increasingly urbanized society; bureaucrats in the 1920s attempted to impose an urban value system on America's dwindling rural population. The modernization message put forth by government officials, farm journalists, and advertisers consistently emphasized that adoption of new household technology would bring "city convenience" to the farm home and thereby make women's life on the farm approximate that of urban women. Attempts to "urbanize" farm women, though, met with only limited success in the 1920s. With the decline of Progressivism and the diminished influence of the social "uplift" wing of the Country Life Movement, farm women of the 1920s lacked a vehicle by which to express their alternative vision of women's experience on the farm, but they nevertheless resisted attempts to turn them into replicas of the urban housewife. Survey results showed that farm women continued to value their role as farm producers throughout the decade. They frequently rejected adoption of "city conveniences" that would tie them to their farmhouse kitchens in favor of acquiring communication/transportation technology that would aid them in their role as farm producer and lessen their sense of isolation. Government officials, however, did not view farm women's resistance to mechanized housekeeping as insurmountable, and indeed during the next decade, under the auspices of Franklin Roosevelt's New Deal, officials would develop a new set of strategies designed to gain farm women's acceptance of the modern domestic ideal.

When Stauffer, a resident of rural Monticello, Wisconsin, wrote to Franklin D. Roosevelt to complain about low farm prices, she intended to speak for all midwestern farm women.[1] Focusing on possessions that farm women lacked, such as a functioning bathroom, Stauffer contrasted farm women's economic status with her perception of the greater affluence of urban women. After twenty years of exposure to the urban domestic ideal, farm women used a ready reference point when attempting to demonstrate the extent of their poverty—their lack of modern equipment. Frequently employing this rhetorical device, women made their opinions known to national leaders, the editors of farm life publications, and other individuals whom they saw as possessing the potential to ease their distress during the Great Depression. Farm women also praised New Deal programs and leaders whom they viewed as coming to farm people's aid during the depression—even though New Deal projects resulted in only limited economic reforms in the American countryside.

After the stock market crash of October 1929, the rest of the nation joined America's farm families in the financial despair that farm people had been experiencing for a decade. Most midwestern farm people blamed the Great Depression on "Hoover, the Republicans, and business," perceiving that Hoover and his Republican predecessors had favored businessmen, and ignored farmers, throughout the 1920s. In Hoover's mind, nothing was fundamentally wrong with American agriculture. All it

3

"A Chance to Live as the City Sisters"

The Great Depression and the New Deal

Mr. President, we don't even live decent. . . . [O]ur bath room is out of order, . . . our buildings need paint and repairs badly, . . . [we] can't pay our doctor, grocer, feed bills. . . . Please try to see our side of the story; we women feel as tho we are in the game also, as we help with the farm labor and save hiring help. I know you are doing the best you know how and are too busy a man to be bothered with this letter but please try to understand my plea. . . . We would like to have a chance to live as the city sisters and not be made to live as a peasant or slave.
—Mrs. Fred Stauffer (1933)

needed was a dose of sound business practices. Toward that end, he secured passage of a bill to create a Federal Farm Board, whose function was to make farm marketing more efficient, particularly by encouraging the cooperative marketing of agricultural products. The congressional Farm Bloc succeeded in tacking onto the bill a $500 million appropriation that the board was to use in making direct purchases of crops in order to stave off price declines. This measure, however, proved inadequate in relieving America's agricultural depression, and Hoover refused to consider any type of price-support system to aid the nation's farmers. Farm people also resented Hoover's effort to relieve depression conditions by creating a Reconstruction Finance Corporation to provide loans to financial institutions, insurance companies, and other businesses. To farm people, this move seemed once again to favor big business at the farmers' expense.[2]

Farm people voiced their complaints against the Hoover administration, and farm women wrote perhaps the most passionate letters that the administration received. As historian Robert McElvaine has suggested, the fact that society deemed it appropriate for women—but not men—to plead for help may account for the fact that so many farm women wrote vivid letters to government officials during the depression. Generally more literate than farm men, farm women also managed the domestic economy, making them the logical family members to write letters that described the difficulties of farm families in procuring food, clothing, and domestic equipment.[3]

Farm women filled their letters to members of the Hoover administration with accusations that Hoover was neglecting farm people while devising futile plans to revive American business. Stating that conditions in the rural Midwest were "not bad, just deplorable and then some," Mrs. J. L. Weege of rural Wimbledon, North Dakota, was typical in her criticism of the Hoover administration and what she saw as the Department of Agriculture's incompetence. In a March 1932 letter to Hoover's secretary of agriculture, Arthur Hyde, Weege charged that the administration's policies, and the impractical advice of the USDA's Extension Service, were useless in the face of declining farm prices and the rising cost of farming machinery:

As far as I can see, the farmer's ambition is done for. He no longer anticipates a future. . . . The Government is trying to inject life into a dead corpse by pumping it full of Federal loans, but the farmers [*sic*] of today . . . no longer cares, and as for our 4 H Club boys and girls . . . [they will] be even more embittered than the present farmers that they have been fooled so bad. I heard over the Radio the Iowa farmers are planning on a farmer's holiday for a year. . . . I am afraid that will come as to try to produce a crop only means to go deeper in debt to produce a free living for our Country's people, while the machine factories raise their prices. . . . I am not a fortune teller but believe our Country will reach a period where they will have to guarantee the farmers a cost of production price and 6 per cent on their investments . . . and no agricultural, so called, Educations [sic] that comes from the department of Agriculture can do the impossible; neither can a farmer.[4]

Weege's letter reflected the attitude, common among midwestern farm people, that American farmers produced food at such low prices that they virtually fed the nation "for free." In the early 1930s, midwestern farm families sold hogs for two cents a pound. They had to sell a good cow for five dollars and a dozen eggs for as little as five cents. Radical organizations, such as Milo Reno's Iowa-based Farmers' Holiday Association, suggested that farmers go on strike and shut down production entirely in order to force a rise in the price of farm products. In response, farmers in Buffalo County, Wisconsin, poured their milk on the roads. While local creameries closed down, farm women churned just enough butter to feed their own families and fed the skim milk to the hogs. In Sioux City, Iowa, farm women and men involved in the Holiday movement barricaded roads to prevent the delivery of milk to the Roberts Dairy Company. As Weege's letter suggests, many midwestern farm people saw direct government intervention as the only long-term solution to farm people's financial distress.[5]

Weege's criticism of the Department of Agriculture and its extension programs, including its 4-H Clubs for young people, indicated that the Extension Service had not adjusted its services to farm people in response to the worsening economic situation. In the early 1930s, Extension Service personnel still argued that the strategies of cooperative marketing and farm modernization would make American farm production more efficient and economically sound. Extension Service policymakers still saw farm women as primarily interested in the modernization of the farm home. In January 1930, extension home economist Grace E. Frysinger reported to the director of extension, C. W. Warburton, that the "farm homemaker [was] interested in increased farm income as a means of bettering home equipment and home conditions and she [would] urge cooperative marketing activities as a means to this end."[6]

Women's letters to the secretary of agriculture, however, indicated that their concerns during the early years of the Great Depression reached far beyond the goal of modernizing their kitchens. Although historians have largely failed to recognize their efforts, farm women played a major role in urging depression-era leaders to rethink existing economic theories and political policies. For example, in her April 1932 letter to Arthur Hyde, Gertrude Jefferies demonstrated a relatively sophisticated understanding of the local political and economic situation in her rural Missouri neighborhood. Jefferies disagreed with Hoover's "trickle down" policy of aiding big business and large financial institutions as a means toward improving the economy as a whole. In her opinion, the Hoover administration should "start at the bottom" and work to bolster American agriculture:

> I write to ask if you can see any *prospect* of things getting any better for us? It is just *terrible*. Eggs & cream are not *worth* anything. Hogs have gone down until they are not bringing anything either. A lot of our prices are *fixed* Interest, Taxes, Insurance. . . . I don't *honestly* believe you will see much lasting *prosperity* in this Country until the Farmer has a chance to get on his *feet*. . . . When you start to build a house you start with the *foundation*, and go up. You don't start at the attic. *Agriculture* is the *Basic* Industry. Its [*sic*] the only Industry that God *Ever Created*. And when you *Save* agriculture, you *Save all*. Just try it and see. I have served on the Republican Central Committee for a good while, until *lately*, So I know a little about *politics too*.[7]

Gertrude Jefferies was not the only disgruntled Republican farm woman who criticized the policies of the Hoover administration. Her fellow Missourian M. M. Clayton wrote to Herbert Hoover himself, giving him an account of the farm situation "First Hand from One who Is in a position to know":

> For thirty-Nine years myself and husband have farmed, worked from 4:30 A.M. until 9:30 P.M. in mid-summers busy season, from 5:30 A.M. until 7:30 P.M. all other times. And never in our life have we faced such a time as your administration has thrust upon us. . . . I among thousands of others . . . rushed to the polls and voted for you. Then what do you do? hand us a farm board that is a curse to every American farmer. . . . You appropriate money to the International Harvester Co. That again does not one cent do the farmer any good. . . . [D]on't think people are going

to put you in [office] again. . . . [T]he people with any back bone are going to vote for a Democrat and take a chance. And the other kind are not going to vote at all [because] they are disgusted.[8]

Clayton's handwritten postscript, apparently written several days after she had typed the body of the letter, created a dramatic finale to her story: "I am actualy destressed [sic]. My poor husband is sick. My poor son Herbert Clayton is sick. . . . [T]he masses are suffering while you all live in Luxury." There is no record that any member of the Hoover administration ever replied to Clayton's letter.[9]

Secretary of Agriculture Hyde directly replied to at least one midwestern farm woman—Mrs. Wellman Bruner of Wabash County, Indiana. When she wrote to the secretary, Bruner was a forty-five-year-old wife and mother who performed the typical tasks of a midwestern farm woman, including occasionally driving the family's gasoline tractor in the farm fields. She also chaired the Social and Educational Department of the Wabash County Farm Bureau and wrote to Hyde under the organization's letterhead. Bruner presented herself to Hyde as a loyal Republican who nevertheless was beginning to distrust her party's competence in confronting the farm depression. Bruner also criticized the policies and advice emanating from the nation's land-grant colleges. In her letter, Bruner attempted to speak for "thousands of inarticulate women, living upon farms, upon whom this [depression fell] heaviest":

We do not go to picture shows. Mr. Bruner has never heard a sound picture, and farmers [sic] cars are all candidates for the junk-heap. If this condition continues we feel we will have to discontinue our electric lights. . . . We have no radio . . . and we are living the average farm life. . . . As I go about my work tomorrow, symbolical of the days of labor of farm women, feeding chickens, milking cows, taking a paint brush and helping paint the barn, there will be a prayer in my heart that you may properly present, to the people of our party, the dignity and worth of agriculture in the national life . . . to the end that we have equality and an American standard of living upon the farm.[10]

Like the comments of the other farm women writing during this period, Bruner's remarks centered to a large degree on the lack of modern equipment in her home and the failure of farm people to achieve "an American standard of living." As these letters also indicate, however, farm women's interest in political and economic issues reached beyond their simply wanting to have homes that better resembled those of urban women. These women wanted economic justice and a voice—however limited—in the policy-making efforts that affected their lives. In focusing on their lack of specific pieces of equipment—in Bruner's case, her lack of a radio and an adequate automobile— farm women gave tangible examples of their poverty and a way to articulate to leaders like Hyde that they did not want to be poor any longer.[11] Bruner's comments, coming as they did from an officer of the conservative Farm Bureau, demonstrate the extent to which the depression affected farm women of all economic ranks and political philosophies.

Like earlier officials in the Department of Agriculture, however, Hyde did not seem to understand the broad scope of farm women's needs and concerns. He did answer Bruner's letter, possibly because she held an office in her local Farm Bureau and wrote the letter on bureau stationery. Hyde's response, though, generally dismissed Bruner's arguments and defended Hoover administration policies in vague and general terms: "You will pardon me if I say that I think you are wrong in your suggestions that agriculture has been betrayed by the Republican party, and in your criticism of the Land Grant Colleges. . . . I want to assure you the leadership of the Republican party is thoroughly alive to the situation and will do as much and go as far to remedy it as human beings can do."[12]

Midwestern farm people remained skeptical of the Republicans' resolve to aid agriculture, however, and in the 1932 election, Hoover failed to carry any of the midwestern farm states—not even his birth state of Iowa. During the campaign of 1932, Hoover's opponent, Governor Franklin D. Roosevelt of New York, had been vague about what his New Deal would do for American agriculture. Most midwestern farm people decided to "take a chance" nevertheless and supported his candidacy. Upon taking office in March 1933, he did not disappoint them. One of his first actions was to propose passage of an Agricultural Adjustment Act to aid the nation's farmers. Roosevelt sent his agricultural recovery bill to Congress on 16 March, and it quickly became law.

Based on the idea that overproduction lay at the heart of the farm depression, the Agricultural Adjustment Act provided for creation of an Agricultural Adjustment Administration (AAA) that would establish strict production quotas. These restrictions would cut total agricultural production and thus raise farm prices. In order to compensate farmers for their smaller crops, the AAA would pay them a certain amount per restricted acre. The money for these payments would come from a tax placed on processors of agricultural products—millers, meat packers, textile manufacturers, and others—and a portion of these payments was to be made to tenants and sharecroppers as well as farm owners. These programs would cover only major cash crops and large livestock—products that were generally men's responsibility—and would not affect women's butter-and-egg business. Farmers' compliance with AAA programs would be voluntary, and the programs would be administered at the local level by the Extension Service's county agents.[13]

The act received widespread support from major farm organizations, which Congress consulted as it hammered out the final legislation. In particular, farm organizations applauded the fact that agricultural processors, the so-called middlemen whom they had often criticized for contributing to farmers' financial woes, would be the source of government payments to American farmers. Farm leaders also praised the economic theory behind the AAA. In opposition to the concept of "trickle down" economics, the AAA promoted the idea that by saving farmers from disaster and putting money in their pockets, it would enable farm people to help stimulate the rest of the economy and reduce unemployment. Although popular with farm organization leaders, the new farm program did have a glaring inadequacy: The AAA benefited middle-sized and large farming operations at the expense of lower-class farmers. For small farmers working poor land, acreage reduction could mean an end to their marginal farming operations altogether. For many poor tenant farmers, acreage reduction meant their removal from land that their landlord took out of production, and, particularly in the South, farm owners frequently pocketed the AAA payments meant for tenants and sharecroppers. Although later New Deal farm programs would attempt to aid the nation's poorest farmers, in 1933 the focus was on saving farmers who were higher on the socioeconomic ladder and thus in a better position to help revive the American economy.[14]

The man who oversaw implementation of the Roosevelt administration's agricultural policies was Secretary of Agriculture Henry A. Wallace of Iowa. The grandson of Commission on Country Life member Henry Wallace, and the son of President Harding's secretary of agriculture, Henry C. Wallace, Henry A. Wallace was also the former editor of his family's farm life periodical—*Wallaces' Farmer*. Wallace soon recognized that despite the support of the nation's major farm organizations, and even with Americans' general optimism about Roosevelt administration programs, the AAA would meet resistance from farmers who were accustomed to planting their crops "from fence row to fence row" and who balked at the notion of cutting back production at a time when people were starving in American cities. Wallace admitted that these production cuts "were not acts of idealism in any sane society" but were necessary during this period of national emergency.[15]

In particular, Wallace was interested in winning farm women's support of the AAA. Like earlier farm reformers, he viewed women as a stabilizing force in rural America. Like President Roosevelt himself, Wallace frequently turned up on radio broadcasts and in newsreel reports in an attempt to persuade Americans to support New Deal policies, and he directed many of these appeals specifically to farm women. Perhaps because of their frequent use of the mass media, Roosevelt and Wallace seemed to farm women to be particularly accessible public figures. In addition, both Roosevelt and Wallace seemed to identify genuinely with the nation's farm people. Although a New York patrician, Roosevelt, who owned a rural estate on the Hudson River, fancied himself a "gentleman farmer." Wallace, a graduate of Iowa State Agricultural College and a well-known farm spokesman for many years, made every effort to demonstrate that he had not lost touch with his roots in the Midwest. Farm women also perceived that they had a friend in the president's activist wife, Eleanor Roosevelt, a compassionate woman whose frequent actions on behalf of disadvantaged people convinced farm women that she was on their side. As a result of their trust in individual members of the Roosevelt administration and their optimism about New Deal programs, farm women wrote to members of the new administration in unprecedented numbers.

Women's letters to members of the New Deal, however, displayed many of the same rhetorical devices farm women had used in earlier years. For instance, the writers of these letters continued to focus on their lack of modern equipment as a way to demonstrate that they were living in poverty. Once again, moreover, their letters showed that farm women were well aware of economic and political conditions beyond their farmhouse kitchens. A letter from Mrs. Jake Caffman of Kankakee County, Illinois, written to President Roosevelt within a month of his inauguration, was typical of those that officials received during the early months of the New Deal. Since 1925, Caffman's large family had been farming 240 acres of rented land. Caffman shared her experiences with Roosevelt in a letter that made suggestions on how he might further aid the nation's farmers but applauded the efforts he had already made:

We do not take no newspaper or have a radio since times got so hard. Can't afford it. Only news we get is ever [*sic*] two weeks out of the *Prairie Farmer*. But [I] see where 400,000 farmers and elevator men and what not are going to fight [the AAA]. . . . [Y]ou can't please them all. . . . It take[s] real labor with lots of sweat and worry to raise a crop, so if you can do any thing to bring about better prices for the farmer, do so. I have a lot of confidence in you. There were 6 of us to vote for you and help you, so help us if you can. If this letter is not thrown in the scrap basket, I ask you to give it a little place in your mind. . . . You have made a good start so far and I think you are a man who . . . know[s] how to do these things right.[16]

Caffman signed her letter "Your Friend, Mrs. Jake Caffman." Farm women, however, did not reserve their feelings of familiarity for the president. Letters to Henry A. Wallace also demonstrated a "personal touch." As the AAA crop reduction programs went into effect during the spring and summer of 1933, women's reactions to the AAA varied, but their attitude of personal connection to Wallace did not. Mary Drees of Delaware County, Iowa, wrote to the secretary of agriculture offering her personal services to help sign up neighboring farmers for the AAA's corn and hog reduction programs.[17] Her fellow Delaware County resident Elizabeth Gavin, although a lifelong Democrat, was more skeptical of the AAA but nevertheless wrote to Wallace in familiar terms: "I am a widow seventy years old, and am facing foreclosure on a 215 acre farm which is mortgaged for $16,000. This farm is said by every one to be one of the best in Delaware Co. Would you please write me a line of advice or encouragement if at all possible? This is a personal letter to you, Mr. Wallace."[18]

Farm women reserved their most impassioned personal pleas, however, for Eleanor Roosevelt. Sensing that they could speak to her "woman to woman," farm women often addressed specific women's issues to her. A letter from Viola Bourret of rural Stickney, South Dakota, was typical of those that Eleanor Roosevelt received during the first year of her husband's administration. Noting that AAA programs did not cover women's poultry and small-scale dairy production, Bourret wrote to Eleanor Roosevelt asking the Roosevelt administration to rectify this problem:

I have been thinking about the situation here in the middle west, and of a plan to help, but to get this plan before the President was another problem. I could not write to him because I felt that the letter would be classed as unimportant by a secretary, and so I decided to try writing one to you. . . . So far the men have had all the attention paid . . . for reducing wheat acreage and . . . for selling of pigs, but it is not getting us any where here. . . . [E]verything which we have to buy has gone up and the things we have to sell are going down in price: eggs, cream and chickens. This is the women's share of farm and small town money. . . . So why not pay the women for their chickens and have them put them in cans or else put a price on them so that they will meet the price of things that we have to buy? . . . You might be surprised to know that there are people in the United States who have not had a new dress for several years. I might say that I haven't had one for almost a year and a half and there are many women right in this community who are much worse off than I am. If the men cannot think of helping the women of the Country then surely we must intercede for ourselves. So Dear Lady . . . Will you intercede for the women here? . . . I know that you are not running the Ship of State but I do know that you are a helper. I voice the opinion of thousands of women here and could get a thousand signers for this letter in a short time.[19]

Bourret's letter differed from women's letters to male members of the Roosevelt administration and revealed characteristics that were unique to letters written to Eleanor Roosevelt. Bourret's letter demonstrated her trust in Eleanor Roosevelt's innate sensitivity. Bourret believed that Eleanor Roosevelt, unlike a correspondence secretary, would immediately acknowledge the worth of Bourret's letter. She also recognized that Eleanor Roosevelt could be trusted to champion women's issues and spoke to Mrs. Roosevelt in terms that she believed only another woman would understand. Rather than focus on her lack of mechanical equipment, Bourret wrote about not having a new dress. Finally, Bourret focused on farm women's role as producers and marketers of specific farm products. Bourret trusted that Eleanor Roosevelt, unlike male members of the New Deal, would recognize that women too were farm producers.

Impoverished farm women also found an ally in Democratic congresswoman Virginia E. Jenckes of Indiana. During the early months of the New Deal, Jenckes was perhaps the most influential midwestern farm woman in the nation. Elected from Indiana's Sixth District on Franklin Roosevelt's coattails, Jenckes came to Washington in 1933 as a feminist and a champion of American agriculture who attempted to bring women's concerns into the formation of agricultural recovery programs.[20]

Jenckes had owned and managed 1,100 acres of Indiana farmland since her husband's death in 1921. Low prices for corn and large livestock, however, had led her to raise her own turkeys, peaches, and sweet potatoes to pay household expenses for herself and her young daughter. Jenckes's entrance into politics was a direct result of her experiences as a farm woman. Concern about flooded farmland had led her to organize the Wabash-Maumee River Improvement Association and thus become a major figure in western Indiana politics. Under headlines such as "The New Woman in Action," the Indiana press had closely followed Jenckes's 1932 campaign and had portrayed her as empathizing with the midwestern farm woman "who raises chickens and gets low prices for eggs; who milks cows and cannot find market for her milk; and who when she does find good customers for these products can't buy new curtains or blankets or radios with her money as farmers' wives are supposed to do but has to use it to help pay the family taxes."[21]

In reality, Jenckes was more prosperous than most of her counterparts, but she nevertheless served as an effective spokeswoman for more typical farm women during her six years in Congress. As one of the few females in Congress, and as the first congresswoman elected from Indiana, Jenckes frequently caught the attention of the national and midwestern press. The fact that she also had a penchant for wearing colorful hats and for sending whimsical gifts to her political mentor, President Roosevelt, further ensured that Jenckes's words and actions often found their way into the nation's newspapers. Jenckes's enthusiastic comments about the AAA, rural electrification, and the use of agricultural products for "non-agricultural purposes"—including the production of alcohol, gasohol, and cornstalk paper—gained widespread attention.[22]

Jenckes was a strong supporter of the Roosevelt administration's agricultural policies and, as a large landowner, felt threatened by the more radical measures of the Farmers' Holiday Association. Worrying that farmers in Indiana would follow the lead of radicals in Iowa and Wisconsin, Jenckes sought to head off further farm strikes in the Midwest by issuing an emergency telegram to the governors of Minnesota, Iowa, Wisconsin, and the Dakotas and to the presidents of the Farmers' Holiday Association, the National Farmers' Union, and the Indiana Farm Bureau. Jenckes's 1933 telegram not only expressed her strong support for the AAA but also voiced her belief that farm women were a pacifying force in rural America: "I . . . am making a special appeal to the women on the farms. I am familiar with the hardships they are enduring. I appeal to them to counsel their men to have patience and to stand by the President."[23]

Jenckes's telegram indicates that she recognized the central role that women were playing within agricultural organizations of the era, particularly those on the left side of the political spectrum. Whether they "stood by the President" or opposed New Deal policies, women used participation in farm organizations as a way to express themselves politically. In the Midwest, the two major organizations during this period were the radical Farmers' Union and the conservative Farm Bureau.[24]

In contrast with the Farm Bureau, the Farmers' Union did not have a separate women's association, and it offered women an equal voice in the formation of policy. Membership was on a family basis, and each family member over the age of sixteen, whether male or female, had an equal vote within the organization. Unlike the Farmers' Holiday Association, the Farmers' Union did not formally advocate violent resistance to government policies, although some Farmers' Holiday members—including Holiday leader Milo Reno—were also affiliated with the Farmers' Union. Unlike the Farm Bureau, the Farmers' Union did not contain members who fretted that the New Deal was leading American agriculture toward socialism. In fact, among the major midwestern farm organizations, the 100,000-member Farmers' Union was the most supportive of New Deal farm policies, particularly those designed to aid small and low-income farmers. An estimated 95 to 98 percent of Farmers' Union members voted for Franklin D. Roosevelt in 1932.[25]

Membership in the Farmers' Union not only allowed farm women an opportunity to work toward farm reform but, with its policy of female equality, allowed women numerous outlets for their political and organizational skills and other talents as well. For Jean Stillman Long of Dunn County, Wisconsin, the Farmers' Union allowed her the first opportunity to get "out of four walls" and away from the watchful eye of her domineering mother-in-law. Using the talents she had developed as a teacher before her marriage, Long traveled through Wisconsin and Minnesota directing educational plays for the Farmers' Union. Because she was undertaking these activities for the cause of agricultural reform, Long's husband and mother-in-law could not fault her for leaving behind her domestic tasks to devote time to "the theater."[26]

Even women who belonged to the conservative Farm Bureau, however, pushed for greater inclusion in the formation of New Deal farm policies. Like the Farmers' Union, the bulk of Bureau membership was centered in the Midwest. At the time FDR took office in 1933, Bureau membership numbered a little less than 200,000, making it the nation's largest farm organization. In contrast with the Farmers' Union, the Farm Bureau was interested primarily in issues that affected larger, more prosperous farmers. As a result, the bureau largely focused its efforts on promoting economic policies favorable to large farmers. Any attention to social issues took place within the women's association, the Associated Women of the American Farm Bureau Federation, an institution that lacked the political clout of its parent organization. In the words of a midwestern observer who harked back to the two-pronged rural reform efforts of the Progressive Era, "Matters dealing with home conveniences, housing, church, health, rural schools, libraries, safety, nutrition and rural youth . . . [are] left to the women's group. . . . Without question more could be accomplished if there were greater mutual sharing among the men's and women's groups in the consideration of both economic and social issues."[27]

Women who agreed with this assessment and were dissatisfied with the bureau's gendered division of labor pushed for greater participation in forming economic policies that affected farm people. For example, a group of Farm Bureau women meeting in Ames, Iowa, in 1934 made a motion requesting that Secretary of Agriculture Wallace "use farm women in council and in the administration of the farm adjustment program."[28] One Iowa bureau member, Mrs. Ellsworth Richardson, even wrote to Wallace offering "to drop every thing" she was doing if she could work with him, "and at a modest salary too." Richardson assured Wallace that Iowans had long forgotten the Farmers' Holiday strikes of the previous year and now had unlimited faith in Wallace's programs. Nevertheless, she believed those programs could be strengthened by the greater inclusion of farm women in policy-making positions. Richardson also indicated that farm women remained skeptical about the extent to which Extension Service advice was applicable to the real-life situations of most farm women:

[F]arm women are really insisting that some one truly representing farm women be used in the AAA program. . . . Can there not be found some place where a farm woman can bring the farm woman's view point and influence into the program? We really feel that there should be a farm woman placed in an advisory capacity in the Extension Division of the Dept. of Agriculture; the educational work of the Colleges and extension are [sic] too often out of step with real farm problems. We have a number of wonderful women that would do credit to the noble program you have started. We want to help you keep it always true to the farm needs.[29]

Director of extension work C. W. Warburton balked at women affiliated with the Farm Bureau gaining undue influence within the Department of Agriculture. In reference to Richardson's letter, Warburton informed Secretary Wallace that he believed home demonstration agents were already adequately looking out for farm women's interests:

> The women members of our extension staff are rural minded and are well informed on the Agricultural Adjustment program. . . . Perhaps there is a place in the Agricultural Adjustment Administration for some competent woman writer to prepare publicity material particularly directed to women readers, pointing out the ways in which the Agricultural Adjustment Administration benefits rural homes, but other than this I do not see how any one woman could make a large contribution to the program.[30]

As Warburton's comments indicate, farm women received no direct representation within the New Deal agencies designed to aid farm people. And as the 1930s progressed, much of the pro–New Deal propaganda that the USDA distributed was aimed at convincing women that the AAA and other programs would "benefit rural homes." Ignoring abundant evidence to the contrary, USDA officials continued to act as though farm women were almost exclusively concerned with housekeeping matters. As in previous administrations, the USDA under Henry A. Wallace focused much of its effort toward farm women on the concept of farm home modernization.

A major forum for the USDA's propaganda of this type was *Wallaces' Farmer*, a publication founded by Henry A. Wallace's family and one that he himself had edited for many years. A favorite strategy for the editors of *Wallaces' Farmer* was to coax women to use their families' AAA payments to purchase modern machinery. The families whom the AAA most benefited—those in the middle and upper ranks of the rural socioeconomic scale—were also the farm families most likely to attain the domestic ideal that their urban counterparts already enjoyed. Officials hoped that women in these families would use government payments to purchase manufactured household equipment and thus help their families remain satisfied with farm life and also help revive American industry. These farm women consumers might also become customers of the appliance manufacturers who advertised in *Wallaces' Farmer*.[31]

Early in the Roosevelt administration, the editors of *Wallaces' Farmer* published a number of letters from women who indicated that they were willing to support cutbacks in farm production—but not at the expense of farm modernization. As in the past, the editors of *Wallaces' Farmer* saw women wielding indirect political power within the farm family, and they believed women should use that influence to promote compliance with AAA policies. In the words of an editorial appearing in the fall of 1933, "There is a great responsibility on farm women these days to keep informed on reduction plans and to use their influence to get farm people 100 per cent behind them."[32]

Wallace and other members of the New Deal also used the long-established "Farm and Home Hour" as a forum for extensive coverage of news and discussion about the AAA. During this period, Elizabeth Wherry wrote about the improved music and informative features on the "Farm and Home Hour" and praised radio as a depression-era morale booster that, free of charge, could bring "song, jest, symphony, news, the outside world, and good fellowship" to distressed farm families. She noted, however, "There's the initial cost of the receiving set and keeping it up, but it's worth it. After all, the few dollars thus spent in keeping up our morale and our batteries would not pay off the mortgage anyway."[33]

In this spirit, Mrs. J. A. Huss of Sac County, Iowa, wrote to *Wallaces' Farmer* in February 1934 to report that she had spent a portion of her family's AAA corn loan check to buy a new radio, which, in her words, "brought the universe to our home." In commenting on Huss's letter, the editors of *Wallaces' Farmer* noted that the $35 million in AAA corn loan money paid to Iowa farm families thus far "must have brought new hope and happiness to thousands of farm folks who ha[d] endured so many privations" in the previous few years. Throughout the first two years of the Roosevelt administration, *Wallaces' Farmer* printed similar letters of support from farm women, arguing that, in all likelihood, "farm women [would] have as much to say as farm men in deciding whether the corn-hog contract campaign [would] go over in every farm community."[34]

As presented on the pages of *Wallaces' Farmer*, women's arguments in favor of the AAA took a variety of forms. A woman from Palo Alto County, Iowa, wrote that, in the long run, the AAA would benefit American industry: "Give the farmers some money and see what they'll do with it. . . . [I]f the farmer got enough money, he might even buy a new car. Give the farmer some money and see him start the wheels of industry."[35]

Emphasizing their role as producers, women also argued that cutbacks in grain and large-livestock production allowed greater investment in the materials necessary for home production. A South Dakota woman reported that she used $75 of her family's corn loan money to invest in a sewing machine, fruit jars, and fruit trees. With these purchases, she could help clothe and feed her family inexpensively.[36]

Jennie Sheldon of Fremont County, Iowa, also suggested that AAA payments allowed the purchase of items that contributed to her family's economic welfare:

> With the money we borrowed from the government . . . we decided to purchase three practical things for our home. The first was a power washing machine, because it would save so much time and hard labor. Next, we enclosed our porch with windows. . . . The third thing we bought was a radio, turning in our old-fashioned one on a moderately priced modern model. Some people might call this a luxury, but I don't, and our experience has proved that it is a practical necessity for a farmer who has livestock and grain to sell.[37]

By the time of the 1936 presidential campaign, however, a *Wallaces' Farmer* editorial argued that the economic situation was sufficiently improved that women could invest in equipment that did not necessarily contribute directly to the farm family economy. Based on letters farm women had recently written to *Wallaces' Farmer*, the front-page editorial, entitled "Mother Will Spend Part of AAA Check," argued:

> These women want a new sink and drain in the kitchen, a bathroom and complete water system . . . a new range, a power washing machine . . . a new radio . . . and plenty of other things to make housework easier and to make the home more attractive. . . . She's turned in her egg and butter money to help with the taxes, or rent, has made over her old dresses, has continued to wear her 1930 hat. . . . [I]t's time to give mother her due.[38]

Letters to *Wallaces' Farmer* in the weeks immediately preceding the 1936 election indicated that some farm women did use AAA checks to purchase such household equipment. Some women also credited the AAA with raising farm prices to a level at which farm families could afford a variety of household improvements. Recognizing this, a *Wallaces' Farmer* editorial that appeared one month before the 1936 election urged that farm families spend a portion of the increased income that had been "the joyous lot of a good many farmers" that year to purchase a new radio. Not mentioned in the editorial's list of the radio's informational and entertainment functions was its role as a conduit for New Deal campaign messages.[39]

Two weeks later, a letter from a Hardin County, Iowa, woman measured the success of New Deal policies by the number of household improvements in her rural neighborhood: "In our community we know of new furnaces in farm houses, new cupboards, new rugs, electric refrigerators. . . . As a farm woman too busy to study either politics or economics, I just 'feel' that these new things have come because of increased incomes, and that increased farm incomes are the result of the Roosevelt-Wallace program."[40]

As in 1932, midwesterners repudiated one of their own in the 1936 presidential election. They went to the polls to defeat the Republican candidate, Kansas governor Alf Landon, in one of the most decisive losses in political history. Midwestern farm women, like the vast majority of American voters, demonstrated their overwhelming approval of the Roosevelt administration's policies—including FDR's agricultural recovery programs.

The results of *Wallaces' Farmer* polls conducted later in the 1930s, however, indicated that farm women were less enthusiastic than farm men about the Roosevelt administration's second AAA. The Supreme Court had declared the original AAA unconstitutional in 1936, arguing that Congress had violated the Tenth Amendment in passing legislation that dealt with agricultural commerce, an area of concern constitutionally reserved for the states. The Court had also ruled that the law's processing tax was a penalty designed to aid farmers rather than to provide for the general welfare as the Constitution required. In 1938, therefore, the Roosevelt administration created a new AAA, which emphasized farmers' implementation of soil conservation practices. The new AAA statute authorized the secretary of agriculture to decide how much acreage should be planted each year in staple crops and provided compulsory quotas that limited production—after approval by a vote of two-thirds of the farmers who produced a specific crop. With this new legislation, the principle of parity-price supports became national policy.

In an informal *Wallaces' Farmer* poll conducted late in 1938, members of the periodical staff asked women in Iowa, Minnesota, Missouri, and Nebraska their opinion of the new AAA. Approximately one-third were in favor of the program, another third disapproved, and a final third had no opinion. The editors of *Wallaces' Farmer* attributed women's apathy and disapproval to their lack of information about the intricacies of the new AAA's conservation program and to the fact that not all women had access to their families' loan checks. On the other hand, the editors noted that the lure of government payments did not seem to influence women in "rough land counties," who "talked most about the benefits from soil conservation and very little about the AAA checks."[41]

In other words, the *Wallaces' Farmer* strategy of stressing home improvements had largely failed. Government checks often went to other farm improvements or to paying overdue debts. Results of the *Wallaces' Farmer* poll indicated that some men never even consulted their wives about ways in which to spend money obtained through the farm program. In areas where the land had been ravaged, women were more interested in reviving the soil than in improving their homes. Some women voiced their opposition to government intervention in general, and others bemoaned the killing of baby pigs that had taken place under the earlier reduction program. In publishing the results of the 1938 poll, *Wallaces' Farmer* even printed remarks critical of Henry A. Wallace. A Redwood County, Minnesota, woman summarized her opinion of the new AAA succinctly: "Secretary Wallace is crazy."[42]

The editors of *Wallaces' Farmer*, however, did note a hopeful pattern among the responses to their poll. Both women who had a favorable view of the AAA and those who held a negative opinion frequently stated that they would be interested in attending AAA meetings. In other words, the editors of the Midwest's major farm periodical had finally acknowledged the argument that women themselves had been making for five years—that they too would like to be involved in the formation of New Deal farm policy. In this case, that involvement would be at the local level. In the words of a Madison County, Iowa, woman, "I talk it over with my husband, and would like to attend the AAA meetings if women were invited."[43]

Responses to the poll suggested, however, that women's participation in AAA meetings was hampered not only by the lack of a specific invitation to do so but also by notions about appropriate gender roles. A Saline County, Missouri, woman stated, for instance, that she would like to attend the meetings herself but that "other women" did not go. The remarks of a Redwood County, Minnesota, woman, however, were perhaps more telling: "I would like to go to AAA meetings if other women went, but I'm afraid people would think I had turned into a farmer."[44]

Based on such responses, the editors of *Wallaces' Farmer* began to use a new strategy to convince women to support the AAA. The editors abandoned the farm home modernization argument in favor of a campaign to educate women about the merits of the AAA conservation program itself. In an editorial entitled "Invite the Women to AAA Meeting," which appeared two weeks after the results of the 1938 poll had been published, the editors of *Wallaces' Farmer* presented their new strategy. Women should no longer encourage their husbands' participation in the AAA in an attempt to reap the advantages of a government check. Instead, women should be full partners in their family's cooperation with the AAA program. In making their argument for women's full participation in the AAA, however, the editors could not resist employing traditional gender-role stereotypes. Women would be worth tolerating at meetings not only because their influence on their husbands was significant but also because women's culinary skills might attract greater male participation at meetings: "Our tip to every committeeman who wants to know how to get a crowd out is this: Ask a committee of women to provide doughnuts and coffee after the business meeting, and then let the news leak out."[45]

Nine months later, the new strategy of encouraging women's participation in AAA meetings seemed to have garnered mixed results. In random interviews with midwestern farm women, *Wallaces' Farmer* found that although meetings were now open to farm women, many still did not choose to attend, and women generally remained less favorable than men toward the AAA. Although women's participation in AAA meetings prompted a Decatur County, Iowa, woman to proclaim, "Now that we understand the farm program we think it's fine," many other women continued to hold the view of a Bureau County, Illinois, woman: "We want to run the farm as we please. We don't need to have the government tell us what to do."[46]

A month later, *Wallaces' Farmer* published the results of a more systematic poll conducted in September 1939, which showed that 75 percent of Iowa farm men and 69 percent of Iowa farm women said that they had generally approved of the New Deal's farm aid legislation. When asked whether the AAA program of production controls and commodity loans should be retained now that American farmers could possibly profit from the war in Europe, 61 percent of the men but only 54 percent of the women answered affirmatively. The editors apparently thought that the margin of difference between men's and women's favorable attitudes toward the AAA was not insurmountable, for in the same issue of the magazine they encouraged women's participation in Home Conservation Committees that had been formed in ten Iowa counties "not because [women] want[ed] a part in running [the AAA]—they already [had] enough to do—but more to study it and to help promote an understanding of the entire plan." According to *Wallaces'*

Farmer, these AAA study clubs were important; it explained, "[Although] rural women know that the AAA program has brought relief to farmers, . . . it is a detailed program and sometimes it is pretty hard to explain to a friend in town or to an unbelieving neighbor just why it has helped to make farm income more dependable." Once again, the chief focus of attempts to win farm women's support for the AAA was on their influence over other members of rural society.[47]

By the summer of 1940, farm women for the first time rated New Deal farm policies as favorably as did men. According to the results of a *Wallaces' Farmer* poll in June 1940, 66 percent of Iowa farm men and 66 percent of Iowa farm women approved of the AAA. The failure of the war in Europe to raise American farm prices was a primary factor in elevating women's approval rating for the AAA, but perhaps the greater inclusion of women in AAA meetings and study clubs had also had an influence on the survey's results. A *Wallaces' Farmer* poll conducted on the eve of the 1940 presidential election, however, possibly suggested that women's support of New Deal farm policies still lagged somewhat behind that of men. According to the poll's results, 56 percent of Iowa farm men intended to vote for Roosevelt, while 53 percent of Iowa farm women were so inclined. The editors reported that the major factor that respondents cited in their decision whether or not to support Roosevelt was their attitude toward his farm policies.[48]

In working to make the AAA a success, Henry A. Wallace actively sought the support of farm women. As secretary of agriculture, and in his association with *Wallaces' Farmer*, Wallace only looked for women's support of the AAA, however, when the program appeared to be in peril. When farm men initially balked at the idea of reducing production, Wallace and his supporters looked to farm women in their role as consumer to encourage their families' participation in the AAA. When that tactic did not appear to work, AAA advocates pushed for women's greater inclusion in local AAA meetings, activities, and policy making. The goal, however, remained the same: Farm women would persuade farm men to participate in AAA programs. New Dealers viewed farm women as valuable allies only to the extent that women could exert "behind-the-scenes" influence and encourage farm men's compliance with AAA programs.

While the AAA largely benefited families in the middle and upper ranks of rural society, aid to the nation's poorest farm families arrived with the creation of the Farm Security Administration (FSA). The FSA began life as the Resettlement Administration in 1935 but was reorganized as the Farm Security Administration under the Farm Tenant Act of 1937. FSA activities included aiding migratory farm workers to improve their housing and helping tenant farmers—who numbered roughly half of those people farming in the Midwest—to buy their own land. By the time of its demise in the mid-1940s—the result, in part, of Farm Bureau charges that the agency was "wasteful of funds, socialistic in trend, and badly in need of new administrative talent"—the FSA had helped 870,000 farm families rehabilitate their homes and had lent funds to 41,000 farmers to purchase their lands.[49]

The FSA's greatest legacy, however, was its catalog of visual images of depression-era farm life. Under the direction of Roy Stryker, the FSA's photographic section provided employment for some of the era's most talented photographers—Walker Evans, John Vachon, Russell Lee, Arthur Rothstein, Marion Post Wolcott, and Dorothea Lange. Their job was to document the problems of America's farm people and thus create public support for the FSA's programs. And among the best-known FSA photographs were those of rural women.[50]

In addition to providing viewers with dramatic images of America's impoverished farm women, the FSA photographs reveal important information about the material conditions of the women in those photographs. In particular, many of the photographs, along with the captions written by the photographers who made them, provide information about the technological experiences of midwestern farm women. For example, Russell Lee's 1938 photograph of a black FSA client at her back porch washboard shows a careworn, middle-aged woman using the only laundry equipment available to most residents of New Madrid County, Missouri (see Figure 3.1). John Vachon's 1940 portrait of a sturdy young FSA client driving a tractor in Grant County, Illinois, is aesthetically pleasing and would have made an appropriate cover illustration for the 1940 McCormick-Deering implement catalog (see Figure 3.2). Vachon's caption for the photograph, however, indicates that the young woman's mastery of "male" technology was considered unusual and worthy of special comment: "She and her mother run the farm without the assistance of any men."[51]

Several of the FSA photographs illustrate the uneven diffusion of technology on midwestern farms. Russell Lee's series of photographs of the Schoenfeldt family of Sheridan County, Kansas, shows people who, as late as 1939, were still living in a sod house. The family matriarch, however, had availed herself of one piece of relatively inexpensive technology that had been a favorite of Extension Service advisers for twenty years. In his portrait of the

Fig. 3.1. Russell Lee's photograph of a farm woman at her washboard shows the type of laundry equipment used by most residents of rural New Madrid County, Missouri, in 1938. (Courtesy of FSA Collection, Library of Congress, Washington, D.C.)

Fig. 3.2. FSA photographer John Vachon found it noteworthy that this young woman and her mother ran a farm in Grant County, Illinois, "without the assistance of any men." (Courtesy of FSA Collection, Library of Congress, Washington, D.C.)

Fig. 3.3. As late as 1939, the Schoenfeldts of Sheridan County, Kansas, lived in a sod house, but Mrs. Schoenfeldt owned a modern pressure cooker, "of which she [was] very proud." Photograph by Russell Lee. (Courtesy of FSA Collection, Library of Congress, Washington, D.C.)

home's interior, Lee reveals Mr. and Mrs. Schoenfeldt standing in front of a freshly whitewashed wall, covered with Catholic iconography and other keepsakes, and Mrs. Schoenfeldt—grease-stained apron, disheveled hair, and all—is posing with her most prized possession, "her pressure cooker of which she is very proud" (see Figure 3.3).[52]

Vachon and Lee's photographs of depression-era North Dakota, however, are perhaps the most dramatic FSA portraits of life in the midwestern Farm Belt. Not coincidentally, North Dakota was the midwestern farm state that the depression and drought of the 1930s had most affected. During the 1930s, nearly a third of the state's population received relief benefits, and by 1940, half of the residents of seven western North Dakota counties were "on relief." During that same period, North Dakota led the entire nation in the proportion of farm homes that abandoned electric service. Between 1934 and 1939, the number of electrified farms in the state dropped 36.5 percent because farm families could no longer afford to run electrical equipment. In 1940, 94 percent of North Dakota farm homes lacked running water, and 89.8 percent relied on outdoor privies.[53]

At the same time, however, North Dakota farm families led all others on the midwestern plains in the ownership of radios. In 1940, 87.2 percent of North Dakota farm families owned radios, primarily battery-powered models. In contrast, in the plains states of Kansas and Nebraska, only 73.2 percent and 76.7 percent of farm families had radios. Perhaps the greater need for radio as a communication tool on the more widely spaced and isolated farms of North Dakota accounted for the higher percentage of radio ownership among the state's farm families. Perhaps Elizabeth Wherry's theory about radio as a depression-era morale booster also came into play for the beleaguered residents of North Dakota.[54]

The depression-era experiences of Margaret Lien illustrate in one woman's life the problems of poverty, distance, and lack of modern technology on the plains of North Dakota. All five of her children were born in her farmhouse, but because the local doctor could not get there in time, four of the children were delivered by a midwife who traveled 3.5 miles from her own farm. Following these births, Lien's husband Ben traveled 5 miles to the nearest telephone to call the doctor for postnatal treatment. According to Lien, "If [Dr. Hilts] was around, why fine. If he was out in the country, or busy with somebody else—well, we had to wait. But he would come. If it was summer he came by car. In the wintertime he would come by car as far as Sorlie's. Then he came to our place with a team sled." Payment for Dr. Hilts's services was $35, a fee that the Liens could not afford when their third child was born in December 1932. Dr. Hilts suggested that the family pay him with a butchered pig. When Ben Lien went to deliver the pig, however, the doctor thought that it was worth more than $35 and proposed another exchange. As Margaret Lien told the story, "He wanted to know if Ben would take that battery-operated radio he had. It was an old Zenith, and here Ben came with the old radio. Dr. Hilts even bought a new battery. But, anyway, that was our first radio."[55]

As this exchange of goods, services, and technologies demonstrates, life was difficult for North Dakota farm families, a fact well illustrated by a series of photographs that Russell Lee made in the autumn of 1937 in Williams County, on the state's western border. Lee's exterior portraits are dramatic. His photograph of Mrs. Olie Thompson shows a sunburned woman in a print dress and straw hat standing behind a team of horses pulling a wagon filled with large barrels (see Figure 3.4). Lee's portrait of Thompson returning

Fig. 3.4. Russell Lee's photograph shows Mrs. Olie Thompson of Williams County, North Dakota, hauling water from a local spring in September 1937. (Courtesy of FSA Collection, Library of Congress, Washington, D.C.)

from her daily trip to a local spring provides a startling visual image of a problem that plainswomen had complained of more than twenty years earlier in David Houston's survey—that they often had to haul water from distances of up to 5 miles.

Lee's interior shots are even more informative. His portrait of a Williams County farm kitchen shows a variety of well-worn pieces of small equipment—and a window frame stuffed with rags to prevent the intrusion of dust storms (see Figure 3.5). His photograph of the interior of one of the county's "better homes" shows a middle-aged couple in a living room illuminated by an old-fashioned oil lamp; they are sitting on a ragged couch in front of a wall covered by brown wrapping paper. A vegetable crate serves as their makeshift end table. Near the edge of the picture, however, resting on a battered table, is the family's radio (see Figure 3.6).

Lee's portrait of a young woman and her four small children, however, is perhaps the most memorable of his Williams County photographs—and one that tells a story very similar to that of Margaret Lien. According to Lee's caption, the photograph shows "Mrs. Shotbang with her four children she delivered herself. Husband broke his foot early this spring, about the time the baby was to be born. They ran short of coal and bed clothing and Mrs.

Fig. 3.5. Rags prevent the intrusion of dust storms into the kitchen of a Williams County farmhouse. Photograph by Russell Lee. (Courtesy of FSA Collection, Library of Congress, Washington, D.C.)

Fig. 3.6. Russell Lee's 1937 photograph reveals the living room of one of the "better homes" in rural Williams County. (Courtesy of FSA Collection, Library of Congress, Washington, D.C.)

Shotbang had to take care of the newly born baby and the rest of the family. She cut fence posts for fuel but the family almost froze. There were no mattresses on the beds this past winter, only quilts over the hard springs." Lee's photograph shows the very young–looking Mrs. Shotbang and her disheveled children—sitting in front of the family radio (see Figure 3.7).[56]

The photographs by Lee, Vachon, and other FSA photographers helped publicize midwestern farm women's continuing lack of many types of modern equipment during the New Deal era. On the other hand, the photographs also provide visual evidence of the types of technology that impoverished farm women had acquired and thus lend some insight into the technological priorities of midwestern farm families. For example, the fact that the people in these photographs often arranged themselves around the family radio indicates the extent to which that piece of equipment played a major role in their lives. Indeed, in many of the FSA photographs, the radio appears to have been the focal point of activities within the farm home, serving as a sort of secular altar (see Figure 3.8).[57]

Fig. 3.7. Members of the impoverished Shotbang family cluster near the family radio in 1937. Photograph by Russell Lee. (Courtesy of FSA Collection, Library of Congress, Washington, D.C.)

The photographs' major contribution, however, is their documentation of continuing economic crisis on midwestern farms. Although critics of the FSA charged that its photographers sometimes staged the situations they photographed or purposely sought out particular subjects or settings that supported the agency's political agenda, the poverty that the photographs documented was real. The FSA photographs demonstrate that even after implementation of New Deal farm reforms, many midwestern farm families were financially incapable of achieving mechanized farming and housekeeping. The farm people shown in the FSA photographs, while often photographed posing with some piece of modern equipment, were actually those whom mechanization

Fig. 3.8. A North Dakota farm couple sit in front of their "secular altar"—the family radio—in 1937. Photograph by Russell Lee. (Courtesy of FSA Collection, Library of Congress, Washington, D.C.)

had harmed rather than benefited. These were the small farmers who could no longer compete with the nation's large, mechanized farming operations. These were the tenant farmers, hired hands, and sharecroppers whom tractors had displaced or would soon remove. Minority farmers were particularly vulnerable, as illustrated by Arthur Rothstein's dramatic photographs of evicted black sharecropping families lining the highway in New Madrid County, Missouri (see Figures 3.9 and 3.10). The FSA relocation and assistance programs were able to aid only a minority of America's poorest farmers; many of the people shown in FSA photographs would no longer be farming the land by the end of the Roosevelt administration. Their loss was not mourned by those who believed that these people were no longer necessary in the mechanized world of modern farming. In fact, among many members of the Department of Agriculture, the Farm Bureau, and the U.S. Congress, open hostility had always existed toward FSA programs designed to keep these people on the land. Although these institutions decried the movement of farm people to the

Fig. 3.9. Displaced sharecropping families line the road in New Madrid County, Missouri, in January 1939. Photograph by Arthur Rothstein. (Courtesy of FSA Collection, Library of Congress, Washington, D.C.)

cities, apparently that sentiment only applied to middle-class farmers. As several stirring photographs by FSA photographers show, by the time the FSA's opponents finally succeeded in killing the agency, many of the nation's poorest farm people were already standing in line for jobs at urban textile factories, sawmills, and food-processing plants.[58]

Nevertheless, for those people whom the agency aided, the FSA had allowed them to stay on the farm for at least a few more years. Grateful for their second chance, these small farmers fought the agency's demise but were powerless in the face of the large farming interests who opposed the FSA. The words of one Iowa farm woman summarize the opinion of many FSA clients: "The FSA has changed the whole world for us. We hope and pray that when congress starts to eliminate anything, it will be the large farm operator, who is crowding out the small operator, and not the FSA."[59]

Although the FSA's legacy was profound in terms of the dramatic images its photographers created, the agency's impact on the economic well-being of tenant farmers and migrant farm workers was limited. Its aid to the nation's poorest farmers came late and ended too soon. Ultimately, the New Deal

Fig. 3.10. A black sharecropper, her child, and their belongings on the highway leading out of New Madrid County in 1939. Photograph by Arthur Rothstein. (Courtesy of FSA Collection, Library of Congress, Washington, D.C.)

program that would have the greatest long-term impact on the nation's farm families was not the Farm Security Administration but the Rural Electrification Administration (REA), established in 1935.

Initially, however, the REA benefited a relatively small group of people—primarily those farm families in the middling ranks of the socioeconomic system and those who lived in rural areas that had a critical population mass. In the Midwest, this meant that the REA had a greater impact on families who lived in the more densely populated prairie Corn Belt than on those who resided in the Great Plains Wheat Belt. Although its initial impact was not felt evenly throughout the region, the REA was a popular program in the Midwest. Its major champion in Congress was Senator George W. Norris of Nebraska, and its chief spokesman within the executive branch was midwesterner Henry A. Wallace. Both men frequently spoke of the advantages of rural electrification for America's farm women, who twenty years earlier had requested a government-sponsored rural electrification program in David Houston's survey. In a speech to farm women in 1936, Wallace even argued that the Roosevelt administration had them foremost in mind when creating the REA because, in his words, "Women make a more important contribution to farming than they do to any other single industry"; thus they needed electric power to perform the "duties of the farm mother and housewife [which were] multitudinous beyond enumeration."[60]

Under the REA, rural neighborhoods organized to install high-line electricity, a service available to only 8 percent of American farm families prior to the establishment of the REA. Most farm families who used electricity still relied on undependable wind- or gasoline-powered home generators. Unlike high-line, central-station power, home electric plants could not run machinery twenty-four hours a day, and home plants rarely powered major domestic appliances because their capacity was too low and because running electric-powered barn equipment took priority. REA high-line electricity thus represented an improvement over the electric power systems that most farm families used. In order to establish REA electricity in a neighborhood, however, residents had to guarantee that an average of three families per mile would use the REA lines. Construction of a mile of REA line cost $1,000, as opposed to the $2,000 that installation of non-REA high-line power would cost. Each family on an REA line would therefore pay approximately $333 for its portion of the construction of electric lines. If a farm family took advantage of the REA loan plan, though, it did not have to pay this amount in a lump sum and could instead make payments over a period of several years. With the REA, then, for the first time midwestern farm families could reasonably afford dependable high-line electricity, providing they found neighbors who were willing to cooperate in paying for its installation and use.[61]

Individual farm families could also obtain REA loans for wiring their houses and farm buildings and for purchasing appliances and equipment. The REA strongly encouraged the purchase and use of a number of appliances and estimated that the combined cost of power-line construction, wiring, and appliances averaged $600 per farm family. At 3 percent interest, a family could pay off their debt over twenty-five years by paying $3.50 a month the first year and less in each succeeding year.[62] According to REA administrator Morris L. Cooke, farm families would find the extra investment in household appliances to be worthwhile: "The more irons, refrigerators, heaters and other appliances that are in use, the greater is the quantity of electric energy required. Thus, a large load is built up, which, in turn, makes possible better service at less cost."[63]

REA proponents argued that the use of more appliances would not only benefit farm families in terms of convenience and lower electric rates but would also benefit the American economy as a whole. According to the author of an article published in *Wallaces' Farmer* shortly after the creation of the REA, "Besides contributing a great deal toward increasing comforts on the farm, an important effect of the program will be the creation of considerable business for the lumber, copper and other industries, and for the manufacturers of electrical and sanitary equipment and appliances."[64]

Once again, members of the Roosevelt administration and other supporters of farm reform viewed women as key to encouraging farm people's acceptance of this New Deal innovation. In a March 1936 discussion of rural electrification presented on the pages of the Country Life Movement's monthly publication, *Rural America*, one participant noted, "[There is] a very definite feeling that the farm woman holds the key to the situation. Because she determines to considerable extent the standard of living in the farm home."[65]

The editors of *Wallaces' Farmer* played their part in encouraging women to publicize the advantages of rural electrification. In the fall of 1937, they offered prizes for the best letters describing how electricity had changed women's lives. First prize went to Mrs. L. C. Davis of Tama County, Iowa, who described electricity as a "good fairy" who "waved her magic wand" across Davis's path. She went on to describe how her electric range, refrigerator, vacuum cleaner, iron, cream separator, toaster, and washer "all help[ed] to make life comfortable." Mrs. George Carroll of Black Hawk County, Iowa, told *Wallaces' Farmer*, "Five days ago, I had the thrill of my life when I pushed a button and had running water in my kitchen. The electric pump is in the basement and pumps water from a well near the house." Alice Cole of Boone County, Iowa, reported, "Electricity has completely changed our home. . . . We have big washings, and it used to take us all day, but this quick electric way gets us thru in about four hours."[66]

Other letters indicated that rural electrification had encouraged farm families to stay in the countryside. Mrs. Arthur Jennings of Marshall County, Iowa, valued her electric lights, washing machine, refrigerator, and radio, but her new electric water pump promised to "outshine them all." With running water in the bathroom and kitchen, she reported, the Jennings family would now enjoy "the advantages of both the city and country." Mrs. Fred Anderson of Johnson County, Nebraska, told *Wallaces' Farmer* that three months of electric power had changed her son's attitude about farm life: "Recently our son said, 'This is the best place of all. I believe I'll stay on the farm.'" Mrs. Ed Reiste of Dallas County, Iowa, wrote about the wonders of her new electric range and added, "[The] farm woman of yesterday envied the city woman. . . .

But now, with our modern homes, I think the city woman may well envy her farm sister."[67]

In an August 1938 issue of *Wallaces' Farmer*, Elizabeth Wherry devoted her "Country Air" column to a discussion of rural electrification. Wherry praised the convenience of an electrified farm home but also recognized the difficulty many farm families still faced in obtaining that ideal:

> The biggest thrills of the year certainly belong to the farmers who have just hooked up to the REA. . . . Yet one ponders all these desirable advances. We should have them—for our comfort, efficiency and well-being, and to keep the people who are employed in the making of all modern commodities on full-time, self-respecting jobs. But the first cost, the operation and maintenance of these things indicate a necessity for some medium of exchange. Services cost money. We can't raise our own electricity some year when we are a bit hard run. . . . [But] there's no sense in going back to self-sufficient days in an interdependent commercialized world.[68]

Wherry's recognition that many farm families still could not spare even $3.50 a month to electrify their homes and fill them with appliances suggests the premature nature of Mrs. Reiste's comment that farm women had achieved technological parity with those who lived in cities. Recognizing this, *Wallaces' Farmer* editorialists began to amend their arguments in favor of rural electrification. Although these writers still supported electrifying farm homes, they noted that some farm families would have to delay that process. Nevertheless, they continued to support the idea of "Power in Kitchen and Laundry." In a September 1938 editorial so titled, the author noted that only 18.5 percent of Iowa farm homes had high-line electricity but stated, "[This situation] need not keep mother from having labor-saving power machinery, since much of it can be secured with gasoline motor equipment."[69]

The editors of *Wallaces' Farmer* continued to maintain that the ultimate responsibility for acquiring power equipment in the farm home lay on women's shoulders. In the same editorial, the author virtually blamed women for the lack of power equipment on midwestern farms:

> On too many farms mother has been given the short end of the stick when it comes to substituting machinery for hand labor. Often that is her own fault. She dislikes to ask for anything for herself. She is impressed by the argument that machinery for use in the field and barn will pay for

itself, plus a profit. She hasn't stopped to figure that household machinery will do the same thing, particularly if you figure that a happy, healthy homemaker is worth something to the family.[70]

In the minds of USDA officials, the happiness of the farm woman and farm home continued to be related to the issue of rural-to-urban migration. In 1940, REA economist Robert T. Beall stated a familiar theme: "Increased income and improved living standards resulting from the use of electricity on the farm may exert a favorable influence on the problems arising from the migration of rural youth to urban centers."[71]

The majority of midwestern farm families, however, continued to function without high-line electricity. Particularly on widely spaced farms in the plains states, where obtaining the requisite three customers per mile made the possibility of obtaining REA power seem remote, farm families despaired of having high-line electricity any time in the near future (see Table 3.1). As the 1930s neared an end, the editor of *Capper's Farmer* noted the REA's slow progress and warned plains residents and other readers that they "should be realistic about rural electrification and should not expect miracles to happen."[72] Statistics for 1940 demonstrated, though, that in midwestern homes being served by the REA, the majority of families were enthusiastically using small electric appliances, particularly irons and radios. Statistics also demonstrated that REA families in the Midwest led those in all other parts of the country in ownership of electric water pumps, cream separators, and particularly washing machines.[73] The higher number of water pumps and cream separators perhaps reflected the concentration of dairying operations in the Midwest. Washing machines were popular in the Midwest because farms there still depended upon large numbers of field workers whose dirty work resulted in heavy loads of laundry. The proximity of midwestern farms to the nation's major washing machine manufacturers may have also been a factor in the appliance's popularity among farm families in the heartland.

Acknowledging the popularity of electric lighting and certain electric appliances among those farm families who had REA power, New Deal supporters continued to use the image of the grateful, "empowered" farm woman in their propaganda, even though she as yet represented the experience of a minority of midwestern farm women. In a *Wallaces' Farmer* editorial entitled "'I've Got Lights,'" which appeared a month before the 1940 presidential election, the author quoted a farm woman's supportive comments about President Roosevelt and his new running mate—Henry A. Wallace:

Table 3.1 Percentage of Farms Electrified, 1940

Illinois	26
Indiana	37
Iowa	23
Kansas	11
Minnesota	17
Missouri	8
Nebraska	13
North Dakota	2
South Dakota	4
Wisconsin	36

Source: Robert T. Beall, "Rural Electrification," in *The Yearbook of Agriculture*, edited by Gove Hambidge (Washington: Government Printing Office, 1940).

A farm woman in Hardin [C]ounty, Iowa, switched on the lights in the kitchen, took a pitcher of cold milk out of the electric refrigerator, and paused to say: "If they hadn't done anything more than the REA, I'd vote for Roosevelt and Wallace. I hear Wilkie is promising to do just as much; but I heard a lot of promises like that before I got the lights in. And a light switch in the kitchen is a lot better than a promise over the radio."[74]

On the pages of *Wallaces' Farmer*, electricity was thus presented as a panacea for farm women's problems. Hyperbolic statements that described electricity as a "good fairy" whose magical powers were released by the "touch of a button" gave the impression that women's household work would virtually disappear with the acquisition of high-line electric power. Electrically powered machines would now quickly perform work that had once taken women hours to do. Such statements not only exaggerated the extent to which electric power would transform housekeeping but more subtly reinforced the notion that women's domestic labor—so easily replaced—was less important than the work farm men performed.[75] REA propagandists exaggerated the extent to which electric power eased women's work and at the same time reinforced existing gender hierarchies. Their rhetoric thus supported one goal of New Deal agricultural policies—keeping the patriarchal farm family in its place on the farm.

As it had always been, women's work was central to the midwestern farm economy of the 1930s. In fact, in their role as farm producer, women were key to the survival of many midwestern farms during the depression era. As they indicated in their letters to federal officials and farm publications, women stepped up their productive efforts, their bartering activities, and their attempts to repair and reconstruct clothing, furniture, and equipment in order to extend the farm family budget. Farm women therefore sought a voice in determining federal policies that would affect life on the farm. With its vision of farm family life divided strictly between men's farm work and women's housework, however, the federal government remained largely resistant to women's direct suggestions about federal economic policies that affected family farms. Even in the face of the Great Depression, the federal government remained committed to its Progressive Era ideal of industrial agriculture and rural homemaking. Nevertheless, federal officials did view farm women as significant in their role as housewives and consumers and attempted to win women's support of New Deal policies that would potentially improve women's access to modern domestic technology.

Farm women's own recognition of the symbolic value of domestic technology apparently took on a different character during the depression years. Their letters to government officials indicated that during this time of economic crisis, women were less concerned with equal status within the farm family than they were with basic economic survival. Their discussion of their lack of modern household equipment now served less to demonstrate their lack of equality with men than to represent what they perceived as greater poverty than that experienced by people in American cities. While New Dealers saw farm women's acquisition of new domestic equipment as a way to keep families on the farm and stimulate American industry, women saw acquisition of such equipment as a tangible symbol of a greater economic prosperity that would more closely resemble that of urban people. Thus, a Wisconsin woman wrote about acquisition of modern technology as a "chance to live as the city sisters," while an Iowa woman measured the success of Roosevelt/Wallace economic policies in terms of the pieces of new household equipment that her neighbors had purchased. Measuring their prosperity, or lack thereof, in these terms was a perfectly reasonable rhetorical device for women who knew that the government officials and farm editors with whom they corresponded viewed women chiefly in terms of their domestic responsibilities.

Although they largely lacked a direct voice in determining agricultural policies, women did use the ballot box and their role in voluntary farm organizations to support most New Deal policies. Their motivations for supporting the New Deal, however, were more varied than simply wanting to improve their access to modern domestic technology. Farm women wanted economic justice for themselves and their families. They wanted a fair reward for their hard work and recognition of the importance of agriculture to the national economy. Although officials viewed women's role on the farm more narrowly than did the women themselves, officials nevertheless recognized that farm women were a political and economic force that could not be ignored. Officials carefully monitored farm women's support or rejection of government policies and, although underestimating the complexity of farm women's concerns, attempted to influence and placate the farm woman voter.

The 1930s ended with midwestern farm women generally in a better position materially than they had been when the Great Depression began. More of them lived on electrified farms, most had radios, and programs such as the AAA and the FSA had helped some of them remain on their own farms. As the FSA's photographers demonstrated, however, large segments of the Midwest's farm population remained in poverty and despair. In its brief life, the FSA did aid some farm families at the bottom of the socioeconomic scale, but government aid came too late to help most of the farm families in that category. Even in those farm families at the middle of the scale, most women lacked much of the equipment they reportedly desired.

New Dealers, then, achieved only a partial success in their attempt to have women acquire modern equipment and thus make them more satisfied with life on the farm and involve them in stimulating industrial production. The New Dealers' attempts to change American farm life—limited though they were—represented the boldest attempts yet by the federal government to aid farm people in any significant way, and these programs, along with FDR's lofty rhetoric, did have an effect on farm women's morale. The desperate tone of farm women's statements made early in the depression gave way to comments of at least guarded optimism by the end of the 1930s. Most of the changes that New Deal proponents promised midwestern farm women, however, were not a reality as the decade of the thirties came to a close.

A final legacy of Roosevelt's New Deal was the wealth of research left behind by its rural sociologists. These scholars worked for the USDA's Bureau of Agricultural Economics (BAE), an agency that was formed in 1922 to conduct economic research but greatly expanded its activities during the New Deal era. Along with the FSA, it was one of only two agencies within the Department of Agriculture that attempted to aid farmers at the bottom of the socioeconomic scale, and it was also the only federal agency that conducted sociological research. Under the direction of Carl C. Taylor, BAE sociologists produced a number of path-breaking studies.[1] Among the most important BAE studies were those that resulted from Taylor's ambitious attempt to study economic, social, and cultural stability in differing types of agricultural communities. In 1940, he sent social scientists to six geographically diverse rural communities, including two in the Midwest—Irwin, Iowa, in Shelby County, and Sublette, Kansas, in Haskell County.[2] As the BAE's investigation of these two communities demonstrated, on the brink of American involvement in World War II, women in Haskell County had adopted many of the practices that USDA personnel prescribed, while those in Shelby County resisted change and maintained their traditional productive role on the farm.

Taylor himself was a native of Shelby County, Iowa, and co-wrote the report on farm life there with a young sociologist named Edward O. Moe, who did the field

4

"The Man Operating the Farm and the Wife Operating the Household and the Garden"

Technology and Gender Roles, 1940

Raising chickens was a lifesaver during the depression.—Nellie Christensen, Shelby County, Iowa

About all we done was farm wheat.—Marguerite Rooney, Haskell County, Kansas

work for the study. In 1940, Moe and Taylor found that descendants of the predominantly Scandinavian and German farmers who had settled Shelby County were continuing many of the practices that their ancestors had established in the nineteenth century. Since that time, Shelby County, situated near the Iowa-Nebraska border, had been the site of general grain and livestock farming, with 160-acre farms as the rule. Although Shelby County farm families produced corn and hogs for market, they also produced much of what they consumed on the farm. According to anthropologist Sonya Salamon's typology, the residents of Shelby County were yeoman farm families who viewed farming as a way of life rather than a business. Underlying this system of agriculture was a division of farm family labor along gender lines. Moe and Taylor described this division of labor as "the man operating the farm and the wife operating the household and the garden." Their description, however, was an oversimplification, as much of their own research demonstrated. As the experiences of Nellie and August Christensen indicate, a more complex gender-role relationship existed in Shelby County.[3]

In 1927, twenty-four-year-old Nellie Ohms ended her career as a rural schoolteacher to marry August Christensen, a local farm laborer who had begun renting a farm from his father. For decades, Shelby County residents had expected young men to progress up the farming hierarchy by first working as hired hands, then renting, and eventually owning their own farms. By 1927, however, only 50 percent of Shelby County farm operators owned the farms they worked, and it had become difficult for young farmers even to begin farming on rented land without parental help. As a result, young people increasingly left predominantly agricultural Shelby County to seek economic opportunities elsewhere. Nellie and August Christensen, therefore, felt fortunate to enter into a cash and crop sharing arrangement with August's father that allowed them to support themselves on the land. This arrangement was common in Shelby County, where in 1930, 39.2 percent of farm tenants were related to their landlords. Survival strategies such as this ensured that by the time of Moe and Taylor's research, following two decades of agricultural depression, the concept of the family farm as home and workplace remained intact.[4]

Shelby County farm women played a major role in maintaining family farming as a way of life. For example, the farm to which Nellie Christensen moved when she married was very similar to the one on which she had grown up in Shelby County, and the chores she performed were familiar to her. Women's work in Shelby County had never been strictly confined to the house and vegetable garden. Shelby County farm women, including Nellie Christensen, periodically worked in the farm fields, particularly in corn picking and haying seasons. In deference to traditional notions about appropriate gender roles, however, women characterized such labor not as "real work" but as "helping" their husbands.[5]

The gradual adoption of gasoline-powered farm equipment, a process that began approximately a decade before Moe and Taylor's research, encouraged women's greater participation in field work in some families. Although not all farm families in the county owned tractors in 1940, the machine's impact on Shelby County farming could not be denied. Of the 2,188 farms in the county in 1930, 763 had tractors. By 1940, 1,300 out of 2,148 farms reported tractors, and some farms had discontinued the use of horses altogether. In talking to farmers about their use of the tractor, Moe and Taylor noted the reasons given for adopting tractor farming: " 'It saves time,' 'it eliminates some of the harder work,' and 'it makes possible a better job of farming.' "[6]

Subsequent research has called into question the notion that adoption of the tractor automatically resulted in more efficient farming, but its use did have an impact on gender roles and further blurred the boundaries between the farm and the farmhouse. While the adoption of mechanized farming prompted some farm families to involve wives and daughters in field work to a greater extent, in other farm families, male members simply took on a greater proportion of the field work themselves, perhaps eliminating the work of women and girls altogether but also reducing the need for hired men. In 1930, hired laborers accounted for 79 percent of workers, exclusive of the farm operator himself, who regularly performed field work on Shelby County farms. Unpaid family workers made up the other 21 percent of Shelby County field laborers. In 1940, hired hands accounted for only 58 percent of farm laborers, with family members making up the other 42 percent.[7]

Moe and Taylor recognized that the tractor reduced the need for hired hands and thus limited agricultural opportunities for young men, but they neglected to note a related change in women's work. Moe and Taylor probably subsumed the care of hired hands, if they thought about it at all, under the general category of women's household work, but care of hired help transcended strict divisions between housework and farm work. For example, Nellie Christensen, who had no children of her own, not only mended one young farm hand's work clothes but also sewed his personal garments, including his baseball uniform. In the two decades preceding introduction of the tractor in Shelby County, women's care of hired help accounted for one-quarter of total expenditures for farm labor in the county, with cash wages making up the other three-quarters of labor costs. Even those day laborers who did not "live in" with the family often expected the farm woman to serve them at least some meals on a daily basis. By decreasing the need for hired hands, adoption of the tractor lessened the farm woman's daily labor to some extent. When Nellie and August Christensen purchased a secondhand gasoline tractor in the late 1930s, Nellie's work life noticeably changed.[8]

Adoption of the gasoline tractor helped diminish women's work in other ways, again blurring the line between house- and farm work. Moe and Taylor wrote that on Shelby County farms, a "frequently mentioned advantage [was] the belt power supplied for grinding, pumping, and corn shelling." By attaching a belt between the tractor engine and water pump, a woman could more easily obtain well water for domestic chores. Women could employ the tractor in this way, however, only when no one was using it in the field.[9]

Shelby County women generally viewed adoption of the tractor in a positive light—even though its purchase might preclude the acquisition of new domestic equipment. Many of these women wanted their families to acquire tractors rather than household machinery because they recognized that by changing the nature of field work and the composition of the farm labor force, adoption of the tractor would lessen women's household labor. At least since the time of David Houston's 1913 survey, farm women had complained about the care of hired help. Now, adoption of new field technology allowed them to decrease the time and effort spent in feeding, clothing, and housing hired labor. That the tractor could also be used to pump water for women's household and gardening chores further illustrates that adoption of the tractor affected farm life in ways that cut across strict boundaries between the farm and the farmhouse.

Perhaps because farm families viewed adoption of new field technology as benefiting both the farm business and the farm home, acquisition of modern field equipment definitely came before the purchase of household appliances. According to Moe and Taylor, "If one of these farmers believes a [farm] machine to be an advantage, he will own one somehow. Conveniences for the house, however, can await the accumulation of extra funds." In 1940, when 60.5 percent of Shelby County farms had gasoline tractors, only 42.1 percent of Shelby County farm homes had electricity, supplied primarily by local cooperatives under the Rural Electrification Administration. Only 31 percent of farm homes in the county had running water (see Figure 4.1). Farm families wanted improved household technology, but, according to Moe and

Fig. 4.1. Note the old-fashioned pump and cob-burning stove in the kitchen of a farm-owning Shelby County family in 1941. Photograph by Irving Rusinow. (Courtesy of BAE Collection, National Archives, Washington, D.C.)

Taylor, the cost of such improvements was "the forbidding factor." REA officials estimated that the combined cost of power-line construction, wiring, and appliances averaged $600 for each family that subscribed to REA service. The editors of *Wallaces' Farmer* estimated that self-installation of modern plumbing equipment in the typical Iowa farmhouse cost about $500—approximately the price of a small tractor. For farm renters, a landlord's wishes also played a role in determining whether or not a farmhouse would have modern equipment. Even August Christensen's father was reluctant to invest in improvements on a house he did not live in himself and that might provide only a temporary residence for his son and daughter-in-law.[10]

According to Moe and Taylor, farm families most desired electricity. As local informants reported, "Every farmer would like to have electricity on his farm, especially for lighting." Moe and Taylor noted that farm women wanted electrical household appliances, including irons, vacuum cleaners, and toasters. Fifty years after the Moe and Taylor study, Shelby County farm women

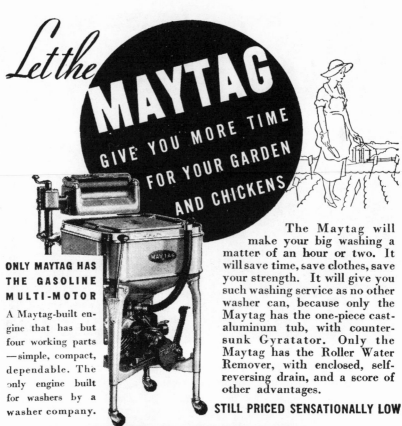

Fig. 4.2. A 1935 Maytag advertisement tells farm women that acquisition of a washing machine will allow them more time for farm production. (Courtesy of *Wallaces' Farmer*)

recalled the eventual acquisition of electricity and electrical appliances as the most significant change in their lives—outdistancing even the impact of gasoline tractors. For Nellie Christensen, the most treasured acquisition was an electric refrigerator, which "saved steps to the cave"—the cellar where she had previously stored perishable foods. Appliance advertisers of the era promised Iowa farm women that such equipment would, in the words of a 1935 washing machine ad, "give you more time for your garden and chickens" (see Figure 4.2). As one midwestern farm woman stated, however, farm

Fig. 4.3. Demonstrating women's interest in field technology, Mrs. Jake Thompson reads a booklet entitled *Planters for the Corn Belt* in her Shelby County parlor in 1941. Note the nearby radio. Photograph by Irving Rusinow. (Courtesy of BAE Collection, National Archives, Washington, D.C.)

families "needed the new [farm] machinery in order to make money to buy washing machines" (see Figure 4.3).[11]

Farm machinery, therefore, remained the chief priority, for women and men, although Moe and Taylor noted that in 1940 some informants believed that traditional patterns were showing signs of "breaking down and that farmers [were] as likely to go into debt for home conveniences as they [were] for farm machinery." Perhaps this change reflected a new recognition of economic realities. Although Shelby County farm families were dependent on the cash sale of hogs and corn for their income, they consumed 9.7 percent of the total value of farm products produced in the county. As Moe and Taylor observed, "This approximate 10 percent is important. It often represents the margin between profitable and unprofitable farming and stands as a tie between the less self-sufficient agriculture of today and the more self-sufficient agriculture

Fig. 4.4. Mrs. Thompson poses with one of her chickens in front of her Shelby County farm home in 1941. Poultry work was one of many ways in which Shelby County women contributed to the farm family economy. Photograph by Irving Rusinow. (Courtesy of BAE Collection, National Archives, Washington, D.C.)

of yesterday." And the production of this crucial 10 percent of farm products fell largely to women.[12]

Shelby County farm women tended vegetable gardens, canned vegetables in the summer, and canned and preserved meat in autumn. Farm women also washed, ironed, mended, baked, and frequently made clothing at home. Such work benefited not only family members but hired help as well. In addition to their production for the household, Shelby County farm women raised chickens, milked cows, separated cream, and then sold eggs and cream to local creameries and stores or traded those products directly for such items as coffee or flour. Women's work, therefore, went beyond the production of some foods for household consumption and accounted for a greater proportion of the farm family economy than the acknowledged 10 percent (see Figure 4.4).[13]

Low cash incomes in the 1930s placed greater emphasis on women's gardens, home-produced goods, and handicrafts. During the depths of the Great Depression, when hogs were two cents a pound and her husband and other Shelby County residents sought a solution in the radical Farmers'

Holiday movement, Nellie Christensen's poultry raising "was a lifesaver." Under the crop sharing agreement with August's father, chickens and eggs were the only produce raised on the farm that belonged solely to Nellie and August. Nellie stepped up her production of chickens and eggs during the 1930s and used her profits to buy necessary items or traded chickens and eggs directly for groceries.[14]

Nellie Christensen's experience was typical. Because people were increasingly leaving the farm during the depression, the number of Shelby County farms on which women raised chickens fell from 2,001 in 1934 to 1,888 in 1939. The number of eggs produced in the county, however, increased from 1,619,903 dozens in 1934 to 1,999,755 dozens in 1939, or from an average of 809.5 dozens per woman to 1,059.2 dozens per woman. Between 1934 and 1939, the number of farms on which women tended vegetable gardens grew from 714 to 1,696, representing an increase in total value of home-grown and home-consumed vegetables in Shelby County from $5,346 in 1934 to $50,504 in 1939. Although the number of Shelby County farm families who milked cows fell from 2,072 in 1934 to 1,980 in 1939, the number of gallons of milk produced rose from 4,258,569 to 4,565,488 in the same five-year period. In 1939, women from 1,760 Shelby County farms sold or bartered cream, accounting for a total of 1,083,358 pounds of butterfat sold or traded. When possible, Shelby County women acquired modern equipment to aid them in their expanded productive efforts. For example, Nellie Christensen purchased an electric incubator soon after the Christensen farm acquired electricity about 1940, ending her reliance on the dangerous and less efficient kerosene-heated incubator she had been using for years.[15]

Shelby County women received information about modern equipment from Extension Service personnel and from radio broadcasts and newspaper and magazine advertisements. By 1940, 88.4 percent of Shelby County farm families possessed battery-powered or electric radios, and farm programs were very popular. Shelby County women listened to Leanna Field Driftmier's "Kitchen Klatter" program from station KFNF in Shenandoah, Iowa, a station that broadcast farm-oriented programming. Like Driftmier's radio program, Shelby County newspapers urged the use of modern appliances in farm homes. Advertisements in the two county-seat papers, the *Harlan News-Advertiser* and the *Harlan Tribune*, promoted the purchase of gasoline-powered washing machines for farm homes and the use of electric-powered sewing machines and kitchen tools to lighten farm women's work. The Nishnabotna

Farm Women are also *Entitled to* POWER

Why not let mechanical power do your hardest household task—the weekly washing. On more than half a million farms, the Maytag has changed washday to wash-hour,

THE MAYTAG is the only washer with one-piece, cast-aluminum tub. Gyrator washing action, Roller Water Remover and a score of other work-eliminating features.

GASOLINE MULTI-MOTOR

A Maytag engine with a 20-year record of performance. Built for the woman to operate—only four working parts—the simplest washer engine built. Electric models for homes with electricity.   F-12-35

Ask the nearest dealer about easy payment plan

THE MAYTAG COMPANY • Manufacturer • Founded 1893 • NEWTON, IOWA

Fig. 4.5. A 1935 Maytag advertisement told farm women that they too were "entitled to power." (Courtesy of *Wallaces' Farmer*)

Valley Rural Electric Cooperative stressed the safety of modern equipment by reminding *Harlan News-Advertiser* readers that "R. E. A. Members Cook with Wire Instead of Fire!"[16]

The significance of women's depression-era economic contribution, and the importance of their use of modern equipment to enhance productive efforts, were also reflected in a Maytag ad of the era that provided Iowa farm families with a dual message. Featuring an illustration of a farm man driving a gasoline tractor, the advertisement told would-be consumers that "*Farm Women* are also *Entitled* to Power" (see Figure 4.5). Despite such recommendations, farm home production remained undermechanized in comparison with cash-producing field work. In 1940, with tractors on 60.5 percent of county farms, only 18.3 percent of Shelby County farm women possessed mechanical refrigerators and only eight farm homes in the entire county had electric ranges. For the majority of Shelby County farm women, including Nellie Christensen, a modernized farmhouse, and the economic power to lay claim to one, were not yet a reality.[17]

The Shelby County farm families that Moe and Taylor observed in 1940 worked and lived year-round on their farms and hoped to maintain farming as a way of life for the next generation. Women's work was vital to keeping families on the land, and women used available technology to aid directly in production of goods, with their use of electric incubators and sewing machines, or to free up more time for production, with their use of mechanical refrigerators and power washers and their families' reliance on field machinery rather than hired labor. Although adoption of new equipment allowed women to adjust the time and effort they spent performing certain chores, women's work roles remained basically intact and continued to encompass the barn and cornfield, as well as the house and garden, just as they had since the nineteenth century.

If the picture of Shelby County in 1940 is one of women resisting the USDA's notion of separate spheres and continuing their role as farm producer, then the portrait of Haskell County, Kansas, is, superficially, one of women's acceptance of the role of domestic consumer. In reality, the lives of Haskell County women were much more complex. In order to understand the situation of Haskell County women in 1940, however, the history of their community must be considered.

When migrants from the Corn Belt of Iowa, Illinois, and eastern Kansas settled Haskell County, Kansas, in the 1880s, they brought with them the farming practices of places like Shelby County. The semiarid plains of southwestern Kansas proved inhospitable to general grain and livestock farming, however, and this phase of Haskell County agricultural history ended with the drought of the mid-1890s. Cattle ranching rather than farming dominated the county's economy for the next two decades, until a series of events conspired to change life in Haskell County once again. The completion of railroad lines through Haskell County and the introduction of gasoline-powered farm equipment, both occurring in 1912, coupled with the great demand for wheat during World War I, stimulated large-scale investment in growing wheat as a cash crop. During the wheat-boom years of World War I and the period immediately following, hundreds of new residents flocked to

Haskell County. With the exception of a group of Mennonites who settled in northern Haskell County, these new residents lacked any sense of ethnic identity and were generally people whose families had been in North America for several generations. Between 1900 and 1920, the number of farms in Haskell County grew from 86 to 177, and the county's total acreage in wheat rose from 985 to 18,372 acres. Among the new wheat farmers were Marguerite and Harry Rooney, who soon found that the familiar agricultural practices and gender roles of the Corn Belt did not remain intact on the plains of Haskell County.[18]

When Marguerite Rooney came to Haskell County from her home in eastern Kansas, her appraisal of the new landscape could be summed up in four words: "My goodness, no trees." The year was 1918, and the twenty-one-year-old bride had come to live in Haskell County with her husband, who owned a section of land near the village of Satanta. Coming to Haskell County in the midst of the wheat boom, the young woman was startled not only by the stark landscape but also by the wealth she saw around her. After she arrived in Satanta on the Dodge City train, her first stop was the local restaurant, where it seemed to her "all the rich people in town" were dining.[19]

Arriving in Haskell County twenty-two years later, BAE sociologist Earl Bell saw a very different picture. Just six years before Bell's arrival, 95 percent of Haskell County farms had experienced devastating crop failures and a dramatic drop in the value of their farm products. In 1929 the value of farm products sold, traded, or used averaged $8,273 per farm; in 1939 that figure had fallen to $1,326 per farm. During this same period in Shelby County, average value of farm products had fallen only from $4,256 per farm to $2,701. In 1939, 102 farms, or nearly a fourth of all Haskell County farms, had sold, traded, or used less than $250 worth of farm products. In contrast, only 1 farm produced so little in 1929, and 240 farms, more than half the county's farms, had sold, traded, or used more than $6,000 worth of farm products. In 1939, only 7 farms had raised products worth that much. As a result of this economic devastation, the population of the county had fallen from 2,804 persons in 1930 to 2,088 residents in 1940, and the number of farms had dropped from 461 to 423. Based on Bell's study, the BAE in fact concluded that Haskell County represented the most unstable type of agricultural community in the nation.[20]

A major cause of the county's economic instability had been the widespread use of gasoline tractors, which for more than twenty years had plowed up native grasses to make way for wheat-dominated farms that averaged 748

Fig. 4.6. According to BAE investigators, this Haskell County farm in 1941 was "quite typical, with its small buildings and the heavy machinery standing un-protected in the yard." Use of modern field equipment was central to Haskell County farming. Photograph by Irving Rusinow. (Courtesy of BAE Collection, National Archives, Washington, D.C.)

acres in 1940. In that year, at a time when 40 percent of Shelby County farm families did not even own one tractor, farm tractors in Haskell County outnumbered farm-operating families by 401 to 386 (see Figure 4.6). The mechanized "plow up" of Haskell County resulted in disaster when, with the droughts of the 1930s, the high winds of the Great Plains carried the dry, loose soil away in the decade's "black blizzards." Lying behind this technological abuse of the land was an economic theory that dust bowl historian Donald Worster has characterized as the ultimate expression of capitalist agriculture—the attitude that nature itself is capital and that humans have an obligation to use this capital for constant self-advancement.[21]

Bell stated about the residents of Haskell County, "[They] consider themselves, and they are, entrepreneurs." As a result of this attitude, emotional ties to the land were tenuous in Haskell County. Like many others, Harry Rooney

Fig. 4.7. This Haskell County shanty was used in 1941 "only to supply shelter during the . . . short periods of time (planting, harvest, and perhaps occasional listing)" that the operator spent on his land. Photograph by Irving Rusinow. (Courtesy of BAE Collection, National Archives, Washington, D.C.)

had actually acquired his land when he lived outside Haskell County. The phenomenon of absentee "suitcase farmers" was prominent in a county where farming as a business took precedence over farming as a way of life. Soon after her arrival in the county, Marguerite rode out to the Rooney farm in Harry's open-topped Ford, the strong Kansas winds ripping at the trimmings of her hat. When Harry proudly pointed out their section of land, Marguerite's reaction was not enthusiastic: "It was just out on the plain prairie. There wasn't any house or trees. [But] I knew I was married and had to get along." Getting along meant weathering the bad times on a farm about which Marguerite remarked, "About all we done was farm wheat." Early in her marriage, lack of a wheat crop meant that she and her husband could not afford gasoline to drive their Ford, and she walked to her job at a Satanta grocery store, a job necessitated by financial need. Economic dependence on the land was risky in Haskell County.[22]

At the time of Bell's study, 50 percent of the people who farmed Haskell County land did not own their own farms, and among those who did own Haskell County land, 29.9 percent did not live in the county. Mechanized wheat farming required intensive labor only during the summer harvest and fall planting seasons (see Figure 4.7). For those families who lived away from their farms, these might be the only times of the year they actually stayed on the farm, where male family members did the majority of the field work. Because wheat farming was only a part-time job for many Haskell County men, in the year before Bell's arrival, 28.4 percent of Haskell County farm operators had supplemented incomes by working away from their farms for an average of 132 days, and more than three-quarters of these people earned their extra cash in nonfarm work. In contrast, at the same time, only 14.8 percent of Shelby County farm operators worked away from their farms, and only 0.03 percent lived away from their farms. The Haskell County situation in 1940, however, showed improvement over the drought period of the mid-1930s, when 42.2 percent of Haskell County farmers had performed paid labor away from their farms.[23]

In 1940, 327 farm families lived in the open country of Haskell County, but another 59 farm-operating families lived in Sublette, the 582-person county seat, or—as the Rooneys did—in the rival village of Satanta, which numbered 345 persons. Both communities had been founded as railroad towns in 1912. Most of those families who resided on the land were residents of the northern third of Haskell County. The sandy soil of this part of the county was not conducive to large-scale wheat farming, and here, on some of the county's oldest and smallest farms, families practiced what Bell described as "a sort of subsistence agriculture grafted onto cash farming." Many of the residents of northern Haskell County were Mennonites who believed in farming as a way of life and rejected the entrepreneurial approach of most Haskell County citizens. On these northern Haskell County farms, situated several miles from the villages of Sublette and Satanta, families had survived depression and drought by relying on the same techniques used by the residents of Shelby County, Iowa. Women on these farms raised poultry, tended gardens, and had increased their efforts at canning vegetables during the depression. Even with these efforts at poultry and garden production in northern Haskell County, in 1939, women kept chickens on only 56.7 percent of Haskell County farms and tended gardens on only 13 percent of farms in the county. In contrast, women kept chickens on 88 percent of Shelby County farms and tended gardens on 79 percent of farms in the county during that same year. Countywide, in 1939, only 66 percent of Haskell County farm households used any products from their own farms. In Shelby County, the figure was 94.4 percent.[24]

The lives of many Haskell County farm women thus contrasted with those of their Shelby County counterparts. Those Haskell County women who differed most radically from their Corn Belt contemporaries—as Marguerite Rooney did—lived in modern town houses, hired local girls to help do their housework, and spent much of their time attending club meetings and driving 35 or 50 miles to shop or visit in larger towns outside Haskell County, such as Garden City, Liberal, or Dodge City. In contrast with the production-minded women of Shelby County, most Haskell County women turned their attention toward the consumption of goods produced away from the farm, be it the network programs they listened to on the radio or the clothing they purchased in Garden City chain stores. To Bell, nothing symbolized these women's attention to the world beyond the farm better than their extensive use of automobiles.[25]

By 1940, virtually all young and middle-aged women in Haskell County drove cars. As one woman put it, the automobile had come to be viewed as "a necessity" by Haskell County farm women. Ninety-five percent of Haskell County farm households owned at least one car in 1940, and on more than half of these farms, the newest car located there had been purchased since 1936. Although initially viewed as a "male machine" by Great Plains residents, the car had fallen into the hands of Haskell County women by Bell's time. While men worked in the fields, women drove into town for tractor parts. In an economy where families purchased most of the goods they used, women also employed the car for grocery shopping in Sublette or Satanta and for shopping trips to Garden City or Dodge City for a variety of items often unavailable in the smaller towns—furniture, home appliances, women's clothing. Haskell County women remained undaunted by the vast distances on the plains. Driving a farm child to and from town school, which some women did every day, could mean daily 80-mile trips for Haskell County farm mothers.[26]

People in Haskell County also relied on the automobile for their recreational activities. Bell observed, "[A] trip of 150 or 200 miles to see a friend between Saturday evening and Monday morning is not unusual. . . . The people of Haskell County think no more of driving 35 miles (a total of 70) to a movie than Corn Belt people do of going 4 or 5 miles." The Rooneys often traveled to Dodge City, 50 miles away, to visit Harry's brother for the weekend. Bell reported that such activities were common even during crop- and cash-poor "bad years." Because many of them were unencumbered by traditional chores in the henhouse or garden, Haskell County women traveled outside the county frequently. Typical items appearing on the *Sublette Monitor* social page included accounts of women's 100-mile day trips to shop and visit friends and relatives.[27]

Women in Haskell County also used the automobile to attend what Bell characterized as their "honeycomb" of women's clubs. Like Shelby County, Haskell County was dotted with women's organizations, although club members here on the plains often lived great distances from one another. With names such as the Social Hour Club, the Read-A-Book Club, and the Sosuntee Club, these organizations allowed Haskell County women, those who lived in town as well as those who lived in the open country, the opportunity to meet twice a month for community projects and educational and social activities. Because many Haskell County women belonged to more than one club, they might attend half a dozen club meetings in a month's time, usually by car. Marguerite Rooney regularly attended Eastern Star, study club, and bridge club meetings.[28]

Haskell County men did not have analogous organizations. Outside of the Oddfellow and Masonic lodges and informal gatherings at the pool hall, men had little opportunity to gather together in same-sex social groups. Bell noted that while the women of Haskell County had a Republican Women's Club, men had no similar organization. In fact, Bell understood women to be the real leaders of Haskell County, as evidenced by their strong participation in the Haskell County Farm Bureau, the county's major agricultural organization. Bell was also impressed that a dozen women in the county managed successful farming operations after their husbands' deaths, as Marguerite Rooney would eventually do. In general, Bell thought Haskell County farm women were knowledgeable about farm affairs. By 1940, they were the most active participants at county AAA meetings, where they learned about conservation practices that would hopefully spare the county another dust bowl experience. Their attendance at AAA meetings, which was an unusual practice for women in much of the Midwest, was consistent with the findings of a *Wallaces' Farmer* poll, which showed that women who lived in dust bowl conditions were more interested than other farm women in AAA participation. If the county agent wanted to make sure a family member read a particular farm bulletin, he more often gave the literature to the wife than to the husband. On those farms where families kept strict financial records, women were the ones who did the bookkeeping, perhaps reflecting the fact that Haskell County farm women averaged more years of formal education than their husbands. Some women became successful entrepreneurs themselves. With money saved from her grocery store job and profitably invested in a turkey-raising operation, Marguerite Rooney was eventually able to buy her own quarter section of farmland.[29]

Women also demonstrated their leadership skills and put their extra years of education to work by holding positions in Haskell County government. In a county where a cash economy had long prevailed and where teaching jobs were generally reserved for young single women, jobs in county government allowed married women wage-earning opportunities. Throughout the 1920s and 1930s, local women sought or held a variety of county offices: register of deeds, county superintendent, clerk of the district court, county treasurer, even sheriff. In years when the wheat crop failed or other disasters struck, a job at the courthouse might mean survival for local women and their families. Again, women often traveled to these jobs by automobile.[30]

Bell's characterization of women as the "real leaders" of Haskell County, however, exaggerated their political power and reflected his own hostility toward Haskell County males, whom he viewed as lazy part-time farmers. Within the patriarchal structure of Haskell County society, women relied on their "honeycomb" of organizations as a means to socialize and exchange information with other women. Through their participation in this women's network, they could circumvent the boundaries of patriarchal control that guided most aspects of their daily lives. When Bell noted that in Republican-dominated Haskell County women had a Republican Women's Club but that men had no analogous organization, he neglected to note that men did not need such organizations—they already had control of the local Republican party. This theme of patriarchal control is perhaps best illustrated by women's use of the automobile. While Bell saw women's automobile use as an emblem of their independence, it was really a symbol of the extent to which women's activities were defined by their place within the patriarchal family. Their extensive use of automobiles to run errands for farm husbands, to ferry children, to purchase consumer goods for the family, and to travel to jobs that supplemented the family income was merely an extension of women's role as wife and mother. Only when women were not using the car for these purposes could they employ it to attend club meetings or to visit mothers, sisters, and friends in distant communities.

That women's activities were defined to a large extent by their role as wives and mothers does not mean that they lacked leadership skills or talent as agricultural businesswomen. As Bell noted, women's experiences in their network of social, educational, and political organizations had a positive impact on their general level of knowledge and expertise. Acknowledging the leadership abilities of local women, Rolland and Dee Jacquart, the married couple who published the "Official Paper of Haskell County," saw women as key to necessary changes in Haskell County farming practices. In his first *Sublette Monitor* editorial of 1940, Rolland Jacquart looked to the influence of farm women for an end to the exploitative practices of the past and a return to a more traditional agriculture:

> In these days of complicated operation and financing of farms, women are coming to play an increasingly important role. . . . If the farm home were attractive because of a year-around program of diversification, if women encouraged residence on the land, if poultry could be widely adopted, the prairie farms would be dotted with busy, cozy farm homes instead of comparatively empty of men and women excepting in wheat sowing and reaping seasons. More people living on the farms ranks with water conservation as the challenging goals here. The surest way to attain the former is to encourage women in the larger farm life [of Haskell County].[31]

Three months later, Rolland Jacquart presented a familiar argument when he suggested that one way to encourage women and their families to live on the land would be the improvement of farmhouse technology. In particular, he urged the modernization of plumbing and toilet facilities with a return to better times in the postdrought era:

> In spite of mechanization of the farm, enabling operators to live in town and easily transport their machinery back and forth, the number of dwellers on the land will increase with invitation from a series of profitable crops. And improvements likely will be more liveable, less of the rural slum variety with which many were content even back in good times. Farmers comfortably living on the land are second only to diversification as the outstanding agricultural problem of the High Plains. . . . [Current] living conditions on the farms are far from gratifying to most families who live there—the families to whom everybody must look for commercial stability.[32]

Jacquart thus placed into a local context the New Deal goal of keeping farm families on the land by modernizing women's living and working conditions. Jacquart's view of farm women as a stabilizing force in rural society fell in line with the perspective of Henry A. Wallace, Virginia Jenckes, and other New

Dealers from the Midwest. As one of the few Democrats in a position of influence within Haskell County, Jacquart served as the local spokesman for New Deal policies—including the policy of promoting farm families' consumption of household appliances in order to refuel the industrial economy. At the time of Jacquart's editorial, however, the campaign to modernize farmhouses had met with little success in Haskell County.

Although 91.8 percent of the homes in Sublette and Satanta had electricity in 1940, a mere 29.2 percent of Haskell County farm homes had electric power. Only 0.08 percent of these electrified farm homes had dependable high-line power, with the remainder relying on home generators. The REA had made little progress in an area where widely spaced farms prevented the requisite three customers per square mile for REA service. Thirty-six percent of farm homes had running water, as compared with 85 percent of homes located in Sublette and Satanta. Rolland Jacquart's call for improved farm homes, however, was apparently a timely one. According to Bell, many Haskell County farm residents had earmarked the profits from a good wheat crop specifically for farm home improvements. Advertisements appeared in the *Sublette Monitor* for a variety of household appliances: electric ranges, gas furnaces, gas water heaters, gas and electric refrigerators, electric washing machines. A 1939 advertisement for the local lumber company promised that a new Coleman range would provide " 'city-gas' cooking convenience for homes beyond the gas-mains." A year later, advertisements proclaimed, "Canning is Fun with a New 1940 Gas Range," and "[With a kerosene-powered Servel Electrolux refrigerator,] thousands of farm women are today finding life easier and more delightful." The Jacquarts directed such advertisements at women readers, and in a full-page ad appearing in 1935 they referred to the typical Haskell County homemaker as "a Clever Budgeter [who] Reads the Monitor and Believes What She Finds There—And, What's More, Follows Its Information When She Sets Out to Buy!" Most Haskell County women, however, had not yet obtained the equipment they saw advertised. In a county where the gasoline tractor and automobile were universal possessions, only 18 percent of women living on farms had mechanized refrigerators in 1940. No women living on farms had electric ranges, and only 0.06 percent of farm households owned gas ranges. These statistics virtually mirrored those for Shelby County. Lack of appropriate household power and the cost of appliances accounted in part for the absence of such equipment on many Haskell County farms. In 1940, a kerosene-powered refrigerator cost $170, an electric range cost from $85 to $135, and a gas range could be as expensive as $70. The type of farm tractor typically used in the area, however, cost at least $600, and the price of the average automobile lagged not far behind. The main reason for the absence of modern equipment in farmhouses remained the priority given to other types of machinery.[33]

The Haskell County farm families that Bell encountered in 1940 represented the dust bowl survivors. Those families who stayed in the county, like the Rooneys, were often able to do so because of the wage-earning work that women performed at the grocery store, the courthouse, and elsewhere. In 1940, Marguerite Rooney was proud of the life she had helped provide for herself, her husband, and their son. On the whole, Haskell County had been good to her, and Marguerite knew that if she could relive her first day there, she would now "be tickled to death" about moving to Haskell County.[34]

On the eve of World War II, Shelby County women continued to play the roles they had been fulfilling for nearly a century. Their work remained undermechanized, although adoption of the gasoline tractor and electric-powered equipment had altered the work of those women who lived on modernizing farms. More than half the women living on Shelby County farms, however, did not own such equipment. Those women who did have modern equipment used it to aid their families during the depression and help them stay on the land, the goal of most Shelby County families.

The role of the Corn Belt farm woman, however, could not make an easy translation onto the "wheat factories" of the plains. The late settlement and harsh environment of Haskell County, coupled with the lack of a yeoman farming tradition among the county's non-Mennonite majority, meant that most farm women had to create a new identity for themselves. Women in Haskell County modified their activities, relying principally upon the same technology that had transformed the Haskell County landscape—the gasoline engine. Just as the gasoline tractor allowed Haskell County men to create a role for themselves as part-time wheat farmers, the automobile allowed women to fashion a role for themselves more appropriate to the cash-dependent economy of Haskell County. With the automobile, women in Haskell County became cash makers who worked at jobs in town and cash spenders who drove outside the county to buy appliances, clothing, and furniture. Women's role as consumer had become so well established by 1940 that the local newspaper editor saw women using that role for agricultural reform. In Rolland Jacquart's view, women's investment in household appliances could make the Wheat Belt more like the Corn Belt, with year-round, diversified farming and families living on the land.

Farm families in both places, however, continued to hold many practices and customs in common. Most important, traditional gender hierarchies remained in place in both counties. Farm men continued to set the family's labor priorities. In Shelby County, farm women could use the tractor engine to pump water only if farm men were not using the tractor in the field. In Haskell County, when tractors broke down, farm men sent farm women into town for replacement parts. Although farm women's work—whether in the garden or the grocery store—had enabled farm families to remain on the farm in both counties, this work was viewed as "helping out" and not as central to the farm family's very existence.

In 1940, with men driving modern tractors in the field and women purchasing items for the home, many families in Haskell County already appeared to have adopted the gender roles that USDA and Extension Service officials prescribed. For members of the BAE, however, Haskell County's apparent achievement of the New Agriculture was not altogether a positive development. According to these observers, with its heavy dependence on expensive equipment and a single cash crop, Haskell County's agricultural economy was highly unstable and vulnerable to boom-and-bust cycles. In contrast, they viewed the more diversified farm economy of Shelby County to be relatively successful.

The BAE's analysis, however, represented a minority position within the Department of Agriculture. In the view of the majority of USDA policymakers, the life that farm families were living in Haskell County in many ways approximated the way of life they envisioned for all farm families. In their opinion, once implementation of responsible conservation practices had eliminated dust bowl conditions, the industrialized agriculture of Haskell County would be back on "solid ground."[35]

In 1940, most USDA officials remained committed to the New Agriculture and its role for women as housewife/consumer. In standing by this ideal, policymakers ignored the lessons of Haskell County—that women could often only fulfill the role of consumer by in part abandoning the role of housewife to perform wage labor. Department of Agriculture officials also largely ignored Bell's evidence that even the consumer-oriented women of Haskell County remained active players in farm business and land management matters.

As consumers who were interested in the purchase of domestic equipment, Haskell County women in 1940 were what many USDA officials wanted those in Shelby County to become. Only those members of the Shelby

County community who had survived the hard times of the 1930s, however, would remain on the farm and thus potentially able to fulfill the new role that officials prescribed. Ironically, survival in the 1930s had often been dependent upon women's home production, "women's work" that would soon disappear. For women in Shelby County, and elsewhere in the Midwest, the New Agriculture was seemingly just around the corner.

In October 1941, two months before the United States entered the Second World War, the USDA's director of extension work set a goal for America's farm women that would last through the duration of the war.[1] With the argument "Food will win the war and write the peace," Wilson and other USDA officials called on farm women to raise food for the war cause.[2] In meeting that goal, farm women would have to make use of technology that the Extension Service had formerly promoted as masculine machinery—motorized field equipment. Wartime propaganda emphasized, however, that the "tractorette"—the rural equivalent of industry's Rosie the Riveter—was behind the tractor wheel only as a temporary, emergency measure.[3] At war's end, insisted the propagandists, she was to return from the fields to the farm kitchen. Farm women's activities, however, had never strictly taken place within the farmhouse. Women's involvement in wartime field work, therefore, actually represented an expansion of the farm duties they had known before the war.

A first step in the federal government's creation of new technological goals for farm women was the establishment of a Farm Labor Program in 1943. Under the direction of Meredith C. Wilson, the Farm Labor Program promoted women's technological competence in the farm field as well as in the household. A major goal of Wilson's Farm Labor Program was to replace young male workers called to military service with other sources of labor, which eventually included Mexican field laborers

"A Call to Farms"

"Tractorettes" Go to War

The farm homemaker, with her husband, has an important job in the national-defense program—a part in the raising of certain foods for shipment overseas, in feeding her own family . . . in guiding children in the ways of self-reliance and democratic living.—M. L. Wilson (1941)

and German prisoners of war. The Farm Labor Program also worked to recruit a civilian "Crop Corps" composed of the elderly, teenagers, and women. The program hoped to encourage retired farmers to return to the farm "for the duration" and to recruit teenage boys and girls from towns and cities for summer work. Its strategy for encouraging women's participation in field work was twofold: to recruit nonfarm women as wartime farm workers and to convince farm women to expand their existing duties on the farm.

A major development in the program's campaign to recruit women farm workers was its creation of a Women's Land Army (WLA) in 1943. Based on Britain's female Land Army, the American version was headed by longtime Extension Service employee Florence L. Hall and included rural women along with city and town women over the age of eighteen who could present a doctor's certificate of fitness to perform farm work and who were willing to do at least one month of full-time agricultural labor. The Extension Service, under whose authority the Farm Labor Program functioned, assigned these women to work in areas where farm labor shortages existed and where members of the Women's Land Army would receive the locally accepted wage for the type of labor they performed. During World War I, female laborers had also functioned as an emergency land army, but the program had achieved little success in the Midwest.[4] This time around, recruiters made a strong effort to enlist the labor of women in all parts of the country and were able to employ advertising techniques and communication technology that had developed since World War I. In the Midwest and elsewhere, the Farm Labor Program's campaign to recruit workers for the Women's Land Army emphasized women's use of modern farm technology.

While publicity materials for the World War I land army had presented photographs of women using rakes and hoes, propaganda during the Second World War often stressed women's use of mechanized equipment. Crop Corps radio announcements tried to persuade young women that driving a tractor would help America win the war—and would also be an amusing way to spend the summer. A 1943 Crop Corps recruitment poster issued women a "CALL TO FARMS" and featured a drawing of a smiling, jumpsuit-clad young woman who flashed a V for Victory sign as she drove a tractor across a farm field. With her sleeves rolled up and her head covered by a kerchief, the figure on the poster resembled a more willowy version of Norman Rockwell's famous Rosie the Riveter. Like Rockwell's Rosie, the smiling woman on a tractor symbolized women's competence in using heavy equipment to perform "men's work" (see Figure 5.1).[5]

Fig. 5.1. Recruitment posters used the image of a rural Rosie the Riveter to attract women to farm production during World War II. Extension Service Records. (Courtesy of National Archives, Washington, D.C.)

Appeals to women's patriotism and sense of adventure would not benefit the Crop Corps, however, if farmers' resistance to female laborers prevented women from working in the farm fields. Recognizing this, editors of the *Country Gentleman* magazine warned Crop Corps recruiters, "Farmers in your locality . . . may object to the idea of using girls to help in the field. Remind them that war plants didn't want to use them either . . . at first. But that when the girls were given a fair chance, they proved themselves every bit as good as men at all but the heaviest jobs."[6]

According to a Gallup poll conducted in 1943, only 28 percent of midwestern farmers approved of women as wartime hired labor. In contrast, 49 percent of farmers in the South and 42 percent of those in the Far West agreed with the idea of women as field workers. Unlike farmers in the South and West, midwestern farmers were not used to relying on the labor of female workers who were not family members. Perhaps the fact that midwestern recruits would primarily be white women, and not the black, Hispanic, or Asian women who commonly labored in the fields of the South and West, also made midwestern farm operators view the notion of female farm laborers as improper. According to George Gallup, even among those farmers who did approve of women workers, the general attitude was that women were "satisfactory for some of the smaller chores or tasks around the farm, but that for the heavy work of harvesting, planting or caring for livestock, women only 'get in the way.'"[7]

The image of women farm workers presented in much of the popular press did little to challenge this prejudiced attitude toward female laborers. Although Crop Corps posters and radio announcements might promote the idea of competent women aboard powerful tractors, popular periodicals frequently presented more frivolous images. Magazines from *Life* to *Screenland* featured pinup poses of "farm girls" on their covers. Many of these cover girls, however, were professional models who posed with bushel baskets—not tractors—as their most frequent prop. Magazine articles appearing in 1943 included one in *Glamour* entitled "Farmers Wear Lipstick" and a pictorial in *Look* featuring movie star Paulette Goddard "on the farm."[8]

Although this type of publicity glamorized and devalued women's farm work, it was correct in its portrayal of nonfarm women largely performing work by hand. Most town and city women who served in the Women's Land Army, or provided more short-term labor, worked primarily without machinery. Indeed, the author of a 1944 Land Army recruitment brochure emphasized women's hand labor and employed gender-role stereotypes, stating that members of the Land Army had perhaps made their greatest contribution in the harvesting of fruits and vegetables, "where their dexterity, carefulness, and persistence [were] great assets." The author acknowledged that the nature of the work that most women performed—unmechanized piecework—meant that wages did "not provide the strongest incentive for doing farm work in wartime." Wages for year-round Land Army workers averaged from $25 to $50 a month, with the Farm Labor Program providing room and board.[9]

In 1944, the federal War Food Administration reported crucial labor shortages in both the Corn and Wheat belts. In publicity aimed at recruiting urban workers, however, officials argued that the corn and wheat harvests were jobs that required "hard work" and could be "done more efficiently by men." Officials noted that in the wheat harvest "some women [were] being used for driving tractors, shocking bundles, and similar work" as an emergency measure but that in the Corn Belt women's work was largely restricted to hand labor such as corn detasseling, a job characterized as "ideally suited to women . . . a comparatively simple job which inexperienced workers [could] do satisfactorily after brief instruction."[10]

In the Midwest, where Farm Labor Program officials promoted the corn and wheat harvests as "man's work," the Women's Land Army made few inroads in recruiting town and city women as agricultural laborers. The dean of the University of Illinois's College of Agriculture argued, however, that this was not so much the result of Extension Service recruitment practices but of farmers' resistance to nonfarm women as field workers. In addition, the fact that women could earn better wages in the region's defense plants meant that the majority of midwestern women who sought paid wartime employment opted for a factory job. At the state level, Farm Labor Program statistical reports were often inexact, but the best evidence indicates that women recruits never constituted more than 10 percent of the total agricultural work force in any of the midwestern states except Missouri. In Missouri, women made up an average 16 percent of the state's seasonal labor force during the last two years of the war, a statistic, however, that reflected the participation of black women in the state's cotton fields. In contrast, in wheat- and corn-dominated Nebraska and South Dakota, women made up less than 4 percent of the work force placed on farms through the Farm Labor Program.[11]

Even during periods of acute labor shortages, farm people were reluctant to accept nonfarm women, especially as operators of field machinery. In Edmunds County, South Dakota, where the labor shortage was particularly severe during the 1943 wheat harvest, farmer Reuben Kirschenmann explained that he was willing to accept untrained workers on his farm: "I can teach anyone to work on the farm if he is willing to work. . . . I should be glad to get hold of anyone who wants to work, and I should appreciate anybody who tries to help me. Work on the farm with the modern machinery we have now is not hard." Kirschenmann's use of the male pronoun, however, was apparently deliberate. Although he argued that he could teach "anyone" to use modern farm machinery, he drew the line at training nonfarm women. Women household workers, though, were another matter. According to an Extension Service writer, "It would help solve Mr. Kirschenmann's problem if he could hire a girl to work in the house. That would allow his wife to do some of the outside work that a town girl would not know how to do."[12]

A *Wallaces' Farmer* poll conducted in 1943 demonstrated that Iowa farm families were also more likely to accept nonfarm women as wartime household workers than as field workers. Only 19 percent of Iowa farm men were in favor of nonfarm women working in the fields, but 38 percent preferred them as household workers, and 43 percent of Iowa farm men remained undecided on the matter because, according to the editors, they "couldn't think of any place where a 'land girl' would be any good at all." Farm women were even less enthusiastic about the prospect of town and city women working in the fields. Only 10 percent of women favored using nonfarm women in the fields, whereas 59 percent reported that they would appreciate the help of town and city women in the farm home. The remainder of Iowa farm women questioned were undecided on the matter.[13]

The responses of men and women to the *Wallaces' Farmer* poll provide some insight into their objections to town and city women as farm workers. Sexual jealousy apparently contributed to the negative attitude of some farm women toward nonfarm women workers. When asked about the prospect of using nonfarm women in the field, one young husband answered with a grin, "I'd have to look at the girl first, before I decided whether she'd better stay in the house or go out in the field." Taking her husband's cue, "with spirit," his wife countered, "If she is young, she can stay in the house and do the work there. I'll help in the field." Other women questioned nonfarm women's technological competence in the field and demonstrated their own pride in their status as farm women. A Washington County woman stated, "It doesn't require any mechanical training to wash and wipe dishes or scrub the floors, but I think these 'land army' women would have a hard time running a tractor." A Cerro Gordo County woman voiced her skepticism that town or city women could live up to the work standards that farm women had set: "I'd like to see any city girl do half the work I do, either in the house or outside." Men's responses indicated that most of them would prefer to have their own wives working with them in the field. A Jones County farmer summarized this position: "If I have to have a woman helping me in the field, I want my wife, not some green city girl."[14]

As these comments suggest, farm men and women recognized that farm women had skills as farm producers and users of farm technology that set them apart from other women. According to the North Dakota Farm Labor supervisor, another reason that farm men preferred having their own wives and daughters operate farm machinery was that as family members they had an economic stake in the expensive equipment and would therefore treat it with care. In that respect, female family members were preferable to outside male labor at a time when wartime conditions meant that farmers had "found it increasingly difficult to obtain male labor that was worth its salt around machines."[15]

Throughout the Midwest, farm women themselves increased their participation in field work dramatically. Midwestern farm women had always taken on some field work responsibilities. The magnitude of the wartime crisis, however, ensured that more women would be devoting more hours to a greater variety of outdoor tasks on a regular basis. Soon after U.S. entry in the war, propagandists labored to convince farm women that increased agricultural production, and thus women's increased participation in field work, were major components of the American war strategy. A *Wallaces' Farmer* editorial appearing in June 1942 urged farm women to recognize and expand their contributions to the war effort: "Chickens are war work. Orphan pigs are war work. Taking a turn in the field with the tractor at haying time is war work. So is helping at grain harvest. So are canning and looking after the garden. And so is keeping the family well, happy and properly fed."[16] The tasks that the editorialist promoted as "war work," however, were ones that women had already performed on a regular basis before the war.

As the *Wallaces' Farmer* editorial indicates, along with promoting women's increased participation in the farm fields, propagandists also encouraged farm women to step up their gardening and canning activities during the wartime emergency. USDA officials reasoned that if farm families purchased fewer foods and instead produced more of their own, they would help release commercial canning plants and transportation facilities for purposes crucial to the war cause. In 1942 alone, demonstration club members across the country canned over 300 million quarts of food and dried over 40 million pounds of fruits and vegetables. Under the slogan "Feed the Family for Health, Morale, and Victory," home demonstration club members in Minnesota pledged to raise at least 75 percent of their families' food supply for 1942. In 1943, 63 percent of the women who responded to a *Wallaces' Farmer* poll reported that they were going to increase their efforts at gardening, canning, and poultry raising, even though most of these Iowa women had already greatly expanded such tasks during the depression years that preceded the war. Government propaganda publicized such efforts, and USDA officials applauded the "patriotic viewpoint and the constructive attitude" of midwestern farm women who expanded their home production activities. Advertisers of the era also joined the call for increased poultry and garden production. The makers of Pan-A-Min, a poultry feed additive, placed an ad in *Capper's Farmer* that featured caricatures of Hitler, Hirohito, and Mussolini and told farm women to remember that these were the "Faces on the Hen-House Door": "Crafty Hitler, cunning Hirohito, crazy Benito—let them be an everlasting reminder that we need eggs, eggs, and more eggs!"[17]

The majority of wartime propaganda, however, continued to publicize women's work in the field. In July 1942, the editors of *Wallaces' Farmer* profiled twenty-year-old Mrs. P. W. Noble of Cherokee County, Iowa, whose husband had left their rented farm for the army. According to the editors:

> Mrs. Noble had to learn all about driving a tractor, cultivating and milking. But she learned fast, and is doing the work well. She hasn't had to call in a man for assistance except once when the tractor wouldn't start, and a neighbor came over to adjust it. . . . There are lots more cases like this, where farm women who have never milked or driven a tractor have learned in a hurry in order to meet a serious need.[18]

Arguing that the American farm family was a "great and efficient bulwark against the dangerous totalitarian dictatorship philosophy that [was] sweeping the world," Senator Arthur Capper of Kansas called upon all farm family members to fight the Axis by increasing their participation in field production. In particular, he praised female family members who gladly put in fourteen-hour workdays to take the place of sons and brothers gone to war. On several occasions throughout the war, *Capper's Farmer* featured cover photographs of farm women and girls performing field work on midwestern farms. Emphasizing women's use of motorized equipment, the editors frequently presented photographs of women driving tractors and farm trucks and offered advice on what women should wear while driving tractors and operating other field equipment. The editors of *Capper's Farmer* noted that farm women and girls were playing a larger and more varied role on midwestern farms than they had in the previous war because of their use of modern equipment, which required "skill but not great strength in operation." Among the dozens of midwestern farm women whom the editors profiled during the war was Edna

White of Rice County, Kansas, who at the age of forty-five had learned to combine wheat. Writing about her experiences for the readers of *Capper's Farmer*, White told other farm women that running a combine was "more thrilling than sky rides at the World's Fair, and a lot more satisfying."[19]

In her "Country Air" columns of the period, Elizabeth Wherry also recognized that women were contributing to the war cause not only by traditional means, such as building morale and canning more vegetables, but also by their expanded participation in field work. Referring to a November 1942 meeting of Manchester, Iowa, farm women, Wherry noted, "About a third of the group could drive tractors. About a half helped milk. All gardened. Most of them fed hogs, stuck forks, drove the horse to the hay fork, raised chickens and helped in some way with chores. Manpower was scarce. The women undertook this extra work without complaint."[20] As Wherry's description indicates, wartime conditions meant a continuation of familiar productive activities—but on a larger scale.

Wherry completed her discussion of the meeting by voicing her hope that farm families would hire city and town women to do the housework while farm women expanded their work in the barn and fields. Indeed, in the same month that Wherry's column appeared, November 1942, statistics for the Midwest showed that farm women in that region of the country led all others in their increased use of power machinery in the field. The percentage of all farm women performing field work on a regular basis at least doubled in most midwestern states between 1941 and 1942, and the percentage using field machinery increased five times on the average (see Table 5.1).

Recognizing this change, the International Harvester Company of Chicago implemented an ambitious 1942 advertising campaign that featured a photograph of a female tractor driver, or—as the ad's copy referred to her—a "tractorette" (see Figure 5.2). Drawing a parallel between the "tractorette" and women who served in the medical corps or industry, the International Harvester ads described her thus: "a farm girl or woman who wants to help win the battle of the land, to help provide Food for Freedom. She is the farm model of the girl who is driving an ambulance or running a turret lathe in the city." Under the heading "*Both* Working For Victory," International Harvester issued a recruitment poster for the U.S. Crop Corps featuring drawings of a female ambulance driver and a young woman driving an International Harvester Farmall tractor. As part of its patriotic advertising campaign, the International Harvester Company provided free schools where midwestern women could learn to operate International Harvester equipment. The

Table 5.1 Estimated Percentage of All Farm Women Performing
Field Work and Operating Field Machinery on a Regular Basis
in Some Midwestern States, 1941 and 1942

	Field Work		Operating Field Machinery	
	1941	1942	1941	1942
Iowa	10	35	5	40
Kansas	14	32	8	26
Minnesota	22	38	12	28
North Dakota	5	10	5	25
South Dakota	5	20	8	30
Wisconsin	15	50	5	25

Source: U.S. Department of Agriculture, *National Summary of Inquiry into Changes
in the Work of Farm Women and Girls Caused by War Labor Shortages* (Washington:
Government Printing Office, 1942).

Illinois-based John Deere Company also used the image of tractor-driving
women in its wartime advertising. One ad of the era featured a drawing of a
young woman operating a John Deere tractor and flashing the victory sign to a
group of soldiers driving by her farm field.[21]

Farm Labor Program records suggest that farm women's increased participation in field work, which began in 1942, continued through the remainder of the war. State Farm Labor supervisors reported major increases in
farm women's field work throughout the Midwest. Statistics on farm women's
work, however, remained inexact, buried as they were within the figures for
increased family labor in general. For example, the Iowa Farm Labor supervisor estimated that in 1941, family members had supplied 75 percent of the
labor on farms in the state, a figure that rose to 90 percent in 1943. He
surmised that women and children in farm families had probably performed
only 9 percent of the daily work on Iowa farms in 1941 but supplied 36
percent of farm labor in 1943. Supervisors in other midwestern states made
similar general estimates.[22]

In an attempt to isolate better the wartime contributions of farm women,
the Kansas Extension Service sponsored a group of Kansas State College
sociologists in a survey of farm families who lived in eight counties of the
state's wheat-producing region. The sociologists found that the proportion of

Women Join the *"Field Artillery"*
as International Harvester Dealers
Teach Power Farming to an Army of "TRACTORETTES"

Fig. 5.2. International Harvester dealers called on "tractorettes" to serve their country during wartime. (Courtesy of *Wallaces' Farmer*)

women in the area's regular farm labor force had risen from 3.5 percent of the total work force in 1942 to 8.3 percent in 1943. Wives and daughters accounted for the majority of new women in the farm work force. Farm girls, who had accounted for only 0.6 percent of all full-time field workers in 1942, constituted 2.7 percent in 1943. Adult farm women had accounted for only 2.8 percent of the area's full-time field workers in 1942, but made up 4.8 percent of the total daily work force in 1943. In contrast, women from outside farm families made up only 0.8 percent of field workers in 1943. Many of these women came from farm backgrounds and were usually friends or relatives of the local farm families that they aided. Among the total female farm work force in the eight-county area, 90.2 percent were farm women or women who had grown up on farms. This meant that only 10 percent of women working on area farms in 1943 had little or no previous farming experience.[23] This type of statistical data, while useful in demonstrating women's replacement of full-time male labor and describing the composition of the daily female work force, nevertheless failed to acknowledge the field work that women performed on an irregular basis—both before and during the war. By only considering full-time work performed on a daily basis, data such as these continued to underrepresent women's field labor contribution.

The Kansas State sociologists found that among the types of work that women were performing on Kansas wheat farms, operation of mechanized farm equipment led all others. In 1943, operation of farm machinery accounted for 85 percent of the farm work that women performed in the eight-county area. Sociologists reasoned that women performed this type of work "either by preference or because . . . their physical limitations" prevented them from doing work that required great physical strength. Another study of Kansas farm women found that 81 percent of the women in a seven-county area were running more farm-related errands for their husbands, continuing a trend in women's increased automobile use that had begun before the war. In any event, farm women's reliance on the gasoline engine was a major component of their wartime experience.[24]

State Extension Service personnel labored to convince farm women to expand their operation of field machinery and thereby aid the war cause. Extension Service recruitment programs at the state and local levels served to counteract much of the misleading publicity about women's farm work that appeared in the national press. The Minnesota Farm Labor supervisor noted that "there was a constant temptation to newspapers and radio stations to overdo publicity in connection with the Women's Land Army and to over-emphasize their contributions to war food production. Washington posters and newspaper releases tended to glamorize the Women's Land Army with the result that little of [that publicity] was used in Minnesota." Whereas in the past extension personnel had not always been sensitive to women's practical needs when prescribing the use of modern domestic equipment, much of their wartime promotion of the use of modern field technology did seem to acknowledge farm women's own preferences and concerns. Extension personnel in Minnesota and other midwestern states offered pamphlets and seminars on how farm women might reduce their domestic burdens in order to increase their field work and provided farm women with lessons on how to operate farm machinery. Some of the less frivolous publicity surrounding the Women's Land Army also persuaded farm women to operate field machinery. For example, the North Dakota Farm Labor supervisor noted that although farm women in his state were little impressed with the "tinsel and trimmings" of Women's Land Army publicity in the popular magazines, the image of tractor-driving women in some of the more serious WLA propaganda probably encouraged North Dakota women to operate machinery on their own farms, although they, like other midwestern farm people, decisively rejected the term "tractorette."[25]

In the Midwest, then, the WLA made little headway in recruiting nonfarm women to perform field labor, in part because farm men and women resisted the participation of these women in their family farming operations. Believing that farm women possessed unique skills as farm producers and harboring concerns that non–family members would not treat expensive equipment properly, farm families instead preferred that their own female members expand their field activities.[26] And while WLA propaganda was apparently effective in convincing some farm women that they themselves should drive tractors, this publicity merely helped farm people accept the inevitable. Most farm women were already used to working in the fields during busy seasons or emergency periods, when their roles expanded to accommodate "men's work." Even without exposure to government propaganda, they surely would have gone into the fields during the extended wartime emergency. Wartime propaganda, however, did acknowledge the importance of farm women's work to American agriculture and gave their work new status—even though much of this publicity did not provide an accurate picture of farm women's wartime experience.

For example, the results of a *Wallaces' Farmer* poll published in April 1943 indicated that although the International Harvester Company, the Crop Corps, and the popular press usually portrayed female field workers as young women, it was farm women over the age of thirty-five who were more likely to perform field work during the war, because they were less hampered by the care of young children. Women of all ages, however, reported that they were attempting to reduce the time spent performing domestic chores in order to spend more time doing field work. A Purdue University study suggested that farm women reduce their housework by relying more on household equipment and hired help than on their own physical labor. An Iowa extension bulletin advised farm women: "Regear Your Work Schedule to Wartime Demands"; it recommended that women "make the best use of help from the family and neighbors and paid helpers and use commercial products and services to release time."[27]

Taking Extension Service advice or implementing their own common-sense strategies, many farm women did successfully reduce some of their domestic burdens during the war. A South Dakota mother of eleven children reported during the wheat harvest of 1944 that she was putting in fourteen-

and fifteen-hour workdays, a feat that she could not perform without the grudging cooperation of her young sons, who frequently helped with the housework. The woman said of her sons, "[They] dislike housework. And, they are awkward about it, also need quite a lot of encouragement. But it lifts a lot." Iowa farm woman Iona Dinsmore, whose husband was disabled, had gone to work in the farm fields after their hired man was drafted. Borrowing her father-in-law's tractor, she plowed and planted 70 acres of soybeans and harvested them by herself. To lighten her domestic work, Dinsmore hired a lonely young woman from a nearby town whose husband had recently been drafted. In exchange for free room and board and the company of the Dinsmore family, the woman "helped in the house but not outside." Farm women's attempts to hire Women's Land Army personnel as house workers and child tenders, however, were largely unsuccessful. As a Nebraska Farm Labor official explained, "This type of work is not spectacular and did not appeal to town women as a contribution to war food production." On an informal basis, however, ten thousand town women aided their friends and relatives on Kansas farms by performing uncompensated housework and child care during the 1945 wheat harvest. Such incidents were common throughout the Midwest.[28]

Most midwestern farm women had to rely on the help of hired workers, friends, and relatives because they could not depend on domestic appliances to lighten their work load. Although farm income trebled during the war years, appliances remained unavailable in a wartime economy that stressed production of military hardware over domestic goods. Although Extension Service publications advised that farm men and women rely more heavily on mechanical equipment during the wartime labor shortage, farm families could more easily obtain field equipment that directly aided the goal of increased food production than they could obtain modern domestic appliances. Among the items unavailable to consumers during most of the war were mechanical refrigerators, washing machines, electric ranges, irons, radios, and vacuum cleaners. Advertising of the era reflected this reality and also acknowledged women's increased participation in outdoor farm work. A 1943 advertisement for the Sioux City–based Wincharger home electric system pictured a soldier receiving a letter from his mother, who reported that their farm had a "New Hired Hand"—electricity:

> With labor so scarce, Dad and I don't see how we would carry on now without it. Remember what a hard chore milking was?—It's simple now.

The electric milker and I do it and we've beat your old record by fully a third. . . . I haven't gotten a lot of things I want—like a refrigerator, a vacuum cleaner, an iron or washer yet. We're buying bonds and putting them away till these things are available again . . . after Victory.[29]

Advertisements for domestic equipment stressed that it could be used to allow women more time for field work. A 1944 ad for Perfection oil ranges pictured an attractive farm woman cooking on a range as her husband drove by the kitchen window on a tractor. The woman told her audience: "When I saw Jim do five times as much work with his tractor as he'd ever done with the horses . . . and with far less effort . . . I knew it was high time I got rid of the 'horse and buggy' coal stove I was feeding in the kitchen. . . . Our first step was to get a Perfection Oil Range. . . . It gives me so much time I've volunteered as Jim's extra farm hand."[30]

In the same ad, however, the makers of the Perfection range reminded would-be customers that because of the company's "war work, only limited models [were] available" at the time. They also urged the ad's readers to "BUY WAR BONDS AND KEEP THEM!" Many other advertisers of the period employed the same strategy, urging consumers to use war bonds to purchase domestic equipment following the war. In a series of articles appearing throughout the last year of the war, the editors of *Wallaces' Farmer* also urged farm families to purchase new equipment "after victory." Editorial writers encouraged further extension of REA lines and use of electrical equipment, arguing, "Electricity has earned its service stripes in saving labor in war-time. . . . [I]n many a safe deposit box in country banks, an envelope full of war bonds is marked, 'Water System,' or 'Refrigerator,' or 'Milking Machine.'"[31]

An Iowa REA study in the fall of 1944 reported that longtime REA customers were more likely to buy an electric refrigerator after the war than to purchase any other type of electrical equipment. First-time REA customers were expected to buy washing machines and irons as their initial postwar purchases. A *Wallaces' Farmer* poll conducted later that fall indicated that 40 percent of Iowa farm women intended to buy some type of electrical appliance following the war, with refrigerators heading the list of would-be purchases. A majority of Iowa farm women also planned to install modern water systems in their homes. Many women who had delayed obtaining modern household devices, first because of the depression and later because of wartime consumer shortages, now felt they could acquire such equipment. One farm woman reasoned, "After all, Ed's been getting some farm machinery. But I just haven't had a chance to buy a thing. He can wait until I get the kitchen fixed up anyway." Record farm incomes, however, convinced some farm people that choices between farm and household technology no longer needed to be made. In the words of one Iowa farm man, "I don't see why the wife can't get her refrigerator and vacuum sweeper at the same time I buy a new tractor. We can swing it, all right."[32]

As these comments indicate, the modern domestic ideal did not disappear during the war years. Although the image of tractor-driving women received prominent display in the era's prescriptive literature, propagandists did not let farm women forget the supposed advantages of the household equipment they would be able to enjoy at war's end. In fact, the editors of *Wallaces' Farmer*, *Capper's Farmer*, and other farm publications urged that farm women acquire this equipment at least in part as payment for the services they had rendered during the war.

As the war ended, praise for the work that women had performed was widespread. The Extension Service published numerous accounts of male farmers who admitted that farm women had performed admirably. Nevertheless, many of the tensions between farm men and women that had surfaced in the years before U.S. involvement in the war continued even during the war. In particular, women continued to complain that the economic worth of their work went unrecognized. A South Dakota woman remarked bitterly during the last year of the war, "I think that we farm women, putting in 14 and 15 hours daily, are entitled to a little extra money too. . . . If it wasn't for all this home-front work . . . I too could apply for an outside defense job and earn big money."[33]

During the war, farm women had expanded their duties on the farm to include greater participation in field work and increased use of modern field technology. In the process, they helped produce record amounts of crops to feed American civilians and service persons and American allies abroad. In payment, suggested farm editors and government officials, women should finally be rewarded with modern household appliances. This argument made it clear that women were to transfer themselves from the tractor to the cooking range in the postwar era. Extension officials reported that with the war behind them, farm women and home demonstration agents could now return to the business of improved rural homemaking.[34]

Changes that had occurred during the war, however, made it impossible for women to assume a role identical to the one they had played in the prewar era. In a situation that mirrored that of urban women, many farm women remained working at least part-time in positions outside the home. The majority of city and town women who entered the work force for the first time during the war remained there after the war, although they no longer held high-paying jobs in heavy industry. Instead, one-time Rosie the Riveters largely found themselves doing lower-paying "women's work" in offices, stores, and light industry. Likewise, many farm women continued participating in field work on a regular basis after the war, although their status as field workers had changed.

Florence L. Hall reported that in some areas of the country more women were performing paid field labor in 1946 than in 1945. The work that these women were doing, however, was primarily unmechanized seasonal labor. Hall reasoned that women were continuing this type of work for a variety of reasons. She suspected that many of the women engaged in farm labor following the war were those who had been displaced from their wartime industrial jobs but who wanted to remain in the work force. With farm wages at a high level during the postwar era, women saw seasonal farm labor as a means to supplement family income and obtain money to buy household equipment. It was also part-time work that could be undertaken with relatively little disruption of women's household routine and family schedule. Finally, Hall reasoned that farmers were simply more willing to hire female farm workers in the postwar era, based on women's performance record during the war when they had "proved to be quick, skillful with their hands, adaptable, dependable, easy to get along with." Nationwide, women made up 22.5 percent of the regular farm labor force in 1945, a figure that fell only slightly, to 18.3 percent of the labor force, in 1946.[35]

In the Midwest, this situation meant that town, city, and rural women continued to perform paid, seasonal labor, particularly during corn detasseling season. But farm women also continued to perform unpaid work with farm machinery whenever their services were needed. Many used the skills they had put into practice during the war to meet the needs of a postwar labor situation in which increased rural-to-urban migration and the GI Bill offered new opportunities to young rural men and thus continued to decimate the ranks of male farm laborers. Continued high production following the war and greater investment in farm machinery also meant that female family members would be called upon to operate expensive tractors, combines, and other equipment during peak seasons.

An advertisement for Ford tractors that appeared in *Capper's Farmer* during the last months of the war presented a generally accurate portrait of the postwar order on midwestern farms. The ad featured a photograph of a young woman driving a tractor and waving to her mother, who stood in the doorway of her modern farm home kitchen—complete with electric range and refrigerator. Under the heading "Is Woman's Work on the Farm Going to Change?," the advertisement acknowledged women's wartime participation in field work and recognized that women would be using a greater number of modern household appliances in the postwar era. According to the ad's copy, the full mechanization of both housework and field work would guarantee women's continued participation in the field. With their household work made easier, women would cheerfully perform field work and not worry about neglecting household duties. Repeating the decades-old argument that mechanization would keep women and their families on the farm, the Ford ad presented a new twist by focusing on women's use of modern field equipment as well as household technology and argued that with their use of the Ford tractor, women would feel "that same deep satisfaction from making crops grow, from creating wealth out of the soil, that ha[d] held generation after generation of men to the land."[36]

As this ad predicted, women continued to labor regularly in their families' farm fields after the war had ended. By 1946, however, ads such as this one, which presented words and pictures that promoted women's use of modern field equipment, rarely appeared in midwestern farm journals. In the postwar era, women's field work was no longer recognized, publicized, and praised. Women's field work no longer represented patriotic devotion to the war cause, and it contradicted the domestic ideal of the postwar period, which applied to both rural and urban women. In an era when Extension Service rhetoric promoted the idea of women as homemakers, women field workers received little attention. The Extension Service discontinued efforts to decrease women's domestic chores in recognition of their double burden in the home and in the field. Once again, policymakers viewed farm women primarily as housekeepers who were occasional farm "helpers" rather than farm producers. The Extension Service's emphasis returned to improvement of domestic technology in order to make farm women better full-time homemakers. Postwar conditions, however, were not conducive to women's acceptance of that role. Farm women's decades-long resistance to the role of full-time homemaker would continue in the postwar era.

When high school junior Mary Jane Fisher wrote her prizewinning essay on rural electrification for the *Indiana Rural News*, the Second World War had been over for a decade and a half.[1] The changes that had occurred in the rural Midwest during that brief time, however, were little short of revolutionary. As Fisher's essay indicates, dramatic changes in household equipment and farm labor practices had taken place across the midwestern countryside. These changes brought with them alterations in the daily activities of midwestern farm women. Although these women still functioned within a patriarchal system, they were able to fashion for themselves a new productive role that allowed them to maintain some power within the family and resist adoption of full-time homemaking.

The initial stages in the postwar transformation of the rural Midwest had begun even before the end of the war. The fact that midwestern farm incomes had trebled during the war caused many USDA officials to become optimistic that farm home modernization would finally be a reality for families in the heartland. With this goal in mind, USDA officials created the Midwest Committee on Post-War Programs to investigate improvement of farm structures. Early in 1943, a subcommittee composed of members of various USDA agencies, including the FSA, the REA, and the BAE, began a systematic study of farm income as it related to home improvements. The subcommittee's report focused on states in the prairie Corn Belt and reported that increased farm income in the area was not

"They Figured
I Didn't Have
a Part in the
Farming"
The Postwar Era

To a farm girl who has been brought up with many electrical conveniences it is like listening to a fairy tale to be told that once rural homes did not have electricity—that there were no electric stoves, refrigerators, washers, radios, bathrooms or running water—that on an average sized farm it was necessary to keep hired help to care for only a small amount of livestock and to farm a few acres.—Mary Jane Fisher (1961) evenly diffused. According to the report, although average incomes had increased from $500 to $1,500 a year during the war, 50 percent of farm families in the region would not have sufficient wartime savings to improve and repair farm buildings and houses "unless ways and means [were] found to reduce drastically the usual cash outlay required."[2]

Reacting to such evidence, Congress amended rural electrification legislation in 1944 to expand REA services and liberalize REA loan policies, thus allowing more midwestern farm families to acquire REA power and electrical equipment. Even with REA loans becoming easier to obtain and repay, USDA officials still estimated in 1946 that only middle- to high-income farm families would be able to make major home improvements. Officials reported that in the Corn and Wheat belts, which led all other areas of the country in increased farm incomes and wartime savings, only "farm families with the largest savings look[ed] forward to having the conveniences that [were] generally available in cities—central heat, automatic hot water, telephone, electricity, and an all-weather road to the door." These families reported that, second only to "the use of increased incomes for the payment of debts," they intended using their money to reap the benefits of "the anticipated expansion of the rural electrification services." The results of one BAE study indicated, "Purchases of electrical appliances are now expected by [middle-class] rural families in about this order: refrigerators, washing machines, irons, radios, deep freezer units, brooders, churns." In other words, for women in these families, increased income gave them "the opportunity, as one woman put it, 'to get some of the things we've always wanted.'"[3]

Less than two months after the end of the war, a front-page *Wallaces' Farmer* story reported that Corn Belt residents would soon be turning in their war bonds "for things which the farm families need[ed]. . . . They [were] counting on reconversion to bring them new tractors, new refrigerators and a host of other things in from three to six months." According to the results of a *Wallaces' Farmer* poll, 34 percent of farm women interviewed expected to purchase a refrigerator before 1 March 1946. A few months later, another of the periodical's polls showed that 43 percent of women respondents said they were going to buy new stoves "as soon as they were on the market." A University of Illinois study showed that in the waning months of 1945, 72 percent of the middle-class farm families taking part in the study had already purchased new electrical equipment for their homes.[4]

Editors of farm life periodicals encouraged such behavior and added to the list of equipment that the modern farm home required. In a 1946 essay designed to persuade farm families to buy the new home freezers recently on the market, a *Wallaces' Farmer* editor even argued that for the first time acquisition of domestic equipment should take priority over farm expansion: "Corn Belt farm income is staying high. . . . Farm women, fortunately, are saying that some of the new income should go to fix up the farm home. A [*Wallaces' Farmer*] Poll, for instance, says that one-third of Iowa's farm women plan to buy freezers. . . . Buying another eighty [acres] may be buying a headache. But buying better home equipment means less work and more fun."[5]

As it had in the past, *Wallaces' Farmer* served as a forum in which midwestern women discussed their technological priorities. In November 1945, the periodical's Homemaking Department editor, Zoe Murphy, printed letters from women discussing what they wanted to purchase "now that the war [was] over . . . and there [would] be all kinds of new equipment on the market." Most of the women whose letters Murphy published wrote of having their homes electrified and acquiring modern bathrooms, stoves, and freezers. A woman from Dallas County, Iowa, summarized their position: "To farm women, it has seemed it has just been year after year of hard work, with not much coming our way, but now at last we feel free to make some of those home improvements for which we've waited so long."[6]

While the periodical's headlines proclaimed that new household equipment would "Help Homemakers Share in Post-War Mechanical 'Revolution,'" the pages of *Wallaces' Farmer* revealed that not all members of rural society were taking part in that revolution. Letters to the editor demonstrated that several barriers still existed for some farm families. A woman from Page County, Iowa, suggested that the "mechanical revolution" of 1946 applied primarily to people who owned their own farms. Many farm tenants could not yet afford modern household equipment or rented their farm homes from landlords who were not willing to invest in improvements. In the words of the Page County letter writer, "There are five houses within a quarter-mile of our own. One has water and lights—that's our landlord. The other four are like our own—no modern conveniences. I'm not speaking just of our landlord. They are all alike."[7]

Families with a limited income did not necessarily see acquisition of modern household technology as a first priority. A Woodbury County, Iowa, farm woman wrote to *Wallaces' Farmer* in November 1946 complaining about the periodical's policy of unqualified support for the REA. In her family, limited resources would be spent in other ways: "We are supposed to get electricity thru this section of Iowa, but I am not one bit enthusiastic about it. I need a better chicken house and a fence. The mister's needs are many. Then there is the returned soldier son whom we would like to help get started at farming for himself. To me these things are much more important than having electricity."[8]

A Burt County, Nebraska, mother and daughter reported that family politics also stood in the way of postwar home improvements for many farm women: "When Dad got the new manure scoop, the elevator and other modern farm tools, daughter and I approved, feeling that one of these days it would be our turn to enjoy electricity and a few modern conveniences. Just when we thought we had him convinced, what does he do? Orders another new tractor for the boys!"[9]

As these letters to the editor of *Wallaces' Farmer* indicate, the transformation of the midwestern countryside applied only to those farm families who were profiting from changes in the postwar market. Many were not. In the same November 1946 issue in which they presented women's skeptical assessment of postwar modernization, the editors of *Wallaces' Farmer* published BAE statistics showing that although farm income had risen dramatically during the war, so had production costs. The editors, like other farm market observers, worried that farm prices would soon fall as Europe recovered from the war and America demobilized its military machine. In commentary accompanying the BAE statistics, the editors remarked, "If farm income dropped back to 1940 levels and expenses stayed the same, there wouldn't be any net income at all."[10]

For many small farmers, farm profits could not keep pace with production costs, and they were forced to leave the farm. The disappearance of those small farms that could not compete in the postwar economy helped create the illusion that all farm families shared in the era's financial success and achieved the goal of farmhouse modernization. In reality, financial difficulties forced about 10 percent of midwestern farm families off the farm in the first five years following the war.

Minority farmers were particularly vulnerable to postwar conditions that made sustaining small farming operations difficult. African Americans who resided in the Midwest's most famous black farming community, the Nicodemus settlement in Graham County, Kansas, did not share in the postwar prosperity of many of their white neighbors. As a result, the town of Nicodemus practically became a ghost town in the 1950s, when many area families abandoned their farms and searched for economic opportunities in

Table 6.1 Number, Size, and Value of Midwestern Farms, 1945 and 1950

	Number of Farms		Average Acreage		Average Value	
	1945	1950	1945	1950	1945	1950
Illinois	204,239	175,543	154.7	158.6	$17,933	$28,279
Indiana	175,970	166,627	113.8	118.0	$10,197	$16,518
Iowa	208,934	203,159	164.9	168.7	$17,284	$27,563
Kansas	141,192	131,394	344.1	370.0	$13,962	$24,738
Minnesota	188,952	179,101	175.4	183.6	$9,705	$15,686
Missouri	242,934	230,045	145.2	152.7	$6,285	$9,781
Nebraska	111,756	107,183	427.3	442.9	$15,205	$25,939
North Dakota	69,520	65,401	589.8	629.9	$10,189	$18,011
South Dakota	68,705	66,452	626.3	674.0	$11,124	$20,740
Wisconsin	177,745	168,561	132.9	137.8	$8,069	$12,225

Source: U.S. Bureau of the Census, *United States Census of Agriculture: 1954* (Washington: Government Printing Office, 1956).

towns and cities. More recently arrived ethnic minorities, such as Hispanic families who came to the plains as agricultural workers during the World War II labor shortage, could not hope to ascend the agricultural ladder and eventually work their own farms as previous immigrant groups had done. For example, Hispanics who settled in Haskell County, Kansas, during the war had few economic opportunities in an agricultural economy firmly based on heavy capital investment in large-scale farming operations. In the postwar era, these men and women had to rely on seasonal employment in the sugar beet fields near Garden City, jobs in the area's burgeoning oil fields, or employment in local light industry.[11]

Those families—largely white and middle class—who remained on the farm acquired the land of their departed neighbors and thus expanded their farming operations to profit from farm prices that remained high as a result of continued U.S. aid abroad, broadening foreign markets, and the demand for food supplies from a U.S. military force rebuilding for the Cold War. As a result, significantly fewer midwestern farms existed in 1950 than in 1945, but those farms that remained were larger and more prosperous, and a higher percentage of these farms owned modern equipment (see Tables 6.1 and 6.2).

Trends that had begun in the prewar period continued in the postwar era. Farms in the prairie Corn Belt continued to have greater access to telephones and electricity, whereas those in the Great Plains Wheat Belt generally had

Table 6.2 Percentage of Farms with Modern Equipment, 1945 and 1950

	Telephone		Electricity		Tractors	
	1945	1950	1945	1950	1945	1950
Illinois	60.7	65.3	58.8	86.9	64.6	72.7
Indiana	55.3	61.8	69.8	91.7	50.8	63.6
Iowa	79.3	81.9	61.7	90.9	72.3	79.4
Kansas	64.7	68.3	38.4	74.4	66.3	75.3
Minnesota	54.6	59.9	50.5	84.1	68.1	79.8
Missouri	44.9	46.4	31.5	69.2	27.8	43.6
Nebraska	56.5	64.8	41.7	77.7	72.9	81.7
North Dakota	34.0	41.6	26.8	67.6	81.4	89.2
South Dakota	45.3	55.5	27.7	69.1	75.8	84.7
Wisconsin	48.4	59.2	70.0	92.8	61.5	75.6

Source: U.S. Bureau of the Census, *United States Census of Agriculture: 1954* (Washington: Government Printing Office, 1956).

greater access to tractors. Farms in the plains states continued to be much larger than those in the Corn Belt, and plains farms, always more susceptible to boom-and-bust cycles, generally made greater financial gains between the prewar and postwar eras than did Corn Belt farms. At the same time, farms in the border state of Missouri continued to lag behind other midwestern farms economically, following patterns more akin to those of southern farms. Overall, however, those farm families who remained on the land during the postwar period had made significant material gains, particularly in terms of their access to electricity and thus the use of electric equipment. Even adjusting for postwar inflation, their financial worth had improved considerably.

Along with changes in the number of midwestern farms, their size, their value, and their equipment, structural changes occurred in the postwar era that resulted in a decline in farm women's home production activities, such as gardening and canning, processing dairy products, and butchering and preserving meat (see Table 6.3). In the postwar era, the USDA and the Extension Service pushed American farmers toward greater specialization, a policy that both institutions had espoused throughout the twentieth century, with the exception of the depression era. USDA and Extension Service officials reasoned that greater specialization resulted in more efficient farming and thus lower food prices for the consumer. In the postwar era, therefore, many home gardens gave way to large-scale vegetable-growing operations on the West

Table 6.3 Percentage of Farms Engaged in Home Gardening,
Dairying, Butchering, War and Postwar Periods

	Gardening		Dairying		Butchering	
	1944	1949	1939	1949	1939	1949
Illinois	86	70	86	74	77	68
Indiana	84	70	83	71	73	63
Iowa	87	71	90	83	80	74
Kansas	69	53	81	75	66	59
Minnesota	84	68	88	80	77	70
Missouri	91	78	82	78	72	66
Nebraska	80	58	86	79	74	68
North Dakota	76	54	84	75	77	71
South Dakota	74	43	84	76	72	68
Wisconsin	88	72	90	85	72	62

Source: Bureau of Human Nutrition and Home Economics, U.S. Department of
Agriculture, *Rural Family Living Charts, 1953* (Washington: Government Printing
Office, 1952).

Coast, and the practice of milking a few cows on each farm gave way to greater
concentration and expansion of dairy production in the Dairy Belt of the
upper Midwest. In other words, dispersed, labor-intensive food production
became more concentrated and capital-intensive.

Technology also played a role in removing much of women's commodity
production and food processing from the farm home. The establishment of
meat lockers and the introduction of home freezers meant that butchering for
the farm family could be done by professionals who would then store the meat
for the family's use. Smaller portions of meat could be kept in the family's own
freezer, along with fruits, vegetables, and other items. In effect, the home
freezer made canning and preserving unnecessary, and many farm people
testified that they preferred the taste of food that had been frozen to that of
canned food. Farm women also found that lower consumer prices for many
foods in the postwar era meant that they could purchase those items more
cheaply than they could produce the foods themselves. Farm families, who
had always bought at least some of their grocery items, now became more
dependent on purchased foods.

Nevertheless, statistics demonstrate a significant persistence of women's
home production activities in the late 1940s, even in the face of numerous

Table 6.4 Percentage of Farms Hiring Labor, 1950 and 1954

	1950	1954
Illinois	57.5	46.3
Indiana	48.5	41.0
Iowa	64.6	50.8
Kansas	60.7	51.6
Minnesota	63.7	46.6
Missouri	47.1	39.5
Nebraska	61.4	49.0
North Dakota	67.4	54.4
South Dakota	68.8	53.2
Wisconsin	60.7	46.2

Source: U.S. Bureau of the Census, *United States Census of Agriculture: 1954* (Washington: Government Printing Office, 1956).

pressures on women to abandon such labor (see Table 6.3). The value they saw in maintaining such practices caused many women to continue home production even when it was no longer practical. Perhaps they saw it as a hedge against the possibility of another depression—an event that still loomed large in the memories of midwestern farm people. Maybe, too, women's pride in the skilled work they performed in producing and preparing vegetables, meats, and dairy and poultry products prompted them to continue these activities even in the face of overwhelming structural change.

As the postwar era progressed, however, women's traditional productive activities on the farm continued their decline. For example, by 1955, only 39 percent of midwestern farm women baked their own bread, down from an already low 56 percent in 1948.[12] In addition, the proportion of farm families who relied on hired labor continued to shrink as the postwar era progressed, which meant that fewer women were cooking large meals for extra people (see Table 6.4).

As anthropologist Deborah Fink has noted in her study of postwar women in Iowa, the transformation of the egg industry provides an excellent example of the types of changes that led to a decline in women's home production. The increased demand for eggs during World War II, when powdered eggs were a military ration staple, convinced USDA and Extension Service officials that egg production could be highly profitable and should no longer be a marginal activity on American farms. The first step in expanding egg production, they reasoned, was to downplay its image as low-status women's work. Increasingly, postwar Extension Service literature made reference to "poultry men" and the profits to be made specializing in the production of eggs.[13]

The notion of egg production as "women's work," however, did not automatically disappear. A front-page *Wallaces' Farmer* article entitled "Husband in the Henhouse?" appeared in 1948 and announced that 51 percent of the respondents to a *Wallaces' Farmer* poll reported that the wives in their families were still primarily responsible for poultry work. Only 30 percent said that husbands were the primary poultry workers, while 15 percent said the husbands and wives in their families shared the work equally. Another 4 percent said children and hired help did most of the poultry work.[14]

Along with presenting survey results that bolstered the notion of egg production as women's work, the article contained visual images and analysis of the labor involved in egg production that helped to reinforce the idea that poultry work legitimately belonged to women. The front-page photograph accompanying the article emphasized the "femininity" of poultry work, featuring as it did a pretty young woman in a midriff-baring shorts and blouse ensemble delicately carrying a bucket of eggs (see Figure 6.1). The article's author noted that although men might do some of the heavier work in the chicken house, women did the "lighter, every-day chores," such as gathering the eggs. The fact that women performed their poultry chores more frequently than men did helped define egg production as "women's work."[15]

The article foreshadowed changes in the poultry industry, however, with this observation by the author: "Large flocks tend to be more of a 50-50 proposition—the bigger the flock the more luck the woman seems to have in getting her husband to help with the chores." In fact, a movement was under way to displace women from poultry production entirely with the expansion of a few poultry flocks and the resulting demise of many smaller, woman-dominated poultry operations. The five-year period between 1949 and 1954 saw a significant decline in the percentage of midwestern farms that kept poultry flocks (see Table 6.5), and the decline continued throughout the 1950s.

A *Wallaces' Farmer* article published in 1958 contrasted sharply with the periodical's article on poultry work ten years earlier and illustrated the changes that had occurred in egg production over the course of a decade. Unlike the earlier article, this one featured no pastoral photos of a smiling young woman standing in a farmyard. Instead, it featured a photograph of a stern middle-aged man candling and grading eggs with the latest equipment.

ho Does most of the poultry work on your farm? In most cases, it's the Missus.
Like Mrs. Robert Buol, Linn county, Iowa, the women usually do chores
h as egg-gathering. But men do their share, too. If you don't believe it, see page 5,

Fig. 6.1. This photograph accompanying a *Wallaces' Farmer* cover story emphasized
that poultry production was still considered women's work in 1948. (Courtesy of
Wallaces' Farmer)

158   Entitled to Power

Table 6.5 Percentage of Farms Keeping Poultry, 1949 and 1954

	1949	1954
Illinois	72.1	61.8
Indiana	64.8	54.1
Iowa	81.6	75.3
Kansas	71.2	59.5
Minnesota	72.2	68.0
Missouri	66.1	52.1
Nebraska	76.2	71.6
North Dakota	57.7	54.7
South Dakota	75.4	73.2
Wisconsin	58.9	55.5

Source: U.S. Bureau of the Census, *United States Census of Agriculture: 1954* (Washington: Government Printing Office, 1956).

This was modern egg production based on the concept of integration. In the words of the article's author, this meant "the control by one management of two or more of the steps in the chain of producing, processing and marketing agricultural products, at least one of which must be a phase of production."[16]

The national trend toward vertical integration of the egg industry in the 1950s meant that increasingly a single corporation owned the hatchery, feed plant, packing stations, and trucking systems necessary for the large-scale production and distribution of eggs. Typical of these "egg factories" was the Creighton Brothers Corporation in Kosciusko County, Indiana. Profiled in a 1961 *Indiana Rural News* article, the corporation was the biggest egg operation in Indiana and a model of high-tech production: "Electrically operated equipment in the laying houses includes feeders, waterers, refrigeration for egg cooler rooms, lighting, 18 fans in each house, egg gathering conveyor belts, pit cleaners and auger elevators. Thanks to automation and dependable [rural electrification], one *man* is able to take care of 15,000 hens in each laying house" (author's emphasis).[17]

Describing midwestern egg production in the decade and a half following World War II, one observer engaged in understatement: "Integrated quality egg programs, combined with state egg laws, are bringing changes in egg production and marketing practices." In reality, however, egg production had been entirely transformed. The growth of large-scale, integrated poultry operations had displaced women from poultry production. Women with small

The Postwar Era 159

poultry flocks could not hope to compete with large-scale operations that could produce eggs more cheaply and could more easily meet new government requirements regarding the quality of eggs. In the words of an Iowa farm woman, egg factories and egg grading "just ruined the egg business" for midwestern farm women.[18]

In effect, changes in the structure and technology of egg production also ruined the egg business for the Midwest as a whole. For decades, the Midwest, with its small poultry flocks on most family farms, had led the nation in the production of eggs. Iowa, in fact, had led every other state in the union in egg production. Iowa lost that position in 1959, however, and never regained it. The development of egg factories and the removal of many of them to the warmer climates of California and the American South meant the demise of poultry production in the Midwest. The small, dependable, labor-intensive poultry flocks that had been "women's work" and a "lifesaver" for many midwestern farm families during the depression were a thing of the past.

During the postwar era, Elizabeth Wherry continued to serve as a keen observer of changes in farm family life, including changes in farm women's work. In the years following World War II, Wherry remained optimistic about life on the farm, and her faith in technology and the domestic ideal remained intact. A December 1950 "Country Air" column was representative of those of the era:

> I was so happy to visit the young wife at the farm and see her shining new gas stove—a beautiful thing with all the conveniences and gadgets, and as gleaming white as her refrigerator. A far cry from the black bulk of the wood range I had after my first five years of housekeeping. . . . [M]y heart rejoices that incomes of recent years have made these standards possible in many farm homes. Maybe this prosperity, inflation, government aid (or interference if that term suits you better) has been the result of the war shortages, post-war booms and productive peaks. . . . I can't feel too guilty about it if it has reduced barnyard chores, replaced hard-to-get hired men with motors, elevators and new buildings, and given farm women time from housekeeping for more homemaking.[19]

Wherry's columns of the era noted postwar improvements not only in domestic technology but in transportation and communication technology outside the farm home. Her 1954 account of a meeting of Farm Bureau women was typical:

Table 6.6 Percentage of Farm Homes with Television Sets, 1954

Illinois	52.1
Indiana	59.4
Iowa	54.9
Kansas	28.3
Minnesota	33.3
Missouri	31.4
Nebraska	33.9
North Dakota	18.1
South Dakota	17.0
Wisconsin	39.3

Source: U.S. Bureau of the Census, *United States Census of Agriculture: 1954* (Washington: Government Printing Office, 1956).

As I parked my car, I noted with considerable satisfaction the cars parked outside. My car (in the low priced bracket) bowed modestly to the other cars, big and powerful. . . . It wasn't hard to remember back a couple of decades ago when a group of farm women's cars were battered and of models of another decade earlier. . . . What a lot of good things good income has done for all of us! . . . What a lot labor saving devices have done for us! And what a lot our interests have broadened with the extra time provided for us thru science and invention![20]

In her last years as a columnist for *Wallaces' Farmer*, Wherry became interested in a new type of communication technology—television. Her enthusiasm for television mirrored that which she had expressed for radio twenty-five years earlier. In Wherry's words, "What a boon [TV] is to shut-ins, invalids, tired people who'd rather enjoy all evening at home than go out, and to people who are geographically too far from events to go to them easily." Wherry spoke of farm families rearranging their meals and activities around the broadcast time of their favorite programs, just as they had accommodated their daily schedules to radio listening a generation earlier.[21] Indeed, after only a few years on the market, television had become a popular piece of equipment on midwestern farms by the early 1950s (see Table 6.6).

Wherry's discussion of television, however, differed from her earlier commentary on radio in one significant way: She never mentioned programming that was specifically directed at farm people. Her favorite programs—"Omnibus," Ed Sullivan's "Toast of the Town," Edward R. Murrow's "Person to

Person," "Mr. Peepers," "What's My Line," "Dragnet"—were all programs directed primarily at an urban audience. In fact, the major theme of Wherry's postwar columns was that farm women and farm families were increasingly similar to those who lived in towns and cities.

For the most part, Wherry found this to be a desirable change. She praised farm women's new status as "homemakers"—women primarily interested in the "comfort and beauty" aspects of housekeeping. She saw this as a direct result of their use of modern household devices and their movement away from many traditional chores on the farm such as gardening, poultry raising, and the care of hired men. She relished the fact that increased income and decreased labor at heavy chores allowed farm women to achieve a physical appearance identical to that of urban women and commented that farm women were now "well dressed in well-fitting shoes and dresses with smart hats perched atop well-groomed hair."[22]

In a 1950 column, Wherry in fact wondered if farm women any longer differed from their urban counterparts at all:

I asked a friend who after 30 years of housekeeping has achieved a laboratory-type kitchen, just what there was left to remind a farm woman that her life and work were different from the town woman any more. What was there to remind her that there was a special dignity or responsibility still her own as a woman of the land? My friend said: "There is still a closer relation to the husband's occupation than city women are privileged to feel." It's not just table conversation nor extra men to cook for, but the variation of jobs as the seasons turn that a farm woman can see from her windows—her husband's work and her family life are closely allied.[23]

According to Wherry, farm women had finally achieved the technological ideal. Their kitchens were now modern "laboratories," and their lives were more like those of urban women. According to this account, farm women no longer performed tasks that were uniquely their own and thus defined their identity as farm women. Although some farm women might still have "extra men to cook for," increasing mechanization and rural labor shortages were even making that situation a relatively rare one. According to Wherry and her friend, farm women, like urban women, now defined themselves principally through their relationships with their husbands. In those marital relationships, however, farm women still differed from urban women because only farm women could look outside their kitchen windows and observe their husbands at work.

Wherry's observations about farm women had changed drastically since she had first written about the topic in the 1920s. At that time, she saw farm women as active participants in farm life who gardened, raised poultry, and picked corn. Now they were "women of the land" only to the extent that they *watched* their husbands perform varying tasks with the change of season. She no longer viewed farm women as connected to the land or the changing seasons by their own diverse chores. Planting season, chick season, and harvest season came and went as farm women increasingly spent their time performing "homemaking" tasks that were identical to those of urban women. In a rare moment of wistfulness, Wherry wondered if farm women even any longer noticed the natural world beyond their domestic "laboratories": "Do farm women with all the modern gadgets of electricity, clean fuel ranges, smooth floor covering, easy-to-clean plastics and fabrics have time to watch sunsets nowadays?"[24]

In fact, farm women's work was not restricted to housekeeping activities. In deference to the postwar rhetoric of propagandists who preached that women's work *should* be restricted to their newly modernized homes, Wherry exaggerated the extent to which farm women confined their tasks to that arena. Just as the rhetoric of the postwar domestic ideal obscured the reality that an increased number of urban married women were working for pay outside the home, a rural version of the postwar ideal denied the reality that an increased number of farm women were spending more time away from the farmhouse in the years following World War II.[25]

Women's double duty on the farm, which had always existed but had remained largely unacknowledged, was carefully disguised by the "modern homemaker" rhetoric of the postwar era. In response to the fact that many women were actually expanding their work in the farm fields, arguments against women's field work became widespread in the postwar era. Most were based on the faulty premise that such work by women represented exceptional behavior and that most women naturally preferred "homemaking." Voices on both sides of the women's field work debate, however, continued to refer to women's farm work as "helping out" the farm husband, thus reinforcing the notion that field work should not be women's primary concern.

Popular and scholarly studies in the postwar era presented discussions of how farm women were spending the time supposedly set free by modern household equipment. The insightful author of an essay appearing in *Wallaces' Farmer* in 1953 noted that changing housekeeping standards and new activities outside the home had left women with virtually no free time. The author discussed farm women's expanded involvement in community activities but argued that their chief activity outside the farmhouse was their increased participation in field work. For many farm families, women's work in the fields was no longer the result of emergency labor shortages or the function of periodic "busy seasons." Decreasing reliance on hired help had made field work and related tasks typical activities for many farm women. Nevertheless, according to the author, women's primary postwar role remained that of "homemaker":

> What does the "little woman" do with her time now that she has a clean-fuel stove and cake mixes have come on the market? . . . With clothes dryers to save trips to the clothes lines, freezers to bring forth frozen pies and casseroles for hurry-up meals, a great many women hours are spent each year on tractors. Perhaps more important are the hours spent on trips to town for repairs for all the new machinery. . . . And then somebody—guess who—has to take time to make the good rolls, and the angel food cakes and the casserole dishes that come out of the freezer on busy days.[26]

In the decade and a half following World War II, *Wallaces' Farmer* published numerous comments from readers who joined the women's field work debate, and most of the people expressing their opinions were farm women themselves. Their comments centered primarily around the extent to which women who worked in the fields were able to fulfill their "homemaker" role. Even the comments of those women who supported the notion of full-time homemaking, however, acknowledged the necessity of farm women at least occasionally "helping out." In using this rhetorical device, these women were able to deny that they actually performed farm work and could thus claim that they were living up to the postwar domestic ideal. Typical of such comments were those of an Audubon County, Iowa, woman, who remained anonymous but significantly signed her letter as a "Housewife":

> This is written to the women who think they have to get out and work in the fields. I know it's a grand feeling to get out and operate a tractor that a child can handle. But it seems to me that it isn't woman's work. A mother has her place in the home, taking care of her children. How many little

tots have been burned or otherwise hurt while the mother was out milking cows? . . . [But a] woman should be ready and willing to run errands, get machinery repairs, shut off the tank, chase the hogs in case they get out.[27]

By denying that taking in machinery parts for repair, shutting off watering tanks, and chasing hogs were farm chores, a "Housewife" could claim that she was living up to her prescribed role.

Readers' comments to the editors of *Wallaces' Farmer* also indicated some male resentment toward women's increasing participation in field work. Margaret Noll's account of her corn picking experiences in Ida County, Iowa, indicated that her attempts to "help out" male neighbors and family members did not always meet with approval: "I'm never fully accepted at corn picking. It is 'man work.' Remarks such as 'the all-American Drawback' or 'Handicap' reach my ears. Still, picking is the best excuse of the year to be outdoors."[28]

Male resentment of women's work in the field seemed to center around the idea that the line between men's and women's work might blur if women increasingly neglected their homes to work in the fields as an "excuse to be outdoors" or to experience the "grand feeling" of driving a tractor. Men frequently requested and benefited from women's participation in field work, but that did not mean that they wanted women to forget where their primary duties lay. Women's neglect of their household duties was thus a theme of several men's comments to *Wallaces' Farmer* regarding the changing role of farm women in the postwar era. Those men most threatened by women's increasing participation in activities beyond the farmhouse, however, were not husbands, who after all benefited economically from women's work in the field, but a group of men who were economically threatened by women's field work—hired hands. These men also conveniently relied on postwar domestic rhetoric to make their arguments against women's activities beyond the farm home. According to the comments of a Marshall County, Iowa, farm hand who wrote to *Wallaces' Farmer*, women were neglecting their household duties whenever they ventured outside the farmhouse.[29]

Such criticism, however, did not deter farm women from spending more time away from the home. When they were not working in the farm field, they were frequently working for pay in off-farm jobs. Throughout the 1950s *Wallaces' Farmer* published several articles about the new phenomenon of farm women working in off-farm jobs. Initially, the editors took the position that it was acceptable for a young farm woman to work away from the farm—but only as a temporary measure until she and her husband could "establish themselves." The author of a 1950 article entitled "Farm Brides Who Work in Town" made it clear that housekeeping should remain a farm woman's chief concern:

> The labor-saving devices which the farm wife now shares with her city cousin, together with better roads and more dependable automobiles . . . make it possible today for farm women to hold part-time jobs. . . . These young women have proved—often to an openly hostile community— that they can do a good job of homemaking and working. . . . [W]ith the large amount of capital required to start farming today, the wife's income may be a welcome addition to the family finances for a few years.[30]

The article's author noted that "in almost every midwest community" farm women were working as teachers, nurses, hairdressers, factory workers, and retail and office clerks. An Illinois study showed that 10 percent of that state's farm women were holding wage-paying jobs and that most of them were working as retail clerks, teachers, or factory workers—the only jobs available to women in most small towns. Although these jobs provided women with low wages, they could earn more money in town jobs than by making cottage cheese, reupholstering furniture, or selling parakeets—all money-making projects that the *Wallaces' Farmer* homemaking editor suggested farm women undertake in their homes. In the words of one midwestern farm woman, "I'd want a real job. Too many things that you do at home bring in only pin money. I'd want more than that."[31]

As the 1950s progressed, the editors of *Wallaces' Farmer* recognized that farm women of all ages were increasingly becoming permanent members of the heartland's small-town labor force. A 1956 portrait of one small Iowa town showed that farm women made up 25 percent of the community's female work force. Some of these women drove up to 40 miles a day in their round-trip commutes between home and job. None of the farm women interviewed for the article expected to quit her job any time soon. With annual farm incomes in the area averaging $3,029 and the capital investment in a farming operation continuing to rise, farm women could not afford to leave their town jobs behind. For the women profiled in the article, a town job meant their families' survival on the farm. The author's comments on the situation of one particular woman told the story of many of her neighbors: "It isn't for a TV set or a home freezer that Harriet Sellers, R.N. and home-maker, is spending her salary. It's for school clothing, groceries, tractor fuel and farm payments. . . . Practically speaking, it seems that mom has come to town so dad and the kids can stay on the farm."[32]

Noting the phenomena of women's off-farm employment and increased field labor, *Wallaces' Farmer* personnel polled farm families in 1958 to determine the extent to which farm men and women were crossing traditional gender-role boundaries to "help" each other with farm or housework. Seventy-seven percent of male respondents reported that their spouses at least occasionally drove the tractor or worked with livestock. There were, however, some generational variations. While only 64 percent of women fifty and older performed farm work, 82 percent of women between twenty and thirty-four did farm work, and 83 percent of women between thirty-five and forty-nine performed such chores. Editor Zoe Murphy reasoned that such differences existed because an "older woman can't swing up on a tractor as easy as a young one." Changing notions about acceptable gender-role behavior, however, also undoubtedly played a part. Although farm families continued to view women's primary role as that of homemaker, younger women were expanding their activities to include "helping out" on a regular basis by operating modern field equipment.[33]

Noting that "part-time work off the farm ha[d] made a new problem for some families," the poll takers also investigated the extent to which farm husbands were necessarily performing housework. In her discussion of the poll results, Murphy quoted several young women who were holding off-farm jobs and were thus dependent on their husbands to perform some household chores. Even though this was the case, Murphy noted that women performed "men's work" to a greater degree than men took on jobs traditionally defined as women's work. According to Murphy, survey results demonstrated that 38 percent of farm wives provided "substantial help" for their husbands on a regular basis, whereas only 28 percent of farm men regularly took on any household duties.[34]

Two years later, another *Wallaces' Farmer* poll confirmed that the trend of women's increased work in the fields had become a permanent reality. Economic necessity lay behind this phenomenon, as Zoe Murphy indicated in her opening comments about the survey's results:

Farm women have always helped with outside work—chores, chickens, and gardens. But today's farm women are doing more outside work than ever before. Many put in long hours in the fields on a tractor or other machinery thruout the growing season. Wives, plus machinery, have taken the place of hired men or other outside help. "I can make more money for us by working in the fields than many women can by working in town," says a young renter's wife in Washington [C]ounty, Iowa. Then she adds, "The best part is that I can work my own hours."[35]

In fact, one of the most significant findings of the poll was that many farm women enjoyed working in the field. Poll results showed that 24 percent of the farm women surveyed performed field work on a regular basis and another 25 percent at least during busy seasons. Of those women who worked in the field, 46 percent said they liked field work better than housework, another 32 percent said they had no strong preference one way or another, and only 22 percent reported that they did not like doing field work "but it ha[d] to be done." Women who preferred doing field work felt that, unlike housework, it allowed them to work on one task at a time and to see that task to completion. One young farm woman stated, "I like outside work because then I'm only doing one thing at a time. In the house there are so many things going on all at once." Women also favored doing so-called men's work because it was viewed as having greater status than housework and demonstrated women's importance to the family economy. A middle-aged respondent reported, "It makes me feel real important when I can stop my work and help my husband get some of the rush jobs done."[36] Given these attitudes, it is not surprising that many women encouraged continued investment in field equipment rather than in domestic appliances. Perhaps they even viewed further investment in upgrading domestic technology as a trap that could only lead toward greater specialization in the role of homemaker—a role that many women clearly did not prefer.

Murphy's closing analysis of the survey's results emphasized another reality of farm women's postwar experience—that farm modernization had not relieved women of long hours of work on the farm: "When modern appliances were first introduced it looked like an end to the old adage, 'Women's work is never done.' But along with the time-savers inside, came the increased use of machinery outside and women were right back where they started."[37]

Perhaps this was one reason why women remained less enthusiastic than men about life on the farm. The 1940 census had shown that 41 percent of western Corn Belt farm women in their early twenties left the farm for the city, whereas only 27 percent of farm men in that age group migrated to urban areas. A 1947 *Wallaces' Farmer* poll showed that only 46 percent of farm men and women wanted their daughters to marry a farmer, while 66 percent said

Table 6.7 Percentage of Farm Homes Having Modern Equipment, 1960

	Piped Water	Washing Machine	Freezer	Telephone	TV
Illinois	85.2	93.6	66.3	82.8	88.5
Indiana	87.3	93.6	65.3	82.9	87.5
Iowa	87.4	96.3	64.3	91.3	90.6
Kansas	81.6	91.8	50.9	85.2	82.5
Minnesota	78.9	95.8	63.0	79.5	82.2
Missouri	64.7	90.4	48.7	65.0	80.7
Nebraska	88.0	95.6	64.1	80.1	87.6
North Dakota	69.5	96.0	71.4	69.6	87.7
South Dakota	73.2	95.0	63.0	73.7	84.3
Wisconsin	87.8	95.7	63.9	79.1	89.1

Source: U.S. Bureau of the Census, *1960 Census of Housing* (Washington: Government Printing Office, 1963).

they would like their sons to become a farmer. In commenting on the poll's results, Zoe Murphy made a familiar argument: "Perhaps one way to keep girls in the country is to make rural living just as attractive and convenient as city living. More farm homes with electricity and the comforts that come with modern conveniences will make country living more attractive."[38]

As the postwar era continued, however, it became obvious that the roots of women's dissatisfaction did not lie in their lack of modern equipment. Even after they had acquired modern farm homes, women questioned whether life on the farm was a worthwhile existence for young women. The results of a *Wallaces' Farmer* poll conducted at the close of the 1950s indicated that economic opportunities in the city—not lack of farm home conveniences— largely accounted for young women's migration to urban areas.[39] By the end of the 1950s, after all, the majority of midwestern farm homes had acquired modern conveniences (see Table 6.7).

Traditional farm inheritance and partnership patterns, however, had remained intact. Young men inherited management of the family farm, went into business partnership with their fathers, or received family financial support in starting their own farming operations. For most young women, these opportunities were not available. While daughters might inherit the family farm, or some portion of it, they were rarely encouraged to take over actual operation of the farm. Instead, they might become absentee landowners or stay on the farm but have a husband or other male relative serve as the chief farm operator. In the postwar era, farm women's economic opportunities remained limited.[40]

By the early 1960s, however, sociologists noted that women's increased participation in field work and off-farm jobs had had an impact on women's economic decision-making power within the farm family. A 1962 study by an Iowa State University sociologist revealed that women's off-farm employment was "associated with a decline in patriarchal authority patterns and with the emergence of equalitarian authority patterns. . . . Employment of wives generally increases family incomes. The increased economic contribution of the employed wife to her family may alter her status and power relations with her spouse." Both male and female participants in the study reported that women's off-farm employment translated into their increased participation and influence in family purchasing decisions.[41]

In a *Wallaces' Farmer* poll conducted in 1962, 73 percent of the women surveyed reported that their husbands discussed most farm family purchases with them. Once again, however, there were generational differences. Eighty-two percent of the women twenty-one to thirty-four years old reported that they participated in most purchasing decisions, while 79 percent of the women between thirty-five and forty-nine, 64 percent of those between fifty and sixty-four, and only 50 percent of women sixty-five and older stated that they made decisions jointly with their husbands. In her discussion of the poll's results, editor Zoe Murphy noted the increased decision-making power of young women and closed the article with a quote from one of them: "I feel that I help in producing the income and have a right to help in spending it."[42]

A 1962 University of Wisconsin study, however, noted that the extent to which farm men and women equally shared in making decisions varied according to the purchase being considered. While 82 percent of husbands and wives equally shared in making decisions regarding the purchase of major home appliances, only 46 percent of the farm couples surveyed shared equally in decisions concerning the purchase of major farm equipment. For the majority of Wisconsin farm families, men were still the primary decision makers when it came to the purchase of field equipment. Nevertheless, women's overall decision-making power within the farm family was decidedly on the rise and now more closely resembled that of women in urban families.[43]

Greater decision-making equality between husbands and wives was only one way in which farm families were becoming more like nonfarm families in the postwar era. Their homes more closely resembled those of urban people, as did their purchasing patterns. In particular, however, the activities of women in farm families now more closely paralleled those of women in urban families. Like women in towns and cities, farm women frequently held paying jobs outside the home. And with the disappearance of canning, poultry, and dairy work, they increasingly performed household tasks that were identical to those of nonfarm women. Perhaps nowhere was their growing similarity to nonfarm women more apparent than in postwar advertisements.[44]

Increasingly, farm life publications of the 1950s and 1960s published advertisements on their women's pages that were very similar or even identical to those directed at nonfarm women. Ads directed at the female reader of the *Progressive Farmer*, the *National Grange Monthly*, and *Capper's Farmer* greatly resembled those published in *Good Housekeeping, Ladies' Home Journal*, and other mainstream women's magazines. Advertisements for home appliances differed very little, or not at all, from the pages of *Wallaces' Farmer* to those of *Redbook*. American Telephone and Telegraph was one company that continued to run ads specifically aimed at farm women. Even Bell System advertisements of the era, however, demonstrated that farm women increasingly resembled those who lived in cities.[45]

For example, an AT&T ad that appeared in various farm life publications in 1954 presented an image of farm women that had never been shown in prewar advertising: the farm woman as wage earner. The advertisement, headlined "Farm Woman at the Switchboard," profiled Mrs. Clara Schindler, chief telephone operator in Perryville, Missouri. The ad featured photographs of the middle-aged Schindler at her switchboard and in her farmyard garden. The ad's copy referred to Schindler as "a farmer at heart [who] 'knows her onions' [in the garden] as well as at her telephone job." The advertising copy also stated that Schindler's understanding of the special concerns of farm people made her "the right person to have on hand" when a farm call registered on the switchboard. The copy went on to explain, "She's a farmer herself and knows what it's like to have grain that needs combining, or stock ready to truck to market."[46]

Although this ad featured a farm woman in a new postwar role, it also emphasized her unique characteristics as a farm woman. The ad's copy mentioned her knowledge of farm and marketing practices and her skills as a gardener and poultry raiser. As the decade continued, however, Bell advertisements increasingly showed women in settings and situations that did not differ from those of urban women. For example, an ad appearing in several midwestern farm magazines in 1958 showed an attractively dressed young woman sitting in a modern kitchen, chatting on the telephone. The advertise-

Take your choice of attractive decorator colors

Why you <u>need</u> a kitchen extension phone

You're a farm business partner as well as a housewife. In the course of your busy day you take or make many calls to do your part in running the farm.

Since you spend so much time in the kitchen, it makes sense to have a telephone handy. When it rings, you're right there to say "hello." The biscuits won't burn or the pot boil over because a telephone call took you from the kitchen. And while you handle important calls, you can keep a watchful eye on the children.

Your husband will appreciate a kitchen extension.

too. He doesn't really *like* to track through your clean house when you call him to the phone. He'd much rather pick it up where tracks are quickly wiped away.

And when your work is done, it's easy and fun to take a break and chat with a friend on your handy kitchen extension.

The convenience, privacy and protection of extension phones throughout your house—where you work, play and sleep—cost surprisingly little. To order, just call your telephone company business office.

 BELL TELEPHONE SYSTEM

SPRING-A-LING! IT'S KITCHEN TELEPHONE TIME! Drop in soon at your local Bell Telephone business office and see the colorful kitchen phones on display there

Fig. 6.2. In this 1959 Bell advertisement only the view of a farmyard through the kitchen window reveals that this modern domestic scene is taking place in a farm home. Bell System Advertisements. (Courtesy of Ayer Collection, Archives Center, National Museum of American History, Smithsonian Institution, Washington, D.C.)

ment aimed at getting farm families to install more than one phone in their homes. The ad's copy told readers, "Modern Homes Have Handy Phones," and "[An] extension telephone in the kitchen is so convenient when you need that 'telephone break' from your household chores."[47]

A 1959 advertisement again showed an attractive young woman talking on the phone in a modern kitchen, with her two young children in the background licking frosting from an electric mixer bowl. The scene could have been in any urban or suburban home. The only clue that this was supposed to be a photograph of a farm home kitchen was the view of a barnyard through the kitchen window (see Figure 6.2). Although the ad began by telling the farm woman reader, "You're a farm business partner as well as a housewife," the remainder of its copy dealt entirely with women's domestic concerns, such as baking biscuits and tending children, and the need to have a telephone in the kitchen because she spent "so much time" there.[48]

Increasingly, advertising of the period portrayed farm women in modern domestic settings and as consumers whose concerns were not significantly different from those of urban women. At a time when farm women themselves were more likely to be in the field or at an off-farm job, advertisers reinforced the domestic ideology of the era and showed farm women in the kitchen. This advertising also appeared at a time when, according to the results of a *Wallaces' Farmer* poll, the midwestern farm family was much more likely to be found in the living room around the television set than in the traditional center of farm family life—the farm home kitchen.[49]

In its emphasis on the growing similarity between the lives of farm and nonfarm women, however, the advertising of the era presented an accurate portrait of farm women's lives. One reason for this growing similarity was the fact that farm women increasingly were women who themselves had not grown up on farms. As anthropologist Deborah Fink has noted, World War II served as a major turning point in the life of many midwestern farm communities. War-related jobs provided young single women with new economic opportunities beyond the farm, and few of them returned to the countryside at war's end. Military service took young men away from their heartland farms, and the GI Bill provided many of them with a college education following the war—an opportunity that most otherwise would not have had. As a result of these changes, the pool of young women from which a farm man might choose a bride had also changed. He was less likely to marry the "girl next door" and more likely to marry a woman from outside the local rural community. In the years following World War II, many young men returned to their family farms with town-reared war brides and college sweethearts. According to one midwestern study, by 1955 one in every three women residing on a farm had grown up in a town or city.[50]

Those farm women who were born between the world wars and married during or after World War II were not only more likely than earlier farm women to have grown up in a town or city, they were also more likely to live in modern houses and to perform field work on a regular basis. A significant proportion were also apt to hold off-farm jobs. One fact, however, had not changed between an earlier generation of farm women and their own: Women remained less satisfied than men with life on the farm. For the generation of postwar farm women, the reasons they voiced for their dissatisfaction with farm life differed from those of their predecessors. Living in the world of modernized farming and housekeeping, postwar farm women rarely mentioned the lack of modern conveniences as a major reason for their dissatisfaction. Instead, they might focus on their unfamiliarity with farm life, the economic necessity of holding a low-paying off-farm job, or other complaints that were unique to the postwar era. At the base of their criticism, however, lay a familiar reality—the inequality of men and women in the farm family. Although sociologists noted women's greater decision-making power, their increased use of modern machinery, and their expanded cash contribution to the family economy, patriarchy remained firmly intact on midwestern farms. The experiences of several members of the postwar generation of farm women illustrate the forms of patriarchal control that continued in the years following World War II.

Most of the women who were new to farm life agreed with the assessment of a Nebraska woman: "Never in my wildest dreams did I think I'd ever marry a farmer." For Adelaide Krentz, of Long Island, New York, the thought of marrying a farmer had certainly been an unlikely notion. When she married her husband Ernest in 1946 and moved with him to his family's farm in Wisconsin, she had to make some adjustments. She learned to milk cows, to dress chickens for the freezer, and to drive a car in order to run errands for the farm. When Leona Giese left Chicago in 1960 to move with her new husband to his Wisconsin farm, she found that her duties included driving the tractor, keeping the farm books, running errands, and taking a job at the local agricultural co-op to aid the farm family economy. Audrey Hauser left behind her life in small-town Iowa to join her husband on a Tama County farm, where she was his "go-fer" who drove to town for machinery parts. She also occasionally drove the tractor, although her husband criticized her driving.

Hauser felt she only "became a real farm woman," however, when her husband injured his leg and had to stay in the hospital for four months. Although pregnant with her fifth child, she took her husband's place and worked outdoors six hours a day.[51]

The experiences of Lois McKnight perhaps best illustrate those of non-farm women who moved to farms in the postwar era. In her own words, "In 1944 I didn't know anything about a farm." A year later, however, the Denver woman found herself on a Wisconsin farm with her new husband and a newly modernized farmhouse. Her major problem was attempting to fit into a rural community that was not used to the presence of outsiders. Her first mistake was taking a daily horseback ride in the mornings while her husband milked the cows. Her neighbors frowned on her horseback riding, which they considered a frivolous activity. Feeling isolated, lonely, and homesick for Denver, she began spending her mornings chatting with her husband in the milk barn. During these early morning conversations, McKnight learned how to use the milking machine and eventually took over the milking operation entirely when her politically active husband was away attending meetings and conventions.[52]

Another task Lois McKnight shared with her husband and his twin brother was the spring plowing, a job that she disliked but to which she adapted:

It's really boring just going up and down a field back and forth when you're plowing. To kind of alleviate some of the boredom I would put on some of my very best cologne on my wrist and every now and then going down the boring furrow of plowing I would smell that and imagine myself someplace else, anyplace but doing this boring chore. . . . The one good thing, they would let me get off the tractor about ten minutes early [at] noon so I could go in and have food fixed for them.[53]

McKnight's child care responsibilities further complicated her attempts to balance farm work and domestic chores. When she milked the cows, McKnight encircled her young daughter—along with the child's toys and books—with straw bales and created a makeshift playpen on the barn floor. During the spring plowing, McKnight tied the little girl to her, and the child thus rode behind her mother on the tractor seat.[54]

McKnight's major challenge, however, remained fitting into the local farming community. Not understanding the neighborhood customs, she early offended her neighbors by suggesting that they close the local one-room school and send their children to modern town schools. Her suggestion "went over like a lead balloon," and she soon gave up her reform effort. Instead, she worked to have modern plumbing, air conditioning, and other conveniences installed in the one-room building.[55]

A final way in which she emphasized her status as an outsider was her lack of culinary skills. During the first year of her marriage, when wartime shortages prevented her husband from purchasing a modern combine or mechanical corn picker, McKnight had to cook for large numbers of threshers and corn shredders. She realized her cooking talents did not live up to those of her neighbors, and she resented the hard work. And because she was a newcomer, none of the neighborhood women offered to help her feed the hungry field workers. In McKnight's words, "Somehow or other I just didn't fit into this community very well. I was weird. I was different. I didn't make a really big splash. All I wanted to be was a part of it, but I never quite made the grade."[56]

McKnight's unfortunate experience feeding field crews made her happy to use the family's resources to purchase modern field equipment in the first year after the war. It also taught her one of the major lessons of life on the farm—that farm families often sacrificed other needs in order to purchase farm machinery:

[E]verything seemed to have to go for machinery. I realized that. The thought was "I know we need things for the house, but the house doesn't produce income, and if we're ever going to do anything worthwhile, we have to do this for income." I went along with that. I understood that. We discussed what he would have to purchase in the way of machinery. In fact, . . . he cashed in [his] life insurance policy in order to buy the first combine.[57]

In the postwar era, even those young women who had themselves grown up on farms faced problems and situations that their mothers had not known. Rose Marie Dower had grown up on a farm, but after marrying and moving to her husband's Wisconsin farm in 1944, she found that her own experiences differed from those of her mother. In order to save money that otherwise would have been paid to a hired hand, Dower became her husband's chief work partner in the farm fields. Complete mechanization of field work in the postwar era meant selling off the draft animals and a tearful farewell to her favorite horse, Old Dan. Unlike her mother, Dower learned to drive a car, which she considered a "treat" because she no longer had to depend on her husband for transportation. And she froze her meat and vegetables in a modern freezer rather than spending long hours canning and preserving as her mother had done.[58]

Although modern household equipment had released many of these post-war farm women from traditional household chores, they still played a major role in farm production—even though that role frequently went unrecognized. The experiences of Dorothy Von der Sump Hartwig illustrate the problems that farm women faced in the postwar era. Hartwig was born in 1921 and grew up on a farm in Marquette County, Wisconsin. As a girl, her two loves were animals and books. In order to attend high school, she had to board in the small town of Pardeeville and travel 10 miles every Friday evening to spend the weekends with her family. She was a good student and after graduation attended the University of Wisconsin as an accounting major. When her father died after her sophomore year, however, Hartwig quit the university "to stay home and take care of the farm." She soon found that running the farm and caring for her disabled mother were difficult tasks, and she sought a neighbor's advice. According to Hartwig, "One of our neighbors told me, 'Well now, if you could get that Carl Hartwig to come and work for you he'd run [the farm] just like it was his own.' But they didn't tell me he was going to make it his own." She married her hired man the following year.[59]

Hartwig's dedication to the farm did not wane following her marriage, and she continued to perform farm work in addition to her housework. In fact, she greatly preferred farm work to housekeeping, which she considered "nothing but a pain." She occasionally worked in the fields, although field work held little attraction for her after it was no longer performed with horses. She did, however, drive the tractor when necessary. Like most other farm women of her generation, she did the farm bookkeeping and spent a significant amount of time in the car taking machinery parts to be repaired. In Hartwig's words, "I think all farm wives are expected to run when their husbands need them. And I was no exception. You never know, maybe you were in the middle of trying to bake something or the like and, 'Oh, you've got to run to town for parts or you've got to come and help with this, that or the next thing.' There was always something . . . so you just never planned ahead of time."[60] Hartwig's chief farm activity, however, was working with the livestock. With her lifelong interest in animals, she virtually took over the family's hog and cattle business, a situation that many of the Hartwigs' neighbors found unusual. One neighbor "was just totally shocked" to learn that Hartwig, and not her husband, was the one who made arrangements to have the cattle artificially inseminated. Members of her rural neighborhood did not understand this task to be appropriate "women's work." Hartwig's long hours of work with the family's cattle herd, moreover, remained unrecognized: Her prizewinning Holstein cattle were registered in her husband's name.[61]

Hartwig passed along her interest in animal husbandry to her daughter and successfully fought local high school officials to allow her daughter to take agriculture courses in the 1960s. Hartwig was not so successful with the local Future Farmers of America (FFA) chapter, however, which refused to allow the young woman entrance into the organization. Once again, an institution charged with educating members of the farm family apparently defined gender roles more narrowly than did the farm women themselves. In the minds of FFA leaders, women could not be "farmers." Undaunted, Hartwig waged a winning battle four years later to have her daughter admitted to dairy science courses at the University of Wisconsin. Noting that her own contributions often remained unrecognized by neighbors, family members, and government officials who only acknowledged the work of male farmers, Hartwig commented hopefully, "My daughter shouldn't have to go through all this."[62]

Nevertheless, in looking back at her own life, Hartwig could not help feeling bitter: "I figured I probably spent . . . a good eight hours a day, seven days a week in farm activity. I'm not calling housework farm activity; that to me was separate. And yet they figured I didn't have a part in the farming. That still irks me a little I guess."[63]

Dorothy Hartwig was not alone in her resentment of rural patriarchy. Many members of the postwar generation voiced similar opinions. For example, although Lois McKnight appreciated getting off the tractor ten minutes early to prepare lunch, she clearly resented the fact that the noon hour represented recreational time for her husband and brother-in-law and an extended work period for her: "They let me out early off the tractor so I could come in and hustle and get the food ready. While I did the dishes, they could read the noon papers, the day's mail and that sort of thing. I did the dishes. That always bugged me. If I had any energy at the end of the day, then I could read the papers, read my magazines, whatever. But yes, I felt put upon."[64]

As the comments of Lois McKnight, Dorothy Hartwig, and other postwar farm women suggest, men remained in control of women's labor on the farm. They called on women to run errands and work in the field when needed while still expecting women to perform traditional domestic duties—albeit with new domestic equipment. In some ways, men held even greater control over women's work in the postwar period. While women of an earlier era had worked in the garden or poultry house without male supervision, men directed the field work that women performed during the postwar years. They told women where, when, and how to drive the farm tractor.

The work that women performed outside the home, whether on the farm or in a wage-earning town job, remained obscured by a domestic ideal that emphasized their homemaking role. Indeed, with their modern household equipment and the loss of gardens, hired men, and small-scale poultry and dairy operations, farm women of the postwar era did increasingly resemble urban housewives. Not even urban housewives were living up to the postwar domestic ideal, however, as their increased participation in the paid work force attested. Farm women, though, were even further distanced from that ideal. As it always had, farm women's work ranged far beyond the farmhouse kitchen. In the postwar era, the tractor and the off-farm job merely replaced the poultry house and the garden as symbols of women's work beyond the home. Like her earlier tasks outside the domestic sphere, the postwar farm woman's work in the field or in town was viewed merely as an extension of her role as dutiful wife. She performed these tasks to aid the farm family economy, which her husband still controlled, although not to the extent that farm husbands had dominated economic decisions in the past. Farm women had gained some economic and political power in the course of the twentieth century, but rural patriarchy remained intact. The adoption of new technologies had merely altered the forms it took. In the postwar era, men were still the "farmers" and women their "helpers," a perception reinforced by women's own assertion that they were not "farmers" but "farm wives."[65]

This domestic rhetoric played a necessary role at a time when gender boundaries were actually blurring. By continuing to refer to women's work in the fields or in off-farm employment as "helping out," farm husbands could convince themselves that they were living up to their responsibilities as farm men and could deny that their wives were assuming such "male" duties as field work and wage-earning employment. By employing language that suggested women's work outside the home was incidental and not crucial to the farm family's survival, hired hands could strengthen their argument that hired labor was still necessary in the postwar farm economy and that women who encroached on work that farm laborers had previously performed were neglecting their domestic responsibilities. By downplaying their work outside the home, farm women could deflect criticism that they were abandoning household duties and could remain satisfied that they were not deviating from behavior considered appropriate for their gender. Government officials, farm editors, and advertisers could employ domestic rhetoric to deny a reality that contradicted their postwar goal for farm women: to make farm women full-time homemakers and consumers.

After fifty years of advice from government officials, farm editors, and advertisers, increased farm income finally allowed farm women to modernize their houses in the postwar era. Mechanized households, however, did not automatically translate into full-time homemaking for those women who remained on the farm in the 1950s and 1960s. Maintaining a high standard of living on the farm required that farm women continue to work long hours performing a variety of tasks. Modern household equipment and the loss of many home production activities meant that women's domestic labor lessened significantly. In its place, however, women spent long hours driving field equipment and automobiles for farm men and laboring in off-farm jobs where they usually worked for male doctors, hospital administrators, school principals, store managers, or factory supervisors.

Even within this patriarchal system, however, midwestern farm women were able to maintain some degree of power through their wage-earning and farm production activities. As sociologists noted, women's contributions to the family economy allowed them a role in family decision making that likely would have been lost if they had subscribed entirely to the full-time home-making role that propagandists had been pushing them toward for fifty years. Women's motivations for resisting that role were complex and were not related to the development of a feminist ideology or any type of organized challenge to patriarchy. Indeed, as the evidence suggests, patriarchy remained firmly entrenched on midwestern farms. Nevertheless, motivated by economic necessity and faith in their abilities as farm producers, women resisted the erosion of their producer role, even in the face of government programs and an omnipresent domestic ideology that pressured them to conform to the role of full-time homemaker. Like their predecessors in the Progressive Era, farm women of the postwar era saw that as an impractical role to play. While others might not always recognize women's contributions to the farm, and while they themselves might sometimes publicly downplay their role as farm producers in order to conform outwardly to the era's domestic ideology, midwestern farm women knew that they indeed "had a part in the farming."

When Snedden, a professor of education at Columbia University, made these observations in 1932, his task was to predict what life in rural America would be like in 1960. Basing his predictions on existing trends, Snedden reasoned that increased "use of power-driven mechanisms" would mean a continuing decrease in the work force necessary to produce food for the nation's foreign and domestic markets. Significantly fewer farm families would be living on the land in 1960, and those families that remained would be smaller in size. A "survival of the fittest" process would determine which family farms would remain in business. In Snedden's words, "farmers of inferior business abilities" would surely fail in an agricultural production system that "increasingly require[d] capital means—machinery, fertilizers, expert service, taxes, drainage, irrigation, improved breeds." Those farmers who would survive and succeed in 1960 would be engaged in less diversified farming than their 1932 counterparts. Rather than raising a variety of products for the market and home consumption, farm families in 1960 would be "specializing their efforts largely on one or two types of money crop products [and] purchasing their larger staples and marketing their products through cooperative agencies, either corporately controlled by themselves or commercially provided by corporate marketing and manufacturing agencies." Snedden argued that it was "reasonable to anticipate that American farmers of 1960 [would] be substantially

Conclusion

Rural mail delivery, telephone, automobile and good roads, accessible libraries, daily newspapers from cities, town shopping for women, central churches, moving pictures, ra-dio, correspondence school courses, and scores of other modern innovations are in effect steadily urbanizing the cultural outreachings, the fellowship contacts, the large group citizenship of America's soil-tilling and pastoral peoples. So recent are still many of these revolutionary expansions that their effects on generations to be reared fully under their influence can as yet only be estimated.—David Snedden (1932) more prosperous" than those of 1932 and that more of their children would complete high school and attend college.[1]

Snedden's predictions for the future were largely accurate. An agriculture based on specialization, mechanization, and greater capital investment, which agricultural reformers were promoting in Snedden's day, would become a reality a generation later. Except for his nod toward women's expanded role as consumer, however, Snedden's predictions about the future of American farming ignored the part that women would play in the New Agriculture. Snedden, like most farm reformers of the era, hoped farm women would increasingly diminish their productive functions and expand their role as consumers. They viewed women's adoption of modern technology as key to this transformation.

Half a century after D. F. Houston's 1913 survey, farm women had indeed adopted a variety of mechanical devices to ease the physical labor involved in their daily household tasks. As proponents of the New Agriculture had hoped, these women had in some ways become more like urban women. For example, they expanded their consumer activities and increasingly purchased groceries and other items away from the farm. They also performed tasks in common with urban women that reformers had not foreseen, such as their frequent use of the family automobile and their participation in off-farm jobs. In 1913, reformers such as Herbert Quick, Henry Wallace, and Secretary Houston had viewed women's adoption of new technologies as a way to make them full-time "homemakers." Two generations later, farm women had access to the prescribed domestic technology but had been able to hold on to the productive labor that defined them as farm women. Resisting fifty years of propaganda, farm women had not conformed to the role of urban housewife.

The changes that had occurred in farm women's lives between 1913 and 1963 are perhaps best summarized by the experiences of Esther and Jean Hardy of rural western Nebraska. When Jean Winkelmann married Bob Hardy in 1959 and moved onto his family farm, she knew that she would necessarily develop a close relationship with her mother-in-law. Having never before lived on a farm, Jean Hardy looked to her mother-in-law to "show her the ropes," and Esther proved to be a capable guide. She introduced Jean to the neighbors and the local farm women's club and helped her with domestic chores when Jean soon became pregnant. The two women developed a close friendship, living as they did in side-by-side houses a mile away from the nearest woman neighbor. Jean never had a chance to become lonely, and she quickly adjusted to life on the farm.

The home that Jean moved into was fully modern and even possessed one of the first automatic washing machines in the neighborhood. Because she gave birth to a child every year from 1960 to 1962, Jean initially worked primarily in the house and greatly relied on her modern domestic equipment. In contrast, her mother-in-law had lived without modern plumbing for most of her married life, had kept house largely without the use of electric-powered equipment, had cared for large numbers of hired men, had worked in the fields, and had milked cows by hand. In comparing their two situations, however, Jean Hardy noted that she was probably no less busy than her mother-in-law had been. The demise of rural schools and farm-centered social activities meant that Jean spent less time on the farm and more time on the road than her mother-in-law had. With a growing family and ready access to an automobile, Jean became the "family chauffeur," a "time consuming" job that included taking the children to school, taking machinery parts to the farm implement dealer, and doing the family grocery shopping.

As her three children grew older, Jean also spent more time working in the field, a situation necessitated by the shrinking rural labor pool and the greater investment in farm machinery. In fact, her biggest worry when working in the field was that she would somehow damage the expensive modern farm equipment—a concern that her mother-in-law had never known. Indeed, in summarizing the differences between her life and that of her mother-in-law, Jean Hardy believed that Esther's life had been characterized by greater physical labor whereas her own was dominated by greater "mental stress" associated with the large financial investment necessary to maintain a farm in the postwar era.[2]

Although Jean Hardy, unlike her mother-in-law, had access to an array of modern appliances, her life was no less stressful, nor was it more constrained by the parameters of the homemaker role. Both women performed their work within the boundaries of the patriarchal farm family, but neither woman restricted her activities to "homemaking." While Esther Hardy had raised chickens and cared for hired men, Jean Hardy operated farm machinery and drove to town for machinery repairs. Both women participated directly in farm production as well as performing services that supported men's field labor. Adoption of modern household equipment had not significantly altered the fundamental role that women played within the patriarchal farm family.

As the Hardys' fellow Nebraskan Minnie B. Davis had pointed out in 1915, access to modern technology, or lack thereof, did not lie at the base of farm women's problems. The technology merely served as a tangible, countable symbol of women's secondary status on the family farm. It was easy to note whether or not a woman owned a washing machine, a modern cooking range, or an electric iron. In Davis's era, a woman's lack of such equipment served as a highly visible indication of the greater value ascribed to men's work and the dominant role accorded men on the family farm. Less astute observers than Davis perhaps genuinely confused the symptom with the disease and believed that adoption of new technology would solve the problem of women's over-work on the farm. Others undoubtedly recognized the underlying patriarchal structure of American farm life as the source of women's complaints about their work but consciously chose not to reform that structure. Indeed, agri-cultural reformers, male and female, chose an opposite path. They sought to prop up the patriarchal farm family by encouraging women to become mod-ern "homemakers." Reformers hoped that by making farm women more like urban housewives, farm women would be set free from hard, dirty work and would enjoy more leisure time. As a result, farm women would become more satisfied with farm life and help keep the patriarchal farm family intact and on the farm.

As the experiences of Jean Hardy and other midwestern farm women indicate, however, like urban women before them, their adoption of new technologies did not ensure that farm women's work was any less "time consuming" than it had been before their acquisition of new equipment. Ironically, reformers' hope that new technology would help keep families on the farm was also doomed to failure. In fact, their adoption of new farm technology meant that fewer farm families were actually needed on the land. And large-scale investment in the technology necessary for participating in the New Agriculture meant that even those families that remained on the farm often had to look elsewhere for financial support. In a gender/work-role system in which men were viewed as the primary agricultural workers, it was largely women who took off-farm jobs. Adoption of new technologies literally *drove* women away from the farm in many cases, as they used the family automobile to travel to wage-paying town jobs.

Nevertheless, as their use of the tractor demonstrated, farm women con-tinued to play an active role as farm producers. Within a patriarchal system reinforced by government policies that recognized men as farmers and women as housewives, women were nevertheless able to protect and enhance a more meaningful and productive role than the one prescribed for them. While paying lip service to the homemaker role, referring to themselves as farm "helpers," and often deferring to husbands in the family decision-making process, women at the same time defended their role as producer and resisted USDA and Extension Service programs that promoted individual farm home modernization. Women's resistance, first demonstrated during the Progressive Era, continued through the Great Depression and the Second World War. Many farm women sought to defend an existing system in which they were participants and enjoyed some, albeit unequal, power. The women of Shelby County, Iowa, provide a good example of women who did not accept the USDA's domestic ideal and the role specialization and loss of power it would entail. During the Great Depression, women's gardening, dairy, and poultry work "was a lifesaver" and enabled their families to stay on the farm.

With World War II came the means for further mechanization of field work as well as housework. Higher farm incomes meant that the choice between modernization of the house or the farm no longer had to be made by those families who remained on the land in the postwar era. In the years following World War II, women obtained household conveniences but not at the expense of a role in production, a role that the mechanization of field work clearly made possible. Women's degree of participation in mechanized field work varied from one family to the next, and their power within the farm family remained unequal to that of men, but farmhouse modernization had not meant their consignment to the role of full-time "homemaker."

In light of these considerations, women's resistance to the proposals for farmhouse modernization that originated with the USDA, the Extension Service, and publications like *Wallaces' Farmer* makes perfect sense. During the agricultural depression of 1920–40, women's coolness toward domestic modernization resulted from their recognition that investment in farm machinery and land could increase farm income. Women also recognized that investment in farm equipment had specific short- and long-term benefits for themselves as well. Investment in tractors, after all, meant reduced dependence on hired labor and an end to women's grudging care of farm workers who were not family members. Investment in tractors and the loss of hired men also meant women's enhancement of their own value and power as farm family coproducers who used mechanized field equipment.

In the fifty-year period between World War I and the Vietnam War, between the presidencies of Woodrow Wilson and John Kennedy, between the suffrage campaign of the 1910s and the beginnings of a modern feminist movement in the 1960s, a revolution had taken place in midwestern agriculture. The energy of people and animals had been replaced by machine power, diversity had given way to specialization, and labor intensity had been re-placed by capital investment. Although, as Professor David Snedden had noted, many of the results of agricultural modernization could "only be estimated" in the early decades of the twentieth century, reformers could be reasonably certain that at least one of their goals would be met: the preservation of the patriarchal farm family. Their policies throughout the century ultimately culminated in that result. The New Agriculture functioned within the structure of the old patriarchy.

Even within that patriarchal structure, however, farm women resisted efforts to remove them from agricultural production. Motivated by economic necessity, faith in their abilities as farm producers and contributors to the family economy, and the utter impracticality of much of the advice they received, farm women resisted adoption of the full-time homemaker role. For the farm women of 1963, as for their grandmothers in 1913, the scope of their work ranged far beyond the farmhouse threshold.

Notes

Introduction

1. From Jensen's introduction to her collection of farm women's primary documents, *With These Hands: Women Working on the Land* (Old Westbury, N.Y.: Feminist Press, 1981), xxiii.

2. The classic works in American agricultural history ignore farm women altogether or mention them only in passing. For example, see Allan G. Bogue, *From Prairie to Cornbelt: Farming on the Illinois and Iowa Prairies* (Chicago: University of Chicago Press, 1963); Merle E. Curti, *The Making of an American Community: A Case Study of Democracy in a Frontier County* (Stanford: Stanford University Press, 1959); Terry G. Jordan, *German Seed in Texas Soil: Immigrant Farmers in Nineteenth-Century Texas* (Austin: University of Texas Press, 1966); James T. Lemon, *The Best Poor Man's Country: A Geographical Study of Early Southeastern Pennsylvania* (Baltimore: Johns Hopkins University Press, 1976); Fred A. Shannon, *The Farmer's Last Frontier: Agriculture, 1860–1897* (New York: Holt, Rinehart, and Winston, 1945); John Shover, *First Majority—Last Minority: The Transformation of Rural Life in America* (De Kalb: Northern Illinois University Press, 1976); and Robert P. Swierenga, *Pioneers and Profits: Land Speculation on the Iowa Frontier* (Ames: Iowa State University Press, 1968). In recent years, a handful of historians have begun to rectify this oversight by examining the experiences of American farm women in eighteenth- and nineteenth-century agricultural communities. See, for instance, Joan M. Jensen, *Loosening the Bonds: Mid-Atlantic Farm Women, 1750–1850* (New Haven: Yale University Press, 1986); John Mack Faragher, *Sugar Creek: Life on the Illinois Prairie* (New Haven: Yale University Press, 1986); Nancy Grey Osterud, *Bonds of Community: The Lives of Farm Women in Nineteenth-Century New York* (Ithaca, N.Y.: Cornell University Press, 1991); and various essays in Steven Hahn and Jonathan Prude, eds., *The Countryside in the Age of Capitalist Transformation: Essays in the Social History of Rural America* (Chapel Hill: University of North Carolina Press, 1985). Historians have made less progress, however, in extending investigation of farm women's lives into the twentieth century. Scholarship examining the experiences of twentieth-century farm women has largely been undertaken by sociologists and anthropologists. Such works include Carolyn E. Sachs, *The Invisible Farmers: Women in Agricultural Production* (Totowa, N.J.: Rowman and Allanheld, 1983); Sonya Salamon, *Prairie Patrimony: Family, Farming, and Community in the Midwest* (Chapel Hill: University of North Carolina Press, 1992); and Deborah Fink, *Open Country, Iowa: Rural Women, Tradition and Change* (Albany: State University of New York Press, 1986), and *Agrarian Women: Wives and Mothers in Rural Nebraska, 1880–1940* (Chapel Hill: University of North Carolina Press, 1992).

3. Jensen, *With These Hands*, xx–xxi.

4. The mechanization of urban women's work is analyzed in a number of major works, including Susan Strasser, *Never Done: A History of American Housework* (New York: Pantheon Books, 1982), and Ruth Schwartz Cowan, *More Work for Mother: The*

Ironies of Household Technology from the Open Hearth to the Microwave (New York: Basic Books, 1983).

5. See material in Ruth Milkman, *Gender at Work: The Dynamics of Job Segregation by Sex during World War II* (Urbana: University of Illinois Press, 1987); Elaine Tyler May, *Homeward Bound: American Families in the Cold War Era* (New York: Basic Books, 1988); and Alice Kessler-Harris, *Out to Work: A History of Wage-Earning Women in the United States* (New York: Oxford University Press, 1982).

Chapter 1

1. This quotation appears in a U.S. Department of Agriculture report entitled *Economic Needs of Farm Women* (Washington: Government Printing Office, 1915), 15.

2. Richard Hofstadter, *The Age of Reform: From Bryan to FDR* (New York: Alfred A. Knopf, 1955), 23–32. For further discussion of the "backward-looking" nature of Progressivism, see David B. Danbom, *"The World of Hope": Progressives and the Struggle for an Ethical Public Life* (Philadelphia: Temple University Press, 1987).

3. See William L. Bowers, "Country-Life Reform, 1900–1920: A Neglected Aspect of Progressive Era History," *Agricultural History* 45 (July 1971): 211–21. See also David B. Danbom's discussion of Progressive Era rural reform in *The Resisted Revolution: Urban America and the Industrialization of Agriculture, 1900–1930* (Ames: Iowa State University Press, 1979).

4. Commission on Country Life, *Report of the Commission on Country Life* (New York: Sturgis and Walton Company, 1917), 41.

5. See Clayton S. Ellsworth, "Theodore Roosevelt's Country Life Commission," *Agricultural History* 34 (October 1960): 155–72.

6. *Report of the Commission on Country Life*, 103–5.

7. The members of Roosevelt's Country Life Commission were Liberty Hyde Bailey, the chairman, who was an agricultural scientist at Cornell University; Henry Wallace, the editor of *Wallaces' Farmer*; Kenyon L. Butterfield, an agricultural scientist and the father of rural sociology; Walter Hines Page, editor of the *World's Work* and a representative of the urban business community; Gifford Pinchot, the nation's chief forester; W. A. Beard, editor of the California-based *Great West* magazine; and Farmers' Union official C. S. Barrett, the only commission member who had any regular contact with the nation's dirt farmers. For a discussion of Progressive attempts to "modernize" the immigrant housewife, see Virginia Yans-McLaughlin, *Family and Community: Italian Immigrants in Buffalo, 1880–1930* (Ithaca, N.Y.: Cornell University Press, 1977), and material in chap. 7 of Sara M. Evans, *Born for Liberty: A History of Women in America* (New York: Free Press, 1989).

8. *Report of the Commission on Country Life*, 104.

9. Ibid., 29, 105.

10. See William L. Bowers, *The Country Life Movement in America, 1900–1920* (Port Washington, N.Y.: Kennikat Press, 1974).

11. According to Bowers, nearly half of the leaders in the Country Life Movement

were from the Midwest, and the majority of the movement's leaders were editors or journalists. See "Country-Life Reform," 213.

12. Herbert Quick, "The Women on the Farms," *Good Housekeeping* 57 (October 1913): 427, 432. In her examination of disgruntled farm women of the era, including those who eventually left the farm or made it possible for their children to leave, anthropologist Deborah Fink discusses many of the issues that Quick raised in his article. See Fink, *Agrarian Women: Wives and Mothers in Rural Nebraska, 1880–1940* (Chapel Hill: University of North Carolina Press, 1992).

13. Ellsworth, "Country Life Commission," 162.

14. "The Farmer's Wife," *Wallaces' Farmer*, 31 July 1914, 5.

15. For information on the different character of life in Michigan and Ohio, see Martha Mitchell Bigelow, "Michigan: A State in the Vanguard," and R. Douglas Hurt, "Ohio: Gateway to the Midwest," both in *Heartland: Comparative Histories of the Midwestern States*, edited by James H. Madison (Bloomington: Indiana University Press, 1988). Madison's anthology provides a good critical history of each of the midwestern states.

16. "Some Real Women Farmers," *Wallaces' Farmer*, 16 August 1918, 3. Like the women profiled in the *Wallaces' Farmer* article, and like the Alexandra Bergson character, most midwestern women who farmed independently had inherited their farming operations from a deceased husband or father. For further discussion of unmarried women farmers, and the challenges they faced, see material in Fink, *Agrarian Women*.

17. Anthropologist Sonya Salamon discusses immigrant opposition to the concept of farming as a business in *Prairie Patrimony: Family, Farming, and Community in the Midwest* (Chapel Hill: University of North Carolina Press, 1992). See particularly the tables on pp. 93, 124, and 182. In the contemporary Illinois farming communities that Salamon studied, she found that families in "Yankee" towns (those founded by native-born Americans) generally pursued an entrepreneurial approach to farming. In contrast, farm families in communities founded by German immigrants followed what she labels a yeoman farming pattern. Unlike the entrepreneur farmer, who sees land as a commodity and farming as a business in which accumulation of land is a means to increase family wealth, the yeoman farmer views land as a sacred trust to be maintained by achieving continuity of family land ownership and an agrarian way of life in an ethnic community. For further discussion of immigrants' yeoman approach to farming in the Midwest, see Jon Gjerde, *From Peasants to Farmers: The Migration from Balestrand, Norway to the Upper Middle West* (New York: Cambridge University Press, 1985); Kathleen Neils Conzen, "Peasant Pioneers: Generational Succession among German Farmers in Frontier Minnesota," in *The Countryside in the Age of Capitalist Transformation*, edited by Steven Hahn and Jonathan Prude (Chapel Hill: University of North Carolina Press, 1985); and several essays in Frederick C. Luebke, ed., *Ethnicity on the Great Plains* (Lincoln: University of Nebraska Press, 1980). For a discussion of Native American women's resistance to Euro-American farming practices at this time, see Patricia C. Albers, "Sioux Women in Transition: A Study of Their Changing Status in Domestic and Capitalist Sectors of Production," in *The Hidden Half: Studies*

of Plains Indian Women, edited by Patricia Albers and Beatrice Medicine (Washington, D.C.: University Press of America, 1983). See particularly the material on pp. 182–200 of Albers's essay. See also Margaret Mead's discussion of Omaha women in *The Changing Culture of an Indian Tribe* (New York: Columbia University Press, 1932), 27, 168, 172, 179–80. African American sharecropping women are discussed at greater length later in this study, as are the women of Nicodemus, Kansas. A good autobiographical account of black farm life on the North Dakota plains is Era Bell Thompson, *American Daughter* (Chicago: University of Chicago Press, 1946). I would like to thank Mary Neth for introducing me to the Thompson book.

18. For discussion of the writing of white midwestern women, see material in Julie Roy Jeffrey, *Frontier Women: The Trans-Mississippi West, 1840–1880* (New York: Hill and Wang, 1979); Glenda Riley, *Frontierswomen: The Iowa Experience* (Ames: Iowa State University Press, 1981); Lillian Schlissel, *Women's Diaries of the Westward Journey* (New York: Schocken Books, 1982); Elizabeth Hampsten, *Read This Only to Yourself: The Private Writings of Midwestern Women, 1880–1910* (Bloomington: Indiana University Press, 1982); and Susan Armitage and Elizabeth Jameson, eds., *The Women's West* (Norman: University of Oklahoma Press, 1987).

19. For an analysis of women's discussion of technological issues in diary sources, see material in Mary Neth, *Preserving the Family Farm: Farm Families and Communities in the Midwest, 1900–1940* (Baltimore: Johns Hopkins University Press, forthcoming). See particularly chaps. 7 and 8.

20. David F. Houston to Clarence Ousley, 17 April 1916, Farm Women's Bureau File (1916), General Correspondence of the Office of the Secretary (1906–70), Records of the Secretary of Agriculture, Record Group 16, National Archives, Washington, D.C. The U.S. Department of Agriculture published results of the survey in a series of pamphlets. Pamphlet titles included *Economic Needs of Farm Women*, *Domestic Needs of Farm Women*, *Educational Needs of Farm Women*, and *Social and Labor Needs of Farm Women*. Unfortunately, the original responses to the survey have been lost.

21. Gasoline tractors first appeared on the market in large numbers about 1913. Use of this equipment in the Midwest, particularly in the Wheat Belt areas of North and South Dakota, Nebraska, and Kansas, would increase dramatically during the First World War.

22. U.S. Department of Agriculture, *Domestic Needs of Farm Women* (Washington: Government Printing Office, 1915), 40.

23. Ibid., 40–41.

24. Ibid., 37.

25. Ibid., 32.

26. Ibid., 33.

27. U.S. Department of Agriculture, *Social and Labor Needs of Farm Women* (Washington: Government Printing Office, 1915), 70. For a discussion of women's use of the automobile during the Progressive Era, see Virginia Scharff, *Taking the Wheel: Women and the Coming of the Motor Age* (New York: Free Press, 1991).

28. U.S. Department of Agriculture, *Social and Labor Needs of Farm Women*, 63.

29. Ibid., 46.

30. Ibid., 63.

31. David F. Houston, "Report of the Secretary," *Yearbook of the United States Department of Agriculture* (Washington: Government Printing Office, 1914), 38–39.

32. Transcript of the Secretary of Agriculture's Address to Farm Youth, enclosed with memo from W. F. Callander to Bradford Knapp, 17 December 1913, Secretary of Agriculture File (1913–14), General Correspondence of the Extension Service and Its Predecessors (June 1907–June 1943), Records of the Federal Extension Service of the Department of Agriculture, Record Group 33, National Archives, Washington, D.C. For a discussion of women's education in the early republic and the concept of "republican motherhood," see Linda K. Kerber, *Women of the Republic: Intellect and Ideology in Revolutionary America* (Chapel Hill: University of North Carolina Press, 1980).

33. C. F. Langworthy, "Home Betterment" (1913), Home Economics File (1914), General Correspondence of the Office of the Secretary (1906–70), Records of the Secretary of Agriculture, Record Group 16, National Archives, Washington, D.C., 1–2, 6.

34. Florence E. Ward, *Home Demonstration Work under the Smith-Lever Act, 1914–1924* (Washington: Government Printing Office, 1929), 2; Madge J. Reese, *A Ten-Year Review of Home-Management Extension, 1914–1924* (Washington: Government Printing Office, 1927), 3.

35. Theodore Saloutos and John D. Hicks, *Agricultural Discontent in the Middle West, 1900–1939* (Madison: University of Wisconsin Press, 1951), 263–64.

36. Quoted in Ward, *Home Demonstration Work*, 10–11.

37. For further discussion of government policies that promoted rural patriarchy, see Fink, *Agrarian Women*.

38. Sonya Salamon notes that women in immigrant communities were more likely to be actively involved in farm production than women in "Yankee" farming communities. Mary Neth notes that women on smaller, less prosperous farms also were more likely to share farm labor with their husbands than were middle-class farm women. Women such as these were therefore particularly resistant to the USDA's separate spheres ideal. See material throughout Salamon, *Prairie Patrimony*, and Neth, *Preserving the Family Farm*.

39. Although little scholarship exists on the history of farm women's opposition to rural patriarchy, historian Mary Jo Wagner argues that such resistance goes back at least to the Populist movement of the late 1880s and early 1890s. Wagner's evidence suggests, in fact, that women were attracted to Populism because they saw it as a means to achieve feminist goals. By the mid-1890s, however, Populist leaders no longer attempted to accommodate specific women's issues and interests. In their attempt to gain political power on a national scale, Populists sought compromise with the Democratic party and thus abandoned a more radical agenda that included feminist demands. See Wagner's essay, "'Helping Papa and Mama Sing the People's Song': Children in the Populist Party," in *Women and Farming: Changing Roles, Changing Structures*, edited by Wava G. Haney and Jane B. Knowles (Boulder, Colo.: Westview Press, 1988).

40. Danbom, *Resisted Revolution*, 10. I would like to thank David Danbom for elaborating on his argument in correspondence with me.

41. On the need for historians to read women's autobiographical writing closely and carefully, see Katherine Jellison, "'Sunshine and Rain in Iowa': Using Women's Autobiography as a Historical Source," *Annals of Iowa* 49 (Winter 1989): 591–99.

42. Minnie B. Davis to David F. Houston, 1 December 1915, Farm Women's Bureau File (1915), General Correspondence of the Office of the Secretary (1906–70), Records of the Secretary of Agriculture, Record Group 16, National Archives, Washington, D.C. I would like to thank Kim Nielsen for sharing information about Davis's life that she unearthed in her own research on the Non-Partisan League. That material includes a letter that Davis wrote to league headquarters in May 1917 asking for employment on the league's newspaper, the *Leader*. Although the league rejected her services, she did write for the *Farm Journal, Country Life, Country Gentleman*, and other publications.

43. Davis to Houston, 1 December 1915, Farm Women's Bureau File (1915).

44. Ibid.

45. David F. Houston to Minnie B. Davis, 9 December 1915, Farm Women's Bureau File (1915), General Correspondence of the Office of the Secretary (1906–70), Records of the Secretary of Agriculture, Record Group 16, National Archives, Washington, D.C.

46. David F. Houston, "The Agricultural Extension Act," Farm Women's Bureau File (1916); Ada Carroll Wortman to D. F. Houston, 3 December 1915, Farm Women's Bureau File (1915); Clarence Ousley to D. F. Houston, 5 April 1916, Farm Women's Bureau File (1916), General Correspondence of the Office of the Secretary (1906–70), Records of the Secretary of Agriculture, Record Group 16, National Archives, Washington, D.C.

47. Florence E. Ward, *Status and Results of Home Demonstration Work, Northern and Western States, 1919* (Washington: Government Printing Office, 1921), 4, 8; Alma Thompson, interview with Eunice Pagel, Manteno, Ill., 2 October 1981, National Homemakers Oral History Collection, Indiana Historical Society, Indianapolis, Ind.; "County Advisers for Women," *Wallaces' Farmer*, 9 July 1915, 5.

48. Ward, *Status and Results*, 7; "County Advisers for Women," *Wallaces' Farmer*, 9 July 1915, 5.

49. Ward, *Status and Results*, 7, 10; R. L. Reeder, ed., *The People and the Profession: Selected Memories of Veteran Extension Workers* (Washington, D.C.: National Board of Epsilon Sigma Phi, 1979), 26. For further discussion of female extension workers' use of the automobile in this period, see Scharff, *Taking the Wheel*, 143–44.

50. Saloutos and Hicks, *Agricultural Discontent in the Middle West*, 87.

51. "The County Adviser for Women," *Wallaces' Farmer*, 6 August 1915, 16.

52. E. H. Thompson and H. M. Dixon, "A Farm-Management Survey of Six Counties in Indiana, Illinois, and Iowa" (1913), Reports, Speeches, and Articles Relating to Farm Management, Records of the Bureau of Agricultural Economics, Record Group 83, National Archives, Washington, D.C. Thompson and Dixon defined farm income as the difference between farm receipts and expenses. It repre-

sented the amount of money available for the farm family's living, provided the family had no interest to pay on mortgages or other debts. Information on the price of household equipment was obtained from the Spring 1913 Sears, Roebuck catalog.

53. Ward, *Home Demonstration Work*, 11, 16, 33; Ward, *Status and Results*, 3; "Home Demonstrators," *Wallaces' Farmer*, 13 September 1918, 20.

54. Danbom, *Resisted Revolution*, 104.

55. Ward, *Home Demonstration Work*, 16, 33; Ward, *Status and Results*, 3, 5, 15–16, 24.

56. See Saloutos and Hicks, *Agricultural Discontent in the Middle West*, 87–110.

57. Bowers, *Country Life Movement*, 128–34. For an overview of the war's effect on Progressivism, see Danbom's *"World of Hope,"* 210–17.

58. For further discussion of these issues, see Ellis W. Hawley, *The Great War and the Search for a Modern Order: A History of the American People and Their Institutions, 1917–1933* (New York: St. Martin's Press, 1979). See also material in chap. 4 of Neth, *Preserving the Family Farm*.

59. Danbom, *Resisted Revolution*, 142.

60. David M. Kennedy, *Over Here: The First World War and American Society* (New York: Oxford University Press, 1980), 122.

61. Saloutos and Hicks, *Agricultural Discontent in the Middle West*, 266.

62. Studies that examine the controversial relationship between the Extension Service and the Farm Bureau, particularly in reference to extension work in the Midwest, include Samuel R. Berger, *Dollar Harvest: The Story of the Farm Bureau* (Lexington, Mass.: D. C. Heath and Company, 1971); Grant McConnell, *The Decline of Agrarian Democracy* (New York: Atheneum, 1969); Christiana McFadyen Campbell, *The Farm Bureau and the New Deal: A Study of the Making of National Farm Policy, 1933–1940* (Urbana: University of Illinois Press, 1962); William J. Block, *The Separation of the Farm Bureau and the Extension Service: Political Issue in a Federal System* (Urbana: University of Illinois Press, 1960). Under congressional pressure, the Farm Bureau only abandoned its formal relationship with the Extension Service in all states in the 1950s.

63. Emily F. Hoag, "The Advantages of Farm Life: A Study by Correspondence and Interviews with Eight Thousand Farm Women" (1923), Manuscript File (1917–35), Records of the Bureau of Agricultural Economics, Record Group 83, National Archives, Washington, D.C.

64. Ibid.

65. Ibid.

66. Ibid.

67. Ibid.

68. Neth's discussion of the Hoag study appears in chap. 7 of *Preserving the Family Farm*. Like Neth, historian Nancy Grey Osterud notes a high level of cooperation and mutual dependence among the farm men and women she has studied. See Osterud, *Bonds of Community: The Lives of Farm Women in Nineteenth-Century New York* (Ithaca, N.Y.: Cornell University Press, 1991). Osterud's study centers on dairy farming families in New York's Nanticoke Valley. Neth notes that among midwesterners, men and women in dairy farming families shared their work to a greater extent than men

and women on wheat farms or general grain and livestock farms. Deborah Fink's study of Nebraska farm women indicates that women on the grain and livestock farms of the plains could not rely on the type of reciprocal arrangements that Osterud notes for New York dairy farming women. Fink argues that women in Boone County, Nebraska, were often critical of male behavior and dissatisfied with life on the farm. See Fink, *Agrarian Women*. As the research of Osterud, Neth, and Fink indicates, women's satisfaction with life on the farm was dependent upon a variety of factors: geography, type of farming, income level, the expectations they brought to the farming enterprise, and individual relationships with male family members.

69. "Feminism on the Farm," *Nation*, 19 October 1921, 440. I would like to thank Lu Ann Jones for bringing this article to my attention.

70. Ibid.

71. Press release from the Office of the Secretary of Agriculture, 3 August 1922, Home Economics File (1922), General Correspondence of the Office of the Secretary (1906–70), Records of the Secretary of Agriculture, Record Group 16, National Archives, Washington, D.C.

Chapter 2

1. Quoted in Florence E. Ward, *Home Demonstration Work under the Smith-Lever Act, 1914–1924* (Washington: Government Printing Office, 1929), 34.

2. Florence E. Ward, *The Farm Woman's Problems* (Washington: Government Printing Office, 1920), 3–4, 7.

3. Ibid., 7.

4. Ibid., 8–9.

5. Ibid., 12.

6. See Joseph Interrante, "You Can't Go to Town in a Bathtub: Automobile Movement and the Reorganization of Rural American Space, 1900–1930," *Radical History Review* 21 (Fall 1979): 151–68.

7. Gertrude Monteith, interview with the author, Imperial, Nebr., 19 May 1986. For further discussion of farm women's use of the automobile in the 1920s, see Virginia Scharff, *Taking the Wheel: Women and the Coming of the Motor Age* (New York: Free Press, 1991), 142–45.

8. Eleanor Arnold, ed., *Voices of American Homemakers: An Oral History Project of the National Extension Homemakers Council* (Washington, D.C.: National Extension Homemakers' Council, 1985), 187–88.

9. Ward, *Farm Woman's Problems*, 10–11.

10. Ibid., 11; Florence E. Ward, *Status and Results of Home Demonstration Work, Northern and Western States, 1919* (Washington: Government Printing Office, 1921), 6.

11. Ward, *Status and Results*, 5, 8.

12. For a discussion of efforts at cooperative housekeeping in urban areas, and the reaction against such attempts, see Dolores Hayden, *The Grand Domestic Revolution: A History of Feminist Designs for American Homes, Neighborhoods, and Cities* (Cambridge: MIT Press, 1981).

13. "Cooperative Laundry," *Wallaces' Farmer*, 29 August 1913, 28. See Victoria Leto's discussion of laundry technology, including rural cooperative laundries, in her essay "'Washing, Seems It's All We Do': Washing Technology and Women's Communication," in *Technology and Women's Voices*, edited by Cheris Kramarae (New York: Routledge and Kegan Paul, 1988).

14. Dee Jacquart, interview with the author, Sublette, Kans., 5 October 1988; Ora Switzer, interview with the author, Nicodemus, Kans., 29 May 1990. Mrs. Switzer, born in 1903, is the oldest resident of Nicodemus, the most famous of the midwestern "exoduster" communities formed after Reconstruction. The phenomenon of devoting less attention to the needs of minority women also occurred in rural regions with a large Hispanic population, as Sandra Kay Schackel demonstrated in her paper entitled "'I Do Not Know What We Would Do without It': Rural Women and the Agricultural Extension Service in New Mexico," delivered at the Eighth Berkshire Conference on the History of Women, Douglass College, New Brunswick, N.J., 9 June 1990. Joan Jensen has noted, however, that members of the Hispanic community could be effectively reached when Hispanic home demonstration agents were employed. See "Crossing Ethnic Barriers in the Southwest: Women's Agricultural Extension Education, 1914–1940," in Jensen's *Promise to the Land: Essays on Rural Women* (Albuquerque: University of New Mexico Press, 1991), 220–30.

15. Julia Kiene, "The Merry Wives of Kansas," *Capper's Farmer*, February 1929, 50; Helen Mason, "Farm Equipment Helps Her," *Capper's Farmer*, November 1929, 45.

16. Karen Elizabeth Altman, "Modernity, Gender, and Consumption: Public Discourses on Woman and the Home" (Ph.D. diss., University of Iowa, 1987), 145–204.

17. H. E. Wichers, "Considerations in Farmhouse Planning," in *The Better Homes Manual*, edited by Blanche Halbert (Chicago: University of Chicago Press, 1931), 575.

18. Madge J. Reese, *A Ten-Year Review of Home-Management Extension under the Smith-Lever Act, 1914–1924* (Washington: Government Printing Office, 1927), 23.

19. Elmina T. Wilson, *Modern Conveniences for the Farm Home* (Washington: Government Printing Office, 1916), 40.

20. E. L. Kirkpatrick, *The Farmer's Standard of Living: A Socio-Economic Study of 2,886 White Farm Families of Selected Localities in 11 States* (Washington: Government Printing Office, 1926), 17–18.

21. Ibid., 46.

22. Ibid., 57.

23. Ola Powell Malcolm, *Home Demonstration Work, 1923* (Washington: Government Printing Office, 1926), 42–43.

24. Ibid., 44, 27.

25. Kirkpatrick, *Farmer's Standard of Living*, 47.

26. Reese, *Ten-Year Review of Home-Management Extension*, 15, 44.

27. Stuart Ewen, *Captains of Consciousness: Advertising and the Social Roots of the Consumer Culture* (New York: McGraw-Hill, 1976).

28. For further discussion of this issue, see Jane Busch, "Cooking Competition:

Technology on the Domestic Market in the 1930s," *Technology and Culture* 24 (April 1983): 222–45.

29. Skelgas advertisement, *Wallaces' Farmer*, 12 April 1929, 36.

30. Perfection range advertisement, *Wallaces' Farmer*, 25 May 1929, 13; Skelgas advertisement, *Wallaces' Farmer*, 6 September 1929, 29.

31. Skelgas advertisement, *Wallaces' Farmer*, 19 July 1930, 13.

32. Lydia Ray Balderston, *Home Laundering* (Washington: Government Printing Office, 1921), 3.

33. Maytag advertisement, *Wallaces' Farmer*, 10 October 1919, 1996.

34. See Stuart Ewen's chapters entitled "Youth as an Industrial Ideal" and "Consumption and the Ideal of the New Woman" in *Captains of Consciousness*. Also see the chapter entitled "Modern Times" in Nancy Cott, *The Grounding of Modern Feminism* (New Haven: Yale University Press, 1987).

35. Maytag washing machine advertisement, *Wallaces' Farmer*, 12 April 1930, 19.

36. Maytag washing machine advertisement, *Wallaces' Farmer*, 5 July 1930, 11; Sears washing machine advertisement, *Wallaces' Farmer*, 21 March 1931, 16.

37. Voss washing machine advertisement, *Wallaces' Farmer*, 1 March 1929, 27; Thor washing machine advertisement, *Wallaces' Farmer*, 5 April 1929, 25; Maytag washing machine advertisement, *Wallaces' Farmer*, 4 October 1929, 23.

38. ABC Companion washing machine advertisement, *Wallaces' Farmer*, 18 January 1930, 12.

39. Maytag washing machine advertisement, *Wallaces' Farmer*, 1 February 1929, 40; Maytag washing machine advertisement, *Wallaces' Farmer*, 3 May 1929, 20.

40. In their classic study of Muncie, Indiana, in the 1920s, Robert and Helen Lynd found that telephone service was frequently the first luxury that families abandoned during times of economic difficulty. See *Middletown: A Study in Modern American Culture* (New York: Harcourt, Brace and World, 1929).

41. Northwestern Bell advertisement, *Wallaces' Farmer*, 4 January 1929, 10.

42. Northwestern Bell advertisement, *Wallaces' Farmer*, 11 January 1930, 18; Northwestern Bell advertisement, *Wallaces' Farmer*, 10 December 1932, 17.

43. Northwestern Bell advertisement, *Wallaces' Farmer*, 7 March 1931, 14; Northwestern Bell advertisement, *Wallaces' Farmer*, 1 October 1932, 19.

44. Chevrolet advertisement, *Wallaces' Farmer*, 6 April 1923, 23. For further discussion of gender and automobile advertising during this period, see Scharff, *Taking the Wheel*, 115–16, 129–31, 141–42.

45. Plymouth advertisement, *Wallaces' Farmer*, 23 August 1929, 14; Buick advertisement, *Wallaces' Farmer*, 7 December 1929, 23; Chevrolet advertisement, *Wallaces' Farmer*, 4 April 1931, 23; Pontiac advertisement, *Wallaces' Farmer*, 28 June 1930, 16.

46. Carmen D. Welch, "How Much Is Your Wife Worth?," *Capper's Farmer*, October 1927, 14.

47. The two major histories of this phenomenon are Ruth Schwartz Cowan, *More Work for Mother: The Ironies of Household Technology from the Open Hearth to the Microwave* (New York: Basic Books, 1983), and Susan Strasser, *Never Done: A History of American Housework* (New York: Pantheon Books, 1982).

48. Although survey data are thin regarding the impact of modern advertising on midwestern farm women's purchasing decisions during this period, a 1926 survey of small-town women in Kansas, Missouri, Nebraska, and Iowa showed that a large majority of women said that they paid a "good" or "great deal" of attention to advertising and that they preferred the national ads seen in magazines over the local advertisements in newspapers.

49. "Agricultural Broadcasting Plan," included with letter from Frank E. Miller, National Broadcasting Company, to W. M. Jardine, secretary of agriculture, 19 September 1927, Radio File (1927), General Correspondence of the Office of the Secretary (1906–70), Records of the Secretary of Agriculture, Record Group 16, National Archives, Washington, D.C.; Susan Smulyan, "'A Latchkey to Every Home': Early Radio Advertising to Women," paper presented at the National Museum of American History, Smithsonian Institution, Washington, D.C., 3 October 1989.

50. "What the Radio Does: Our Readers Comment on Its Value to the Farmer," *Wallaces' Farmer*, 28 August 1925, 11.

51. I. W. Dickerson, "Why Have a Radio Set: Entertainments, Education, and Profit from the Air," *Wallaces' Farmer*, 20 February 1925, 14; I. W. Dickerson, "Radio and the Farm: Practical Benefits of Radio Not Fully Realized," *Wallaces' Farmer*, 13 November 1925, 8; "Radio Sets on Farms," *Rural America*, May 1926, 14.

52. "Radio Sets on Farms," 14.

53. I. W. Dickerson, "Radio and the Farm," 8.

54. "Radio for the Farm Folks: How the Farm and Home Hour Started," *Wallaces' Farmer*, 17 August 1935, 13; *25th Anniversary of the National Farm and Home Hour* (New York: National Broadcasting Company and Allis-Chalmers Manufacturing Company, 1953), 3.

55. Gayle G. Wherry, correspondence with the author (including photocopy of Elizabeth C. Wherry's obituary), 7 September 1988; Elizabeth C. Wherry, "Country Air," *Wallaces' Farmer*, 31 December 1938, 13; Zoe Murphy, "Country Air," *Wallaces' Farmer*, 5 January 1957, 37.

56. Wherry, "Country Air," *Wallaces' Farmer*, 19 July 1929, 17; Wherry, "Country Air," *Wallaces' Farmer*, 2 August 1929, 23.

57. "Department Uses Radio," *Wallaces' Farmer*, 25 January 1930, 30; Wherry, "Country Air," *Wallaces' Farmer*, 15 February 1930, 46.

58. Wherry, "Country Air," *Wallaces' Farmer*, 6 December 1930, 26.

59. "Radio Kitchen Pet," *Wallaces' Farmer*, 7 June 1929, 16.

60. Wherry, "Country Air," *Wallaces' Farmer*, 31 December 1938, 13.

61. Wherry, "Country Air," *Wallaces' Farmer*, 26 April 1929, 26; Wherry, "Country Air," *Wallaces' Farmer*, 9 November 1929, 40.

62. Wherry, "Country Air," *Wallaces' Farmer*, 15 February 1930, 46.

63. Atwater Kent advertisement, *Wallaces' Farmer*, 19 February 1926, 21.

64. Eveready advertisement, *Nebraska Farmer*, 6 April 1929, 18.

65. Ibid.

66. Radiola advertisement, *Wallaces' Farmer*, 8 March 1930, 30.

67. Betty Hunter, "Household Shopper's Guide," *American Farming*, July 1931, 9.

68. Ibid.

69. Wherry, "Country Air," *Wallaces' Farmer*, 25 October 1930, 23.

70. Reese, *Ten-Year Review*, 2.

71. Maud Wilson, "The Farm Homemaker's Job," *Rural America*, February 1930, 8–9.

Chapter 3

1. Mrs. Fred Stauffer to Franklin D. Roosevelt, 7 November 1933, Farm Relief File, (1) Misc. Farm Relief Plans (1933), General Correspondence of the Office of the Secretary (1906–70), Records of the Secretary of Agriculture, Record Group 16, National Archives, Washington, D.C.

2. Scott G. McNall and Sally Allen McNall, *Plains Families: Exploring Sociology through Social History* (New York: St. Martin's Press, 1983), 187.

3. For a larger discussion of depression-era letters, see Robert S. McElvaine, ed., *Down and Out in the Great Depression: Letters from the "Forgotten Man"* (Chapel Hill: University of North Carolina Press, 1983).

4. Mrs. J. L. Weege to Secretary of Agriculture Arthur Hyde, 11 March 1932, Farm Relief File 2 (1932), General Correspondence of the Office of the Secretary (1906–70), Records of the Secretary of Agriculture, Record Group 16, National Archives, Washington, D.C. In an effort to communicate Weege's ideas clearly, I have altered some of the letter's original punctuation in this quotation.

5. Rangmar and Margaret Segerstrom, interview with Dale Trelevan, Buffalo County, Wis., 29 and 30 September 1976, Wisconsin Agriculturalists Oral History Project, State Historical Society of Wisconsin, Madison, Wis. See Leslie A. Taylor, "Femininity as Strategy: A Gendered Perspective on the Farmers' Holiday," *Annals of Iowa* 51 (Winter 1992): 252–77.

6. Grace E. Frysinger, "Suggestions as to How the Farm Board Might Arouse the Active Cooperation of Farm Women," report included in letter from C. W. Warburton to James C. Stone of the Federal Farm Board, 18 January 1930, Farm Women File (1930), General Correspondence of the Office of the Secretary (1906–70), Records of the Secretary of Agriculture, Record Group 16, National Archives, Washington, D.C.

7. Gertrude Jefferies to Arthur Hyde, 24 April 1932, Farm Relief File 2 (1932), General Correspondence of the Office of the Secretary (1906–70), Records of the Secretary of Agriculture, Record Group 16, National Archives, Washington, D.C. In an effort to communicate Jefferies's thoughts clearly, I have altered some of the letter's original punctuation in this quotation.

8. M. M. Clayton to Herbert Hoover, April 1932, Farm Relief File 2 (1932), General Correspondence of the Office of the Secretary (1906–70), Records of the Secretary of Agriculture, Record Group 16, National Archives, Washington, D.C. In order to communicate Clayton's ideas clearly, I have altered some of the letter's original punctuation in this quotation.

9. Ibid.

10. Mrs. Wellman Bruner to Arthur M. Hyde, 4 June 1930, Farm Relief File (April–August 1930), General Correspondence of the Office of the Secretary (1906–70), Records of the Secretary of Agriculture, Record Group 16, National Archives, Washington, D.C.

11. Historian Noralee Frankel commented on this phenomenon at the Women and the Transition to Capitalism in Rural America Conference, held at Northern Illinois University, 30 March–2 April 1989. I am grateful for Dr. Frankel's insights.

12. Arthur M. Hyde to Mrs. Wellman Bruner, 9 June 1930, Farm Relief File (April–August 1930), General Correspondence of the Office of the Secretary (1906–70), Records of the Secretary of Agriculture, Record Group 16, National Archives, Washington, D.C.

13. In his recent book, *From New Day to New Deal: American Farm Policy from Hoover to Roosevelt, 1928–1933* (Chapel Hill: University of North Carolina Press, 1991), historian David E. Hamilton convincingly argues that in many ways Roosevelt administration agricultural policy merely continued and expanded measures begun under Hoover. The emphasis fundamentally remained on farmers' voluntary cooperation with a government program designed to shore up capitalist agriculture.

14. For a good discussion of the impact of AAA policies on tenant farmers and sharecroppers, see David Eugene Conrad, *The Forgotten Farmers: The Story of Sharecroppers and the New Deal* (Urbana: University of Illinois Press, 1965).

15. Irwin Unger and Debi Unger, *Twentieth Century America* (New York: St. Martin's Press, 1990), 226–27.

16. Mrs. Jake Caffman to Franklin D. Roosevelt, 3 April 1933, Farm Relief File, (2) Comments on the Bill (1933), General Correspondence of the Office of the Secretary (1906–70), Records of the Secretary of Agriculture, Record Group 16, National Archives, Washington, D.C. In an effort to communicate Caffman's ideas clearly, I have altered some of the letter's original punctuation in this quotation.

17. Mrs. Henry F. Drees to Henry A. Wallace, 5 June 1933, Farm Relief File, (1) Misc. Farm Relief Plans (1933), General Correspondence of the Office of the Secretary (1906–70), Records of the Secretary of Agriculture, Record Group 16, National Archives, Washington, D.C.

18. Mrs. Elizabeth Gavin to Henry A. Wallace, 28 June 1933, Farm Relief File, (1) Misc. Farm Relief Plans (1933), General Correspondence of the Office of the Secretary (1906–70), Records of the Secretary of Agriculture, Record Group 16, National Archives, Washington, D.C. In order to present Gavin's thoughts clearly, I have altered some of the letter's original punctuation in this quotation.

19. Viola Bourret to Mrs. Franklin D. Roosevelt, 15 September 1933, Farm Relief File, (1) Misc. Farm Relief Plans (1933), General Correspondence of the Office of the Secretary (1906–70), Records of the Secretary of Agriculture, Record Group 16, National Archives, Washington, D.C. To communicate Bourret's ideas clearly, I have altered some of the letter's original punctuation in this quotation.

20. Virginia E. Jenckes to Alice Paul, National Woman's Party, 10 May 1934, Virginia Ellis Jenckes Papers, Box 1, Indiana State Library, Indianapolis, Ind. (hereafter cited as Jenckes Papers).

21. *Terre Haute Tribune*, 20 March 1932.

22. Virginia E. Jenckes, "The AAA from the Viewpoint of a Farmer Who Is a Member of Congress" (undated speech), Box 3, Jenckes Papers; Virginia E. Jenckes, interview with Tom Krasean, Terre Haute, Ind., 11 and 12 October 1967, Indiana State Library Oral History Collection, Indianapolis, Ind.

23. A copy of Jenckes's telegram is included with a letter from the congresswoman to Stephen Early, assistant secretary to the president, 8 November 1933, Farm Relief File, (1) Misc. Farm Relief Plans (1933), General Correspondence of the Office of the Secretary (1906–70), Records of the Secretary of Agriculture, Record Group 16, National Archives, Washington, D.C.

24. See Mary Neth, "Building the Base: Farm Women, the Rural Community, and Farm Organizations in the Midwest, 1900–1940," in *Women and Farming: Changing Roles, Changing Structures*, edited by Wava G. Haney and Jane B. Knowles (Boulder, Colo.: Westview Press, 1988).

25. DeWitt C. Wing, "Trends in National Farm Organizations," *Yearbook of Agriculture, 1940*, edited by Gove Hambidge (Washington: Government Printing Office, 1940), 964, 974; David Edgar Lindstrom, *American Farmers' and Rural Organizations* (Champaign, Ill.: Garrard Press, 1948), 207–8, 213, 257; Segerstrom interview.

26. Jean Stillman Long, interview with Dale Trelevan, Menomonie, Wis., 16 July and 20 August 1974, Wisconsin Agriculturalists Oral History Project, State Historical Society of Wisconsin, Madison, Wis.

27. Lindstrom, *Farmers' and Rural Organizations*, 181, 196, 200.

28. A copy of the motion was included with a letter from Mrs. Alma H. Jones to Henry A. Wallace, 21 February 1934, Farm Women File (1934), General Correspondence of the Office of the Secretary (1906–70), Records of the Secretary of Agriculture, Record Group 16, National Archives, Washington, D.C.

29. Mrs. Ellsworth Richardson to Henry A. Wallace, 20 February 1934, Farm Women File (1934), General Correspondence of the Office of the Secretary (1906–70), Records of the Secretary of Agriculture, Record Group 16, National Archives, Washington, D.C.

30. C. W. Warburton to Henry A. Wallace, 1 March 1934, Farm Women File (1934), General Correspondence of the Office of the Secretary (1906–70), Records of the Secretary of Agriculture, Record Group 16, National Archives, Washington, D.C.

31. As former historian for the Department of Agriculture Wayne D. Rasmussen makes clear in his study of the USDA and the Extension Service, *Taking the University to the People: Seventy-five Years of Cooperative Extension* (Ames: Iowa State University Press, 1989), farm journals received much of their material directly from the Department of Agriculture and Extension Service during this time.

32. "Everybody's Say-So," *Wallaces' Farmer*, 30 September 1933, 18.

33. "Plan Your Radio Listening: It Pays to Hunt for the Best Programs," *Wallaces' Farmer*, 27 October 1934, 8; Edmund deS. Brunner, *Radio and the Farmer* and *A Symposium on the Relation of Radio to Rural Life* (New York: Radio Institute of the

Audible Arts, 1935), 40–42, 46–47, 53, 57; Elizabeth C. Wherry, "Radio for Winter Nights: Entertainment for the Whole Farm Family," *Wallaces' Farmer*, 11 November 1933, 15.

34. "Good Radios for All," *Wallaces' Farmer*, 3 February 1934, 20; "Everybody's Say-So," *Wallaces' Farmer*, 28 October 1933, 17.

35. "Everybody's Say-So," *Wallaces' Farmer*, 28 October 1933, 17.

36. "Utilizing Money Wisely," *Wallaces' Farmer*, 3 March 1934, 19.

37. Ibid.

38. "Mother Will Spend Part of AAA Check," *Wallaces' Farmer*, 28 March 1936, 1.

39. "When Buying Your Radio," *Wallaces' Farmer*, 10 October 1936, 23.

40. "What Farm Women Think of Politics: Letters Show That Our Readers Have Studied Both Sides," *Wallaces' Farmer*, 24 October 1936, 18.

41. "Farm Women Discuss AAA Program," *Wallaces' Farmer*, 31 December 1938, 1.

42. Ibid., 10.

43. Ibid.

44. Ibid.

45. "Invite the Women to AAA Meeting," *Wallaces' Farmer*, 14 January 1939, 6.

46. "Farm Women Say the AAA Is 'Ridiculous,' 'Wrong' 'Against the Bible' 'A God-Send,'" *Wallaces' Farmer*, 23 September 1939, 1.

47. "Shall We Drop the AAA?," *Wallaces' Farmer*, 21 October 1939, 5; "Women's Side of the AAA," *Wallaces' Farmer*, 21 October 1939, 25.

48. "Do Iowa Farmers Like AAA?," *Wallaces' Farmer*, 15 June 1940, 9; "How Iowa Farmers May Vote," *Wallaces' Farmer*, 2 November 1940, 5.

49. Lindstrom, *Farmers' and Rural Organizations*, 199; Marguerite Gilstrap, interview with the author, Washington, D.C., 18 September 1989. Gilstrap, a longtime employee of the Department of Agriculture, worked for the FSA from 1942 to 1944. For further discussion of the history of the FSA, see Sidney Baldwin, *Poverty and Politics: The Rise and Decline of the Farm Security Administration* (Chapel Hill: University of North Carolina Press, 1968).

50. Perhaps the most famous of all the FSA photographs, and certainly one of the most frequently reproduced, is Dorothea Lange's "Migrant Mother," a portrait of a young migrant farm worker surrounded by her three small daughters. For an overview of Lange's portraits of rural women, see *Dorothea Lange Looks at the American Country Woman* (Fort Worth, Tex.: Amon Carter Museum of Western Art, 1978). For further discussion of Lange's career and the "Migrant Mother" photograph, see Karin Becker Ohrn, *Dorothea Lange and the Documentary Tradition* (Baton Rouge: Louisiana State University Press, 1980).

51. John Vachon, Negative No. 34-61020-D, FSA Photograph Collection, Library of Congress, Washington, D.C.

52. Russell Lee, Negative No. 34-34090-D, FSA Photograph Collection, Library of Congress, Washington, D.C.

53. J. M. Gillette, "Socio-Economic Submergence in a Plains State," *Rural Sociology* 5 (March 1940): 61; John Kerr Rose, "Rural Electrification: A Field for Social

Research," *Rural Sociology* 5 (December 1940): 425; U.S. Bureau of the Census, *Sixteenth Census of the United States, 1940: Housing*, vol. 2 (Washington: Government Printing Office, 1943).

54. *Sixteenth Census of the United States, 1940: Housing*, vol. 2.

55. Eleanor Arnold, ed., *Voices of American Homemakers: An Oral History Project of the National Extension Homemakers Council* (Washington, D.C.: National Extension Homemakers' Council, 1985), 100–101.

56. Russell Lee, Negative No. 34-30812-D, FSA Photograph Collection, Library of Congress, Washington, D.C.

57. In his study of FSA photography, James Curtis notes that Roy Stryker directed photographers to provide images of how rural Americans spent their evenings in the home and wanted pictures of people playing cards, entertaining guests, and listening to the radio. Curtis states that if the image of a new radio in the center of an otherwise shabby rural parlor strikes modern viewers as "high camp," they miss the "significance of the radio and its centrality to the life" of farm families. See James Curtis, *Mind's Eye, Mind's Truth: FSA Photography Reconsidered* (Philadelphia: Temple University Press, 1989), 103.

58. For discussion of the propaganda value of the FSA photographs, see F. Jack Hurley, *Portrait of a Decade: Roy Stryker and the Development of Documentary Photography in the Thirties* (Baton Rouge: Louisiana State University Press, 1972); material in the last two chapters of Maren Stange, *Symbols of Ideal Life: Social Documentary Photography in America, 1890–1950* (New York: Cambridge University Press, 1989); chap. 4 of James Guimond, *American Photography and the American Dream* (Chapel Hill: University of North Carolina Press, 1991); and Curtis, *Mind's Eye, Mind's Truth*. Hurley's discussion of Arthur Rothstein's placement of a nearby steer skull onto a patch of parched earth in North Dakota provides an example of how FSA photographers sometimes altered a given scene in order to enhance the impact of their photographs. The resulting picture dramatically illustrated drought conditions, but Rothstein's manipulation of the scene prompted New Deal critics to charge that FSA employees "doctored" their photographs. Hurley argues that even though photographers sometimes made such changes, they were committed to a "policy of total truthfulness," and their photographs were "propaganda in the best sense—that is, the photographs focused attention on real problems and hinted at real solutions." Guimond too defends the truthfulness of the FSA's depression-era photos, stating that the "FSA images showed that American farmers really were poor. . . . Anyone looking at Russell Lee's picture of the four small children of an Iowa tenant farmer eating a 'Christmas dinner' of corn bread and 'a sort of thin soup' in a room with rough, unpainted board walls, would have realized that stories about rural poverty were not New Deal 'propaganda,' that these farmers really did need help if they and their families were going to survive." Stange and Curtis, however, are more critical of FSA photographers and administrators in their role as propagandists. For further discussion of the use of documentary photography by various New Deal agencies, including the FSA, see Pete Daniel, Merry A. Foresta, Maren Stange, and Sally Stein, *Official Images: New Deal Photography* (Washington, D.C.: Smithsonian Institution Press, 1987).

59. "Pay Up, Said the Bank," *Wallaces' Farmer*, 7 March 1942, 8.

60. Henry A. Wallace, "Contributions of Women to Agriculture," *Rural America*, October 1936, 2.

61. "Electricity for the Farm," *Wallaces' Farmer*, 8 June 1935, 16; "Electricity for the Farmer: How Communities May Get REA Loans," *Wallaces' Farmer*, 28 September 1935, 12.

62. "Rural Electrification," *Rural America*, December 1936, 11.

63. "Electricity for the Farm," 16.

64. "Electricity for the Farmer," 12.

65. Mrs. L. J. Killey, "Summary of Discussion," *Rural America*, March 1936, 9.

66. "Servants on the Farm: Electricity in Rural Homes," *Wallaces' Farmer*, 9 October 1937, 18; "The Modern Miracle," *Wallaces' Farmer*, 23 October 1937, 21.

67. "Servants on the Farm," 18; "The Modern Miracle," 21.

68. Elizabeth C. Wherry, "Country Air," *Wallaces' Farmer*, 13 August 1938, 43.

69. "Power in Kitchen and Laundry," *Wallaces' Farmer*, 24 September 1938, 7.

70. Ibid.

71. Robert T. Beall, "Rural Electrification," in *Yearbook of Agriculture, 1940*, edited by Gove Hambidge (Washington: Government Printing Office, 1940), 793.

72. Ray Yarnell, "Between Thee and Me," *Capper's Farmer*, July 1938, 36.

73. "Percentage of Saturation of Electric Appliances and Plumbing Facilities on REA Projects," *Rural Electrification News*, January 1940, 6.

74. "'I've Got Lights,'" *Wallaces' Farmer*, 5 October 1940, 6.

75. This interpretation is an extension of historian Jeanne Boydston's discussion of the pastoralization of housework in *Home and Work: Housework, Wages, and the Ideology of Labor in the Early Republic* (New York: Oxford University Press, 1990).

Chapter 4

1. For further discussion of the BAE during the New Deal era, see Richard S. Kirkendall, *Social Scientists and Farm Politics in the Age of Roosevelt* (Columbia: University of Missouri Press, 1966).

2. The other communities studied were El Cerrito, New Mexico; the Old Order Amish of Lancaster County, Pennsylvania; Landaff, New Hampshire; and Harmony, Georgia.

3. Edward O. Moe and Carl C. Taylor, *Culture of a Contemporary Rural Community: Irwin, Iowa*, vol. 5 (Washington: Government Printing Office, 1942), 56. Moe and Taylor believed the 350-person village of Irwin, and its surrounding farm families, to be typical of other rural communities in Shelby County and in the western Corn Belt as a whole. See Sonya Salamon, *Prairie Patrimony: Family, Farming, and Community in the Midwest* (Chapel Hill: University of North Carolina Press, 1992).

4. Nellie Christensen, interview with the author, Harlan, Iowa, 12 October 1988; U.S. Bureau of the Census, *Fifteenth Census of the United States, 1930: Agriculture*, vol. 2, pt. 1 (Washington: Government Printing Office, 1932), 975.

5. Christensen interview. For further discussion of women's perception of them-

selves as farm helpers, see Deborah Fink, *Open Country, Iowa: Rural Women, Tradition and Change* (Albany: State University of New York Press, 1986), and Carolyn E. Sachs, *The Invisible Farmers: Women in Agricultural Production* (Totowa, N.J.: Rowman and Allanheld, 1983).

6. Moe and Taylor, *Contemporary Rural Community*, 38.

7. Leona Wiese, interview with the author, Irwin, Iowa, 12 October 1988; Velma Knudson, interview with the author, Irwin, Iowa, 12 October 1988; Christensen interview; *Fifteenth Census of the United States, 1930: Population*, vol. 3, pt. 1, p. 794; U.S. Bureau of the Census, *Sixteenth Census of the United States, 1940: Population*, vol. 2, pt. 2 (Washington: Government Printing Office, 1943), 908.

8. Christensen interview; U.S. Bureau of the Census, *Thirteenth Census of the United States, 1910: Agriculture*, vol. 6 (Washington: Government Printing Office, 1913), 548; U.S. Bureau of the Census, *Fourteenth Census of the United States, 1920: Agriculture*, vol. 6, pt. 1 (Washington: Government Printing Office, 1922), 566. For further discussion of the blurring of the line between women's farm and home work, see Sarah Elbert, "Amber Waves of Gain: Women's Work in New York Farm Families," in *"To Toil the Livelong Day": America's Women at Work, 1780–1980*, edited by Carol Groneman and Mary Beth Norton (Ithaca, N.Y.: Cornell University Press, 1987). For further discussion of the impact of farm mechanization on women's work, see Coralann Gee Bush, "The Barn Is His, the House Is Mine: Agricultural Technology and Sex Roles," in *Energy and Transport: Historical Perspectives on Policy Issues*, edited by George H. Daniels and Mark H. Rose (Beverly Hills: Sage Publications, 1982); Coralann Gee Bush, "'He Isn't Half So Cranky as He Used to Be': Agricultural Mechanization, Comparable Worth, and the Changing Farm Family," in Groneman and Norton, *"To Toil the Livelong Day"*; Katherine Jensen, "Mother Calls Herself a Housewife, but She Buys Bulls," in *The Technological Woman: Interfacing with Tomorrow*, edited by Jan Zimmerman (New York: Praeger Publishers, 1983).

9. Moe and Taylor, *Contemporary Rural Community*, 38.

10. Ibid., 77, 39; *Sixteenth Census of the United States, 1940: Housing*, vol. 2, pt. 3, pp. 48, 71; "Rural Electrification," *Rural America*, December 1936, 11; "Easy to Turn the Faucet," *Wallaces' Farmer*, 30 December 1939, 7; Christensen interview. For a good discussion of the history of gasoline tractors, including information on the general cost of purchasing such equipment, see Robert C. Williams, *Fordson, Farmall, and Poppin' Johnny: A History of the Farm Tractor and Its Impact on America* (Urbana: University of Illinois Press, 1987).

11. Moe and Taylor, *Contemporary Rural Community*, 39; Christensen, Wiese, Knudson interviews; Mary Pries, interview with the author, Irwin, Iowa, 11 October 1988; Alta Weidner, interview with the author, Sublette, Kans., 5 October 1988. For further discussion of Iowa farm women and their use of washing machines, see Katherine Jellison, "'Let Your Cornstalks Buy a Maytag': Prescriptive Literature and Domestic Consumerism in Rural Iowa, 1929–1939," *Palimpsest* 69 (Fall 1988): 132–39.

12. *Sixteenth Census of the United States, 1940: Agriculture*, vol. 2, pt. 1, p. 562; Moe and Taylor, *Contemporary Rural Community*, 77, 42.

13. Moe and Taylor, *Contemporary Rural Community*, 42–43; Pries, Wiese, Knud-

son, and Christensen interviews. For further discussion of Iowa farm women and poultry production, see Fink, *Open Country, Iowa.*

14. Moe and Taylor, *Contemporary Rural Community,* 43; Christensen interview.

15. *Sixteenth Census of the United States, 1940: Agriculture,* vol. 1, pt. 2, pp. 162, 220, 158; Christensen interview.

16. Pries, Wiese, Knudson, Christensen interviews; *Sixteenth Census of the United States, 1940: Housing,* vol. 2, pt. 3, p. 71; H. B. Summers, *The 1940 Iowa Radio Audience Survey* (Des Moines: Central Broadcasting Company, 1940), 61; *Harlan News-Advertiser,* 30 March 1939, 14 March 1940, 17 October 1940. For further discussion of Iowa farm women's use of radio, see Katherine Jellison, "Domestic Technology on the Farm," *Plainswoman* 11 (September 1987): 3–5, 17.

17. Maytag ad, *Wallaces' Farmer,* 14 September 1935, 18; *Sixteenth Census of the United States, 1940: Housing,* vol. 2, pt. 3, p. 71; Christensen interview.

18. U.S. Bureau of the Census, *Twelfth Census of the United States, 1900: Agriculture,* vol. 5, pt. 1 (Washington: Government Printing Office, 1902), 82; vol. 6, pt. 2, p. 164; *Fourteenth Census of the United States, 1920: Agriculture,* vol. 6, pt. 1, pp. 735, 755. Studies of Haskell County include: A. D. Edwards, *Influence of Drought and Depression on a Rural Community: A Case Study in Haskell County, Kansas* (Washington: Government Printing Office, 1939); Earl H. Bell, *Culture of a Contemporary Rural Community: Sublette, Kansas,* vol. 2 (Washington: Government Printing Office, 1942); William E. Mays, *Sublette Revisited: Stability and Change in a Rural Kansas Community after a Quarter Century* (New York: Florham Park Press, 1968); and material included in Donald Worster's *Dust Bowl: The Southern Plains in the 1930s* (New York: Oxford University Press, 1979).

19. Marguerite Rooney, interview with the author, Satanta, Kans., 5 October 1988.

20. *Sixteenth Census of the United States, 1940: Agriculture,* vol. 1, pt. 2, p. 722, and vol. 2, pt. 1, pp. 839, 562, 847.

21. *Sixteenth Census of the United States, 1940: Agriculture,* vol. 1, pt. 2, p. 797; Worster, *Dust Bowl,* 5–6.

22. Bell, *Culture of a Contemporary Rural Community,* 108; Rooney interview.

23. *Sixteenth Census of the United States, 1940: Agriculture,* vol. 1, pt. 2., pp. 192, 791.

24. Bell, *Culture of a Contemporary Rural Community,* 42, 56–58; Louzell Giles, interview with the author, Garden City, Kans., 6 October 1988; Weidner interview. Weidner, born in December 1897, is the oldest native-born resident of Haskell County. *Sixteenth Census of the United States, 1940: Agriculture,* vol. 1, pt. 2, pp. 758, 817, 162, 220, and vol. 2, pt. 1, pp. 839, 562. Mennonites first settled in northern Haskell County in 1916. Some hostility existed between Mennonites and non-Mennonites within the county, particularly over the issue of education. In a county where a high school education was greatly stressed, Mennonites refused to educate their children beyond the eighth grade. There was also some jealousy of the Mennonites' successful diversified farming practices. Non-Mennonites in the county commonly referred to themselves as "white people" when distinguishing themselves from their Mennonite neighbors.

25. Bell, *Culture of a Contemporary Rural Community,* 64–65, 92, 108; Dee Jacquart, interview with the author, Sublette, Kans., 5 October 1988.

26. Jacquart and Giles interviews; Bell, *Culture of a Contemporary Rural Community*, 65, 68–69; *Sixteenth Census of the United States, 1940: Agriculture*, vol. 1, pt. 2, p. 797. For further discussion of farm women's use of the automobile, see Joseph Interrante, "You Can't Go to Town in a Bathtub: Automobile Movement and the Reorganization of Rural American Space, 1900–1930," *Radical History Review* 21 (Fall 1979): 158–60. For a discussion of plains women and the automobile, see Katherine Jellison, "Women and Technology on the Great Plains, 1910–1940," *Great Plains Quarterly* 8 (Summer 1988): 153.

27. Bell, *Culture of a Contemporary Rural Community*, 65; Rooney interview.

28. Bell, *Culture of a Contemporary Rural Community*, 70, 92; Papers included in the Read-A-Book Club, Social Hour Club, and Sosuntee Club collections, all housed at the Haskell County Historical Society, Sublette, Kans.; Rooney interview.

29. Bell, *Culture of a Contemporary Rural Community*, 62–63, 75, 79–80, 90–94, 101; *Sixteenth Census of the United States, 1940: Population*, vol. 2, pt. 3, p. 40; Rooney interview. One of Haskell County's most successful farmers was a widow named Ida Watkins. Her sixty thousand bushels of wheat, produced in the last harvest before the droughts of the 1930s, had earned her the title of the world's "Wheat Queen" and a position as Haskell County's most famous resident. Although Watkins had had no wheat crop during the worst dust bowl years, she had survived that period and was still considered a prominent citizen at the time Bell was doing his research.

30. Bell, *Culture of a Contemporary Rural Community*, 94; Jacquart interview. A similar reliance on county government and other off-farm jobs occurred among western Iowa Corn Belt women in the post–World War II era. See Fink, *Open Country, Iowa*, 161–97.

31. *Sublette Monitor*, 4 January 1940.

32. *Sublette Monitor*, 4 April 1940.

33. Bell, *Culture of a Contemporary Rural Community*, 76; Jacquart interview; *Sublette Monitor*, 4 May 1939, 9 May 1940, 6 June 1940, 18 April 1935; *Sixteenth Census of the United States, 1940: Housing*, vol. 2, pt. 3, pp. 162, 138; *Sixteenth Census of the United States, 1940: Agriculture*, vol. 1, pt. 2, p. 797; *Sears, Roebuck Catalog* (Chicago: Sears, Roebuck and Company, Spring 1940), 573–75, 587. For further discussion of elec-trification and modernization of plumbing facilities on Great Plains farms, see Jellison, "Women and Technology on the Great Plains," 145–57.

34. Rooney interview.

35. As Richard Kirkendall notes in his study of the BAE, many of the same agencies and individuals within the USDA who challenged FSA programs also opposed the BAE. By the mid-1940s, the BAE's critics would succeed in diminishing its influence within the Department of Agriculture and silencing its voice of dissent. See *Social Scientists and Farm Politics*.

Chapter 5

1. Quoted in Florence L. Hall, *On the Homefront in Rural America: Home Demonstra-tion Work Annual Report, 1940* (Washington: U.S. Department of Agriculture, 1941), 2.

2. Meredith C. Wilson, *How and to What Extent Is the Extension Service Reaching Low-Income Farm Families* (Washington: Government Printing Office, 1941), 18.

3. The term "tractorette" was used most prominently in advertising for International Harvester field equipment. Midwestern farm people themselves never accepted the use of this term.

4. Cynthia Beeman, "Farmerettes—The Woman's Land Army of World War I," paper presented at the Fourth Conference on Rural/Farm Women in Historical Perspective, University of California, Davis, 27 June 1992.

5. *Country Gentleman* Correspondence File (1943), Farm Labor Program Correspondence, Records of the Federal Extension Service of the Department of Agriculture, Record Group 33, National Archives, Washington, D.C.

6. Ibid.

7. *Washington Post*, 13 February 1943.

8. "O.W.I. [Office of War Information] Support to Crop Corps Program," Farm Labor Progress Reports (1943–48), Farm Labor Program Correspondence, Records of the Federal Extension Service of the Department of Agriculture, Record Group 33, National Archives, Washington, D.C.

9. U.S. Department of Agriculture, *The Women's Land Army of the U.S. Crop Corps, 1944* (Washington: Government Printing Office, 1944), 5, 8.

10. "Farm Labor Needs in 1944," Occupations File (Agriculture, 1944), Records Relating to Women Workers in World War II, Records of the Women's Bureau of the Department of Labor, Record Group 86, National Archives, Washington, D.C.

11. Dean H. P. Rusk, University of Illinois College of Agriculture, to Illinois senators and representatives, 26 November 1943, State Correspondence File, Farm Labor Program Correspondence, Records of the Federal Extension Service of the Department of Agriculture, Record Group 33, National Archives, Washington, D.C.; Annual Narrative and Statistical Reports of Extension and Other Workers under the Farm Labor Program (1943–45), Records of the Federal Extension Service of the Department of Agriculture, Record Group 33, National Archives, Washington, D.C.

12. "National, State, and Local Farm Labor Stories Published in the *Extension Service Review* in 1943," Occupations File (Agriculture, 1943), Records Relating to Women Workers in World War II, Records of the Women's Bureau of the Department of Labor, Record Group 86, National Archives, Washington, D.C.

13. "When Town Girls Help," *Wallaces' Farmer*, 19 June 1943, 1.

14. Ibid., 1, 15.

15. Annual Report of the North Dakota Farm Labor Supervisor (1945), Annual Narrative and Statistical Reports of Extension and Other Workers under the Farm Labor Program, Records of the Federal Extension Service of the Department of Agriculture, Record Group 33, National Archives, Washington, D.C.

16. "Farm Woman Is Busiest War Worker," *Wallaces' Farmer*, 27 June 1942, 4.

17. Carl Hamilton, assistant to the secretary of agriculture, to Mrs. Paul Edgar, 15 January 1943, Women File (1943), General Correspondence of the Office of the Secretary (1906–70), Records of the Office of the Secretary of Agriculture, Record Group 16, National Archives, Washington, D.C.; Florence L. Hall, *Farm Women on the*

Homefront (Washington: Government Printing Office, 1942), 4; "Farm Women Help," *Wallaces' Farmer*, 17 April 1943, 1; "War Jobs at Home," *Wallaces' Farmer*, 17 March 1945, 28; Pan-A-Min ad, *Capper's Farmer*, October 1942, 40.

18. "She Learned to Milk, to Drive a Tractor," *Wallaces' Farmer*, 11 July 1942, 6.

19. Arthur Capper, "Give the Family Farm a Break," *Capper's Farmer*, February 1941, 1; Capper, "Food Production Must Not Fail," *Capper's Farmer*, November 1942, 1; "The Girl in the Garden," *Capper's Farmer*, June 1943, 16; "Farm Women at Work," *Capper's Farmer*, September 1943, 20; "What Working Women Wear," *Capper's Farmer*, April 1943, 13; "Women at Work," *Capper's Farmer*, October 1942, 8; Edna M. White, "Going to the Fields, Ladies?," *Capper's Farmer*, April 1945, 34.

20. Elizabeth C. Wherry, "Country Air," *Wallaces' Farmer*, 28 November 1942, 15.

21. International Harvester advertisement, *Wallaces' Farmer*, 5 September 1942, 15; International Harvester poster, Farm Labor Program Records (1943–47), Information Division, Records of the Federal Extension Service of the Department of Agriculture, Record Group 33, National Archives, Washington, D.C. The September 1989 issue of *Green Magazine*, a publication for collectors of John Deere memorabilia and antique equipment, featured as its cover story an article about commercial artist Walter Haskell Hinton and the illustrations he created for the Deere company, including his portrait of the woman tractor driver, which he entitled "V For Victory."

22. Supplement to the Annual Report of the Iowa Farm Labor Supervisor (1943), Annual Narrative and Statistical Reports of Extension and Other Workers under the Farm Labor Program, Records of the Federal Extension Service of the Department of Agriculture, Record Group 33, National Archives, Washington, D.C.

23. Annual Report of the Kansas Farm Labor Supervisor (1943), Annual Narrative and Statistical Reports of Extension and Other Workers under the Farm Labor Program, Records of the Federal Extension Service of the Department of Agriculture, Record Group 33, National Archives, Washington, D.C.

24. Ibid.; Annual Report of the Kansas Farm Labor Supervisor (1945), Annual Narrative and Statistical Reports of Extension and Other Workers under the Farm Labor Program, Records of the Federal Extension Service of the Department of Agriculture, Record Group 33, National Archives, Washington, D.C.

25. Annual Narrative and Statistical Reports of Extension and Other Workers under the Farm Labor Program (1943–45), Records of the Federal Extension Service of the Department of Agriculture, Record Group 33, National Archives, Washington, D.C.

26. For further discussion of these issues, see Caron Smith's case study of the WLA in Kansas, "The Women's Land Army during World War II," *Kansas History* 14 (Summer 1991): 82–87.

27. "Farm Women Help"; *New York Times*, 25 January 1944.

28. "Women's Land Army," Farm Labor Program Records (1943–47), Information Division, Records of the Federal Extension Service of the Department of Agriculture, Record Group 33, National Archives, Washington, D.C.; Iona Dinsmore, interview with Mary Allison Farley, Hillsboro, Iowa, 5 September 1985, Iowa Oral History Collection, State Historical Society of Iowa, Iowa City, Iowa; Annual Report of the Nebraska Farm Labor Supervisor (1943), Annual Narrative and Statistical Reports of

Extension and Other Workers under the Farm Labor Program, Records of the Federal Extension Service of the Department of Agriculture, Record Group 33, National Archives, Washington, D.C.

29. Wincharger advertisement, *Wallaces' Farmer*, 16 October 1943, 20.

30. Perfection range advertisement, *Wallaces' Farmer*, 16 September 1944, 29.

31. "What They Will Buy," *Wallaces' Farmer*, 1 July 1944, 19.

32. "They'll Buy New Refrigerators," *Wallaces' Farmer*, 7 October 1944, 22; "It's Mom's Turn Now," *Wallaces' Farmer*, 18 November 1944, 1; "Plan Now for Farm Homes," *Wallaces' Farmer*, 17 March 1945, 1.

33. "Women's Land Army," Farm Labor Program Records (1943–47).

34. Ibid.

35. Florence L. Hall, "Will Women Be a Continuing Source of Farm Labor?," Farm Labor Program Records (1943–47), Information Division, Records of the Federal Extension Service of the Department of Agriculture, Record Group 33, National Archives, Washington, D.C.; U.S. Department of Agriculture, *1948 Rural Family Living Outlook Charts* (Washington: Government Printing Office, 1948), B-3a.

36. Ford tractor ad, *Capper's Farmer*, February 1945, 31.

Chapter 6

1. Mary Jane Fisher, "What Rural Electrification Means to My Community," *Indiana Rural News*, June 1961, 5.

2. Midwest Committee on Post-War Programs, "What Kind of a Rural Housing and Farm Building Program Can We Have in the Midwest after the War?" (mimeographed report, 1944), Post-War Housing and Rural Housing File, General Correspondence (1941–46), Records of the Bureau of Agricultural Economics, Record Group 83, National Archives, Washington, D.C.

3. Arthur Raper, "Uses Being Made by Rural Families of Increased Wartime Incomes" (mimeographed BAE report, 1946), 7–8.

4. "What'll You Buy?," *Wallaces' Farmer*, 3 November 1945, 1; "Who Gets Stoves?," *Wallaces' Farmer*, 20 July 1946, 22; Cleo Fitzsimmons and Nellie L. Perkins, "The Homemaking Plans of 50 Farm Homemakers," *Rural Sociology* 10 (December 1945): 408.

5. "How to Spend," *Wallaces' Farmer*, 3 August 1946, 1.

6. " 'Don't Wake Me Up,' " *Wallaces' Farmer*, 17 November 1945.

7. " 'New Look': Equipment to Help Homemakers Share in Post-War Mechanical 'Revolution,' " *Wallaces' Farmer*, 7 August 1948, 34; "Voice of the Farm," *Wallaces' Farmer*, 16 November 1946, 30.

8. "Voice of the Farm," *Wallaces' Farmer*, 16 November 1946, 30.

9. Ibid.

10. "More Profit—and More Expenses," *Wallaces' Farmer*, 16 November 1946, 30.

11. Ora Switzer, interview with the author, Nicodemus, Kans., 29 May 1990; La Barbara W. Fly, "Into the Twentieth Century," in *Promised Land on the Solomon: Black Settlement at Nicodemus, Kansas*, edited by Gregory D. Kendrick (Washington: Gov-

ernment Printing Office, 1986). The town of Nicodemus is now a National Historic Landmark. For a discussion of Haskell County in the second half of the twentieth century, including brief discussion of the Hispanic community in Satanta, see William E. Mays, *Sublette Revisited: Stability and Change in a Rural Kansas Community after a Quarter Century* (New York: Florham Park Press, 1968).

12. Household Economics Research Division, Agricultural Research Service, U.S. Department of Agriculture, *Farm Family Spending in the United States* (Washington: Government Printing Office, 1958), 46.

13. See chap. 6 of Deborah Fink's *Open Country, Iowa: Rural Women, Tradition and Change* (Albany: State University of New York Press, 1986).

14. "Husband in the Henhouse?," *Wallaces' Farmer*, 7 August 1948, 1, 5.

15. Ibid.

16. Ray Franklin, "Quality Egg Programs May Bring . . . Better Eggs, Lower Marketing Costs, Increased Demand," *Wallaces' Farmer*, 5 July 1958, 14.

17. "Warsaw Chicken, Egg Operation Largest of Its Kind in Indiana," *Indiana Rural News*, September 1961, 3.

18. Franklin, "Quality Egg Programs," 14; Della Tenley Koppenhaver, interview with the author, Martelle, Iowa, 30 January 1989.

19. Elizabeth C. Wherry, "Country Air," *Wallaces' Farmer*, 2 December 1950, 30. For the impressions of other rural women columnists of the period, see Gladys Talcott Rife, "Personal Perspectives on the 1950s: Iowa's Rural Women Newspaper Columnists," *Annals of Iowa* 49 (Spring 1989): 661–82. See also the discussion of Rife's article by Katherine Jellison and Deborah Fink on pp. 683–91 of the same issue.

20. Wherry, "Country Air," *Wallaces' Farmer*, 20 February 1954, 63.

21. Wherry, "Country Air," *Wallaces' Farmer*, 3 May 1952, 35.

22. Wherry, "Country Air," 20 February 1954, 63.

23. Wherry, "Country Air," 2 December 1950, 30.

24. Wherry, "Country Air," 3 May 1952, 35.

25. For an excellent discussion of the postwar domestic ideal and the experience of urban women, see Elaine Tyler May, *Homeward Bound: American Families in the Cold War Era* (New York: Basic Books, 1988).

26. "What Does She Do with Her Time?," *Wallaces' Farmer*, 21 March 1953, 51.

27. "Wife's Place on Farm," *Wallaces' Farmer*, 16 March 1946, 39.

28. Margaret Noll, " 'When I Husk Corn,' " *Wallaces' Farmer*, 17 November 1945, 28.

29. "Voice of the Farm," *Wallaces' Farmer*, 15 February 1947, 52.

30. "Farm Brides Who Work in Town," *Wallaces' Farmer*, 21 October 1950, 48.

31. Ibid.; Zoe Murphy, "Earn Money and Stay at Home," *Wallaces' Farmer*, 3 January 1959, 26; Bureau of Human Nutrition and Home Economics, U.S. Department of Agriculture, *Rural Family Living Charts* (Washington: Government Printing Office, 1951), 11; Zoe Murphy, "What Would You Do?," *Wallaces' Farmer*, 3 December 1955, 34.

32. John Clayton, "Farm Wife Turns Wage Earner," *Wallaces' Farmer*, 20 October 1956, 60.

33. Zoe Murphy, "Does Your Wife/Husband Help?," *Wallaces' Farmer*, 20 September 1958, 60.

34. Ibid.

35. Zoe Murphy, "Women Who Work in the Field," *Wallaces' Farmer*, 3 December 1960, 28.

36. Ibid.

37. Ibid., 29.

38. Zoe Murphy, " 'Don't Marry a Farmer,' " *Wallaces' Farmer*, 3 May 1947, 23.

39. "Why Farm Girls Go to Town," *Wallaces' Farmer*, 15 February 1958, 40.

40. During the postwar era, midwestern farm publications for the first time presented feature stories about young women who were independent farmers. Under the titles "Feminine Farmer Does a Man's Work" and "Two Ex-G.I. Girls Run a Farm," *Wallaces' Farmer* and *Capper's Farmer* both ran stories in the early postwar period about Corn Belt women, apparently all in their late twenties, who had rented or purchased land in their rural neighborhoods. In both instances, these "girls," as the authors of their stories referred to the young women, were viewed as continuing the "masculine" wartime roles they had played either in the military or as replacement labor in the "Crop Corps." The authors of these stories made it clear that although these women were successful farmers, they were considered to be unusual in their role as independent farm operators. Stories about independent women farmers did not appear in either of these midwestern farming periodicals after the early 1950s.

41. Lee G. Burchinal, *Factors Related to Employment of Wives in a Rural Iowa County* (Ames: Iowa State University, 1962), 662, 666.

42. Zoe Murphy, "Decisions . . . Decisions . . . Decisions," *Wallaces' Farmer*, 18 August 1962, 44.

43. Eugene A. Wilkening, *Farm Husbands and Wives in Wisconsin: Work Roles, Decision-Making and Satisfactions, 1962 and 1979* (Madison: Wisconsin University Cooperative Extension Program, 1979), 6, 10.

44. Again, for a discussion of the characteristics of postwar urban families, see May's *Homeward Bound*.

45. Conversation with Carol Zeigler, former fashion and beauty editor for the *Farmer's Wife* magazine, Des Moines, Iowa, 28 February 1990.

46. Bell advertisement (February and March 1954), "Farmers 1951–1956b" Folder, Box 28, American Telephone and Telegraph Series, N. W. Ayer Collection, Archives Center, National Museum of American History, Smithsonian Institution, Washington, D.C.

47. Bell advertisement (April and May 1958), "Farmers 1957–1961" Folder, Box 29, American Telephone and Telegraph Series, N. W. Ayer Collection, Archives Center, National Museum of American History, Smithsonian Institution, Washington, D.C.

48. Bell advertisement (April 1959), "Farmers 1957–1961" Folder, Box 29, American Telephone and Telegraph Series, N. W. Ayer Collection, Archives Center, National Museum of American History, Smithsonian Institution, Washington, D.C.

49. Zoe Murphy, "Farm Families Move into Living Room," *Wallaces' Farmer*,

19 January 1957, 40. Seventy-four percent of respondents to the poll said that their families watched television together on a typical winter evening.

50. See Fink, *Open Country, Iowa*; Christine Hillman, "What's Wrong with Farm Living?," *Wallaces' Farmer*, 16 July 1955, 44.

51. Jean Hardy, interview with the author, Imperial, Nebr., 10 May 1989; Adelaide Krentz, interview with Jean Saul Rannells, rural Montello, Wis., 28 February 1985, Rural Women's Oral History Project, State Historical Society of Wisconsin, Madison, Wis.; Leona Giese, interview with Jean Saul Rannells, rural Montello, Wis., 6 December 1984, Rural Women's Oral History Project, State Historical Society of Wisconsin, Madison, Wis.; Audrey Wolfe Hauser, interview with the author, Coralville, Iowa, 11 April 1989.

52. Lois McKnight, interview with Jean Saul Rannells, Lafayette County, Wis., 9 February 1985, Rural Women's Oral History Project, State Historical Society of Wisconsin, Madison, Wis.

53. Ibid.

54. Ibid.

55. Ibid.

56. Ibid.

57. Ibid.

58. Rose Marie Dower, interview with Jean Saul Rannells, rural Gratiot, Wis., 14 February 1985, Rural Women's Oral History Project, State Historical Society of Wisconsin, Madison, Wis.

59. Dorothy Von der Sump Hartwig, interview with Jean Saul Rannells, Dalton, Wis., 6 December 1984, Rural Women's Oral History Project, State Historical Society of Wisconsin, Madison, Wis.

60. Ibid.

61. Ibid.

62. Ibid.

63. Ibid.

64. McKnight interview.

65. Throughout the Wisconsin Rural Women's Oral History Project interviews, when women were asked whether they considered themselves "farmers" or "farm wives," even those who performed farm work on a regular basis usually defined themselves as "farm wives."

Conclusion

1. David Snedden, "American Rural Life in 1960," *Rural America*, May 1932, 3–4.

2. Jean Hardy, interview with the author, Imperial, Nebr., 10 May 1989.

Index